The Telling:
One Family - Two Centuries
Daniel C. Tabor
ISBN: 978-1-914933-34-9

Second Printing: June 2023

Copyright 2023
All rights reserved. No part of this publication may be reproduced, stored in a retrieval system or transmitted in any form or by any means, electronic, mechanical, photocopy, recording or otherwise, without prior written consent of the copyright owner. Nor can it be circulated in any form of binding or cover other than that in which it is published and without similar condition including this condition being imposed on a subsequent purchaser.
The right of Daniel C. Tabor to be identified as the author of this work has been asserted in accordance with the Copyright Designs and Patents Act 1988.
A copy of this book is deposited with the British Library.

Published By: -

i2i
PUBLISHING

i2i Publishing. Manchester.
www.i2i.publishing.co.uk

Remember the days, consider the years of many generations; ask your father, he will inform you, your elders, they will tell you.

Deuteronomy, 32:7

The whole world is a narrow bridge; the important thing is not to be afraid.

Nachman of Bratslav (1772–1810)

To the memory of my parents

Acknowledgements

Many people have helped me with this project over the years, including those who are no longer alive. Where family is concerned, my biggest debt is to my parents, David and Hanna Tabor. Other family members who I am grateful to, and who answered my questions with patient good humour, are (in the UK): my paternal grandmother Rivka (Rebecca); my aunts, Esther Tabor and Bessie Lush, my cousin David Lush, and Min Tabor and her daughters, Jane Englesman and Hazel Scheinman. In Australia: my maternal grandmother, Melita Stillschweig; in Belgium, Pierre Orfinger; in Finland, Golda Zewi. In Israel, I am grateful to my great-aunt Rosy Strauss, Josef and Daisy Hepner, Josi and Nenette Palti, and their daughter, Ronny Fogel; Paulina Chananowicz and her daughter, Rina; Henry and Vivienne Tabor, Judith and Avraham Dudaie and their son, Ohad; and Margaret Rothschild. In South Africa, Julian Schragenheim; in the USA: Harris and Rosa Weinstein, and my brother, Michael Tabor.

Other individuals have provided support and advice, for which I am grateful. In particular, I would like to thank the following in the UK: Professor Ladislaus Löb, Charles and Brendel Lang and Michael Jolles. In Germany, I am grateful for the assistance I received from: Dr M. Katzemi, (Archiv der Max-Planck-Gesellschaft, Berlin), Professor K. Zilles, (The Cécile & Oskar Vogt Archive, University of Dusseldorf), Dieter Steil and Dr L. Braker (Director of the City Archive) in Geissen, and Dr Gabriel Nick and Regina Lübke, of the Jewish community in Giessen. In Lithuania, we were fortunate in being given a guided tour of the main sites of Jewish interest in and around Vilnius by Dalia Rimkuniene, and thanks also to Galina Baranova, of the Lithuanian State Historical Archive, for her help. I am grateful to Bela Velikovsky and Yuri Dorn (of the Jewish Heritage Research Group in Belarus) for organising our remarkable day trip to Belarus, and to Zhanna Ivanova, the Director of the Oshmiany Museum, and Marina Moisevich (Director of the Smorgon Museum) and her colleague, Nadezhda Markova, for their assistance during our visit. In Australia, I am grateful to Howard Freeman and Susie Ehrmann (Victoria) and Yehuda Feher (New South Wales) for their help and advice. In Israel, thanks are due to

Betty Doari and Nati Taborisky. In the USA, I am grateful for the help received from Professor Bert Lazerow, and Beatrice Caplan. In Canada, I am grateful to Janice Rosen, Archives Director, Canadian Jewish Congress Charities' Committee National Archives, Montreal, and volunteer researcher, Willie Glaser. Thanks are also due to Michal Singer of the Cape Town Holocaust Trust, for enabling me to access documents and photographs from the Schragenheim Archive. I am most grateful to Lionel Ross (proprietor and publisher) and Mark Cripps (senior editor) of i2i Publishing for their support, encouragement and advice.

I am most grateful to Agnes Kaposi for providing critical feedback on a draft of the text. I am grateful to Matthew Rigby-Burr for drawing the maps. I am grateful to the Parkes Archive, University of Southampton, for permission to reproduce the photograph of James Parkes in Chapter 3. I am grateful for the permission given by NS-Dokumentationszentrum Rheinland-Pfalz, Osthofen, to reproduce the photo of Osthofen concentration camp in Chapter 4. I am also grateful to the Royal Society of London for permission to use the photograph of my father, David Tabor, in Chapter 9. I am grateful to the New York City Library (the Botolph Collection of Menus) for permission to reproduce the menu card from Cassel's Hotel, in Chapter 10. Thanks are due to Pierre Orfinger for providing the family photographs reproduced in Chapter 10, and I am grateful to Daisy Hepner for many of the family photographs reproduced in Chapters 11 and 12. I am also grateful to the Government of Israel Press Office, for permission to reproduce, in Chapter 11, the photograph of Revivim taken in 1943.

I would like to thank my wife, Hazel Johnson, Ricca Edmondson and my brother, Michael Tabor, for providing critical feedback on a previous version of this book. Any mistakes in the book are, of course, entirely my responsibility. I am particularly grateful to Hazel for her support and encouragement, without which this project would never have been completed.

Contents

Prologue:	Secret Messages	1
Chapter 1	Golden Years	7
Chapter 2	Home in Notting Hill	31
Chapter 3	A Rarity in Cambridge	59
Chapter 4	Germans of the Mosaic Persuasion	79
Chapter 5	Weimar and After	103
Chapter 6	Newcomers Down-Under	133
Chapter 7	Life in War-time Australia	151
Chapter 8	Coming Together	173
Chapter 9	Jews of the English Persuasion	193
Chapter 10	Mind and Heart	217
Chapter 11	Making the Desert Bloom	233
Chapter 12	Surviving Bergen-Belsen	249
Chapter 13	Innovators and Pioneers	265
Chapter 14	Lest We Forget	279
Chapter 15	Connecting with the Past	291
Epilogue:	Looking Back, Moving Forward	305
Glossary		311
Notes		317
Bibliography		319

x

Prologue

Secret Messages

As a child, I was fascinated by talking to old people, especially members of my family and particularly my paternal grandmother, Rivka. They knew something I didn't, and this intrigued me. I have never forgotten that feeling. If I listened attentively, I would hear what they were trying to tell me. It was like a secret. It wasn't in the words themselves; it was almost in the cracks between the words where I might be able to hear this message, born of a life-experience so different from my own childhood naivety. They had something to tell me, beyond the narrative of this or that particular event, and it was important that I should catch it, particularly as at one level 'it' could never be put into words. I had to listen very carefully, note everything down, and ask lots of questions, so that I wouldn't miss anything. By doing this, I would somehow get closer to understanding what they were trying to tell me, and if only I could catch something of this secret, it would reveal a meaningful pattern in their lives and by extension, perhaps confer meaning on my own life.

Telling stories in this way, especially ones about the family, has long been a tradition of Jewish family culture. Older generations passing on what were, in effect, oral histories of their lives to current generations occurred in my family, and in many others, too. Even if unsaid, what this created was a tradition of ensuring that lives were recorded and thereby remembered, often with pride, and respect for their resilience and tenacity.

So it was, with this thought in mind, that in 2009, I decided to start writing down what I knew about my past and that of my family. That process led to me asking current relatives if I could talk to them about their lives. This book is the result. In a way, it is my contribution to the tradition of the telling of the family history and the analysis of its significance, including for my own life. Hence the title I have chosen for the book, *The Telling*.

The book records the range of conversations I have had with about twenty relatives from my extended family, intermittently over a period of about fifty years. I have also drawn on the family archive I have collected, which consists of interviews, diaries, letters, memoirs, articles and ephemera. I've tried to convey the sense of curiosity and wonder I experienced as a child: feelings which have never entirely left me, even as an adult.

As I wrote, I wanted to communicate the aspects of our family's history and the many individual lives of my relatives that had come to interest and intrigue me. Three themes emerged that seemed particularly important: memory, identity and place, and these themes run through the book.

Reflecting on these themes, and the stories I was told, a number of questions often came to mind: What stories do people tell about themselves and their forebears? What do they transmit to future generations and why? How do these stories change, and how do they shape the ways people see themselves? What did the decisions involved in the telling of all the stories say about the individuals, the family and their lives?

In describing the early years of my father's family in London, there was far more information available to me than when I was writing about his ancestors in Russia. Nevertheless, even in the twentieth century, there are still spaces which the torch cannot illuminate, because of family estrangements, for example, where it is often impossible to establish what happened and why. At times, I became aware of tensions, often under the surface, between what some relatives were willing to talk about and areas they skirted round, concerned perhaps that aspects of the family stories were not entirely 'respectable'. My father, by contrast, was much less inhibited in talking openly about the community he grew up in. Paradoxically, this sense of the different shades of grey in the stories I was told made me more aware of how remarkable the achievements of this first generation of immigrants were.

Where the extended family is concerned, there are stories of considerable poverty and hardship. It is easy to forget how poor many people were over a hundred years ago, and often we do not know much about the lives of very poor people, because they do not leave many traces behind. I have had to be aware of what can and cannot be found out, and sensitive to what can and cannot be said, making decisions about what I felt was appropriate to put in the public domain.

The stories that are told here are from one extended Jewish family, even though at the centre of the book is an account of my late parents' lives. While not detracting from the unique qualities of the personalities whose stories are presented here, in a world of globalisation, massive migrations and far-flung diasporas, I would hope that the questions the book raises are also of wider interest.

***

There were a number of challenges I faced when writing the book.

The first concerned the theme of memory, a topic much written about, particularly in the context of traumatic events such as the Holocaust. How reliable are memories? How can one ever know? But the telling or re-telling of personal stories cannot be separated from forgetting. What do we remember, and what do we forget? As Gabriel Josipovici observes in his book *Forgetting*, every reader has to contemplate specific cases 'of the anguished interconnectedness of the need to forget and the fear of forgetting.'[1]

What is significant about the memories that are presented here, and what has been filtered out or forgotten? One can ask these questions, even if it is not always possible to answer them.

Where the interviews are concerned, they were conducted in the circumstances in which they were recorded. My questions served as a structure or series of prompts, though even these would not determine where the conversations ended up. In turn, I edited these interviews to produce a narrative, including my questions where this seemed necessary.

About half my interviewees did not have English as their first language, and although my mother's relatives (those born in Germany) spoke very good English, their syntax sometimes reflects a different grammar below the surface. My Aunt Daisy, born in Hungary and incarcerated in Bergen-Belsen for several months as a teenager, struggled heroically to communicate in English, experiences that were at times indescribable. Her difficulty in talking about them seemed particularly appropriate and powerful.

How to write about memories of the Holocaust was thus another challenge I faced. This is not a book about the Holocaust, though Jews who have lived through it or were born after the Second World War have all been affected by it. The challenge is, how does one write about the Holocaust, so as to do justice to those who were witnesses?

Zoe Waxman, a historian of the Holocaust, argues that it is important not to universalise or collectivise Holocaust testimony, but instead 'to revive the particular by uncovering the multiple layers within testimony. It is only by exploring the social and historical context of Holocaust testimony that we can appreciate the sheer diversity of witnesses' experiences.'[2] I have tried to be sensitive to the unique and the particular, while placing these testimonies within their social context.

***

The second major theme I addressed in writing the book was that of identity: how, for example, the children of Russian-Jewish immigrants became British Jews, or a Hungarian refugee became an Israeli citizen, processes which are multi-layered, complex and often full of contradictions. They were difficult to discuss in an abstract sense, and I had to decide how to describe these processes in telling each personal story. How identities are constructed within a social context, how this sense of who one is can change in different, often painful circumstances, are revealed in the different life stories.

The French novelist, Amin Maalouf, argues in *In the Name of Identity*, that different – sometimes conflictive – identities can co-exist in the same person, in ways that can often be creative. How individuals negotiate and express this sense of who they are will clearly vary, depending on changing personal circumstances.

Diaries provide one way of recording intimate thoughts and feelings about oneself and others. James Hinton, a historian of twentieth-century British life, has produced a fascinating book, *Nine Wartime Lives*. It describes the experiences of nine different people who kept diaries during the Second World War as volunteers for Mass Observation, the pioneer social research organisation founded in 1937, which aimed to record everyday life in Britain. Hinton notes that the 1940s in Britain was an era of increased democratisation, with greater personal autonomy, especially for women. Keeping a diary (which would be donated to Mass Observation) became a way of constructing 'a coherent sense of their own identities', accompanied by a heightened sense of self-awareness.[3]

In this sense, my father's diaries, especially from the war years, reveal both his sense of identity and his responses to the people he was involved with. I have also drawn on other personal accounts, such as letters and memoirs. For example, the way my maternal grandmother constructed her narrative about growing up in Germany before the First World War was not only a description of her childhood, written for me, her British-born grandson, but also an attempt to remember and explain the values of the community that shaped her – a community that vanished long ago.

The related feelings of loss and displacement, which permeate many of the experiences of my extended family, are also apparent in the writing of W.G. Sebald, especially in *The Emigrants* and *Austerlitz*. In these novels, Sebald reflects on identity and place, the effects of history in its European and imperial contexts, and the disturbing experience of trying to recover painful memories. The themes he writes about resonate with the concerns explored in this book.

***

The themes of memory and identity cannot therefore be separated from the third important theme: place. Many of the people in this book came from places that no longer exist or places whose names and identities have changed out of all recognition. Many places in Eastern and Central Europe have multiple social and geographical identities, which reflect various phases of political domination. For example, Vilnius in modern-day Lithuania has at different times been part of the Russian Empire, part of Poland and is now the capital of an independent country. For Yiddish-speaking Jews, it was known – before the Second World War – as 'the Jerusalem of Lithuania', though of this great religious tradition little remains. The differences are reflected in the different names that have been used for the same place, and the languages that were used by the dominant political cultures (such as Russian, Polish, Lithuanian, and so on).

To say 'the same place' is perhaps misleading, because, as the geographer, Doreen Massey, has pointed out, places are contested through time. She argues that it is more helpful to talk about 'an envelope of space-time', because this enables us to think about places 'not as areas on maps, but as constantly shifting articulations of social relations through time.' In looking at the relationship between a place and its history, she suggests that we need to recognise '… that what has come together, in this place, now, is as a conjunction of many histories and many spaces.'[4] A place is never 'just' a place: it is a place seen through someone's eyes. The social construction of the place and its significance are intertwined in this book with the themes of memory and identity.

A final challenge in writing this book has been deciding what to include and what to leave out. My impulse was to include more and more, to continue to 'excavate' the archive in the hope that the next piece of information would give the whole book a greater significance or confer the meaning that I sought as a child.

However, Edmund de Waal, the potter and writer, has written in *The Hare with Amber Eyes* about the need to let go: how it isn't necessary to tell 'everything'. There are places in memory, he comments, where you do not wish to go with others, and he cites his grandmother Elizabeth's determination to keep some intimacies private by burning hundreds of letters. But it isn't as straightforward as that, as he says, 'The problem is that I am of the wrong century to burn things. I am the wrong generation to let it go.' He reflects on the 'careful burnings by others, the systematic erasing of stories', and the stamping of 'Sara' and 'Israel' in red on Jewish birth certificates.[5]

Suddenly, I am brought up short. One can read about these things, but it did not prepare me for the shock of discovering, in my maternal grandmother's papers, a copy of the letter her father had been forced to write in 1938 'requesting permission' to adopt the name 'Israel', and for his birth certificate to be changed accordingly (there was in fact no choice in the matter).

Hinton has remarked that all biography is a form of 'hidden autobiography' and this is most probably true of my book.[6] I am part of the narrative, and my comments will point to those aspects of each story that I think are significant for the three main themes of the book. Finally, whether or not I found the secret messages that I sought as a child, and if they enabled me to draw any conclusions about my family's life and my own, is something I will return to in the epilogue.

Chapter 1

Golden Years

Rivka was my paternal grandmother. She was the relative who made a significant impact on me when I was a child. At family gatherings, the older relatives told the younger members some of the family stories about their lives, and I was always interested to learn more. Therefore, I think it is fitting and appropriate to begin by sharing Rivka's story, and the memories of her early life in Tsarist Russia. Her sense of place, and the tension between her Jewish identity and the attraction of Russian culture, are intertwined with her narrative.

***

Almost two hundred years after it had been founded by Peter the Great in 1703, St Petersburg had become a grand metropolis, the capital of the Russian Empire and the chief conduit for western influence. It was the centre of Russia's cultural and economic life, and famous for its magnificent palaces, vast squares and sweeping avenues. It was the city of Puskin, Dostoevsky and Tchaikovsky, and many other famous writers, composers and artists.

For a young girl, arriving in St Petersburg from a provincial town hundreds of miles away, the impact must have been overwhelming. I can imagine Rivka, about nine years old, as she arrived in St Petersburg in 1885 by train after a long journey from Vilna (the old Russian name for Vilnius; Vilne in Yiddish), a town in the Baltic states. She was accompanied by her parents, Israel Jacob and Sarah Miriam Weinstein, and as they arrived at the Petersburg Station she was struck by the noise and bustle on the platforms, the smoke and steam of the trains, and the sensation of ceaseless activity. They travelled across the city to visit the apartment of her paternal uncle and aunt, and I wonder what her first glimpses of the city must have been.

From the grime and poverty of her hometown, she was now in a cosmopolitan city of culture, and the seat of power in Imperial Russia. This girl – Rivka – was given a home by her uncle and aunt, whose four children had died in an influenza epidemic. They were delighted to have such an alert and responsive child in their care. She was their niece, but she also took on the role of a new daughter, to replace the children who had been lost, and they adopted her, at least unofficially.

Rivka's parents returned to Vilna; they were elderly, poverty-stricken Jews, deeply orthodox, but apparently untouched by the political and social changes in Russian society taking place at this time, and they were indifferent to the *Haskalah*, the Jewish Enlightenment (the interest in secular knowledge and learning) sweeping the Jewish communities of the Russian Pale of Settlement.

As a result of successive partitions of Poland in the eighteenth century, Russia had acquired vast lands on its western borders and an enlarged population that included, by the end of the nineteenth century, approximately five million Jewish subjects. Jews were confined by law to the lands that had once belonged to an independent Poland and Lithuania, but they were not allowed to live in large cities. Jews had also been forbidden to settle in the Russian interior, though by the second half of the nineteenth century, small groups of privileged Jews, whose skills were considered to be useful to the economy, were allowed to live in Moscow or St Petersburg, with special permits. Periodic outbursts of anti-Semitism, and the pogroms unleashed in 1881 after the assassination of Alexander II, contributed to a mood of uncertainty and anxiety among the Jews of the Russian Empire, and triggered the mass migration of Jews westward over a period of about twenty-five years.

But for Rivka, arriving at the spacious four-roomed apartment of her Uncle Isaiah and Aunt Esther, with servants in attendance, a new world was opening up. Compared to the cramped and shabby conditions of her early childhood, her life was transformed. The apartment was in the district just south of the Nevsky Prospekt, the city's grand central boulevard, where many Jews had already settled, and close to the Merchants' Synagogue, which she started to attend with her uncle and aunt.

When Rivka arrived, she only spoke Yiddish, the language of the *shtetls*, the small towns throughout the Russian Pale, and home to several million Jews, most of whom lived in conditions that had not changed appreciably for hundreds of years. Her uncle and aunt employed a governess, Sophia Davidovna, a kind, friendly woman, who responded to Rivka's eagerness to learn. The first imperative for Rivka was to learn Russian, and she was told by her governess that the Russian spoken in St Petersburg was the "best" Russian. Later, she started to learn French, the language of European culture, and the language of the court.

Russian Pale of Settlement 1835-1917

Sophia Davidovna took Rivka out and about in St Petersburg; they watched skaters on the river Neva in the winter, and occasionally, saw Tsar Nicholas II taking the salute at military parades. This was the period when Tchaikovsky was at the height of his fame, but Rivka did not attend concerts because (as she remembered many years later), Jews did not go to concerts.

But in this new world of Russian culture, Rivka's Jewish heritage wasn't neglected either; a student called Plotkin, living illegally in St Petersburg, came once a week to the apartment to teach Rivka her prayers in Hebrew. She learned Russian quickly, and it was the language she soon spoke with her uncle and aunt, while Yiddish, the language of her past, receded into the background. This was typical of the acculturation that took place among many Jews in St Petersburg at this time. Yiddish-speaking Jews could not have access to the world of Russian culture, and the incentive to learn Russian was a powerful force for the modernisation of Jews in the Russian Empire.

Rivka read Russian literature, and in early adolescence, developed a deep love for Pushkin's poetry that would stay with her all her life. Even in old age, one only had to mention Pushkin's poetry, and she would 'melt'. Her uncle and aunt adored her; she regarded them as her true parents, and they were ambitious for her to be successful. A photograph of Rivka from this period, gazing confidently at the camera, shows an intelligent, young Russian woman of the late nineteenth century; she does not look like a girl from the *shtetl*.

She also learned important lessons in self-reliance from her uncle and aunt. Once, when she was about to go out, she asked a servant to take her coat off the hook and hand it to her. Uncle Isaiah watched without comment, and when the servant went into another room, he said, "Don't ask anyone to do something for you that you can do yourself." It was a lesson in self-reliance that she never forgot. She learnt other lessons from her uncle and aunt about good habits, such as not to swear, cheat or tell lies.

Many Jews who lived in St Petersburg appeared to have had little or no social contact with the city's predominantly Russian population, but unusually for a young Jewish girl at this time, Rivka had non-Jewish friends. Her best friend, Olga Lusterman, was the daughter of a senator in the Duma (Russian Parliament); she kept a photograph of her friend among her most treasured mementoes in old age. Rivka was proud to discover she had cultured relatives, the Marshaks, one of whom, Samuel (Shmuil) Marshak, became a distinguished translator of Shakespeare and an author of children's books during the Soviet era.

By the age of fifteen, her outlook, her intellectual horizons, her sense of who she was and what she might become, were totally different from the young women of her generation who stayed in the confined environment of the *shtetl*. In that world, as a young woman, she would have received little or no Jewish education, as it was mainly the prerogative of men, and she would certainly have had no opportunity to receive a secular education. Many of her female contemporaries would have been illiterate; and both men and women were subject to the severe restrictions on any form of higher education and access to the professions, that were part of the official policy towards the Jews in the Russian Empire.

Her uncle had some sort of official position, but over one hundred and thirty years later, it is not clear what it was. It may be that he collected rents from the estates of the aristocracy. However, the position of Jews in the capital was always precarious, and the main difficulty was getting a residence permit. There were periods when the official approach was relatively relaxed, and residence permits were not checked too closely or consistently. But in the early 1890s, there was another crackdown on Jews who were living there illegally, and it was discovered, at an official level, that Rivka was living in St Petersburg without a permit.

It was a traumatic moment when, as a fifteen- or sixteen-year-old, she was told that she had to return to her parents' home in Vilna. After her departure, she lost touch with her uncle and aunt, and it may be that they too, had to leave St Petersburg. The gate of her "golden years" (as she called them) closed behind her.

In terms of place, St Petersburg left an indelible mark on Rivka, because of the loving relationship with her uncle and aunt, as well as the city's association with the wider world of Russian culture. Many years later, my father commented that Russian was the language where Rivka felt culturally most at home.

***

By the end of the nineteenth century, Vilna was a city of over one hundred and fifty thousand inhabitants, of whom over forty per cent were Jewish. Jews played a significant role in manufacturing, banking and the running of small businesses. In the 1897 census, over seventy per cent of the merchants were identified as Jews. Vilna was also famous in the Jewish world for its rabbinical academies, with their emphasis on the intellectual analysis of biblical and rabbinical texts associated with the Vilna Gaon. He was an outstanding rabbi and scholar of the late eighteenth century and a fierce opponent of the Hasidic movement (a pietist-mystical movement that had originated in eighteenth-century Ukraine).

There were other ideological and political currents at work in the Jewish community in Vilna, as there were throughout the Russian Empire. For example, the Jewish Enlightenment had spread during the nineteenth century from its point of origin in Berlin to outposts in the Russian Empire, such as Odessa, Riga and Vilna, where it was a powerful influence in promoting the secular education of Jews.

Vilna had also become an active meeting ground for Jewish socialists in the 1890s. A convention of Jewish socialists was held in 1895, while in 1897, the socialist *Bund* (Yiddish: league) held its founding convention there, and Vilna became the centre of its activities. At the same time, a revival of interest in Hebrew as a language of literature and an early enthusiasm for Zionism took hold of sections of the Jewish community.

Yet after St Petersburg, Vilna appeared so provincial to Rivka. The broad avenues, paved streets and impressive public buildings of the capital were replaced by cobbled, muddy roads and a pervasive feeling of squalor. The ideological and social changes sweeping through Eastern Europe had not affected her elderly parents, now in their late fifties or early sixties. Her two brothers were about to emigrate to America, and her other siblings had left home. Russian had become her main language, and back home in Vilna, she was told by her mother that she spoke bad Yiddish, with wooden words (*mit hiltzene werte*). She had to relearn Yiddish to communicate with her family.

Rivka felt that her parents, Israel Jacob and Sarah Miriam, were very narrow-minded. For example, when she was about eighteen years old, she read a copy of the New Testament, and when her father saw what she was reading, he threw it on the fire. Her parents did not get on very well together, a state of affairs exacerbated by their poverty. Rivka's recollection was that her parents were always quarrelling, and that her mother, who clearly thought she had married beneath her, would start an argument with the words, "In our family, there were six and thirty rabbis…"

Rivka's father, Israel Jacob, was the eldest of three or four siblings. His father, (Rivka's paternal grandfather) was Hirsch Weinstein, a timber merchant from Minsk, who had moved to Vilna in about 1840. Israel Jacob's sister, Esther Gittel was the aunt who had adopted Rivka in St Petersburg. His wife, Sarah Miriam Kahan (in the Russianised form, Kagan), was the daughter of the state rabbi of Oshmiany (Yiddish: Oshmene), now known as Ashmyany in present-day Belarus, near the border with Lithuania, but then part of the Russian Pale.

Rivka's parents married in 1860, or possibly a couple of years earlier. Israel Jacob was a bookkeeper, a poorly paid source of employment, and the family story records that he considered it below his dignity to be a manual worker, so he sat and studied, living on money from his father, so that his family was always very poor. Rivka's abiding memory of living at home was the extreme poverty: "It was horrible – I hated it."

This experience of degrading poverty was the norm (with few exceptions) throughout the Pale of Settlement. Golda Meir (Prime Minister of Israel 1969-74) described growing up in Pinsk in the early years of the twentieth century in her autobiography, *My Life*. Her account was one that my grandmother would have recognised, as for most Jews in the Pale, life was wretched with little hope of a better future, and the recurring anxiety that they would be the next victims of a pogrom.

Israel Jacob and Sarah Miriam had two sons who survived into adulthood, Avram Zelig and Moshe Shir (who both emigrated to America), and three daughters, of whom the youngest was Rivka. She was born in October 1875 in Troki (known today as Trakai), which was a Karaite settlement near Vilna, where her mother was visiting friends. The Karaites were a distinct sect of Jews who lived by the teaching of the Torah, but rejected the rabbinical tradition enshrined in the Talmud and other post-biblical texts. They co-existed with orthodox Ashkenazi Jews, another indication of the pluralistic society that had existed in the former Grand Duchy of Lithuania over many centuries until its absorption by Russia, Prussia and Austria in the late eighteenth century.

There is little information about where Rivka's family lived. The official records from Troki for 1874–75, record that the family was then living in a nearby village, Popelianka, in the house of Piletski, where I assume, they rented rooms. Israel Jacob's occupation is described as the 'assistant to merchant Gamberg', and his eight-year-old son, Abram, was studying in a *cheder* (a primary school for boys providing a basic education in Judaism and Hebrew) in Petkeniskes village. At this stage, Israel Jacob and Sarah Miriam had five children; the youngest, a son called Hirsch, aged six months in 1874–75, did not feature in the later family narrative, and he may have died in infancy. Rivka had not yet been born. The Troki records for 1890 show that Israel and Sarah Miriam were no longer living there, but there are no records about where they had moved to, though it is probable that they stayed in the area. When in old age, Rivka said that she came from Vilna; it seems that she meant Vilna *gubernia*, the province as opposed to the town.

Rivka (back row, left), in the 1890s, next to one of her brothers, Moshe Shir. In front are her parents and a nephew.

In later years, Rivka was teased by her own children that she wasn't really Jewish but was, in fact, a Karaite (teasing which she rather enjoyed and participated in, according to my father). As a young child, she remembered playing with skittles and wooden hoops, and the excitement of seeing for the first time, a horse-drawn carriage with rubber tyres. But as a sophisticated young woman, returning to the poverty and restrictions of the parental home from St Petersburg, her overwhelming feeling was the desire to get away.

In the last decade of the nineteenth century, the Russian Empire was in political ferment. As a young woman at this time, Rivka attended meetings of the Jewish Socialists, and she went to nocturnal meetings in graveyards with other young Jews to sing anti-Tsarist songs. Cousins of hers, a married couple with the surname Gordon, were exiled to Siberia for revolutionary activities, though it is not known what happened to them subsequently. Though in old age, Rivka spoke of the Tsar with respect, she also said that it was right that the Russian monarchy had been swept away.

Rivka's interest in intellectual pursuits, her love of Russian literature, and her engagement with the wider world, had developed during her formative years in St Petersburg. At the same time, she was much influenced by the rabbinical heritage of her mother's family, of which she was immensely proud.

Rivka's mother, Sarah Miriam, was from a distinguished rabbinical family, and Rivka's maternal grandfather, Rabbi Michael Meir Kahan (or Kagan in the Russian form of his name), was the state or official rabbi in Oshmiany, a small town in Vilna province. He combined this official role, recording births, deaths and marriages, with that of a communal rabbi, serving the religious needs of the local Jewish community. He represented the family's *yichus* (Yiddish: pedigree), and Rivka kept his photograph on her mantelpiece until the end of her days. The small photo, with its faded image, captures the key event for his family: the award of a gold medal by Alexander II to the rabbi, for carrying out his official duties over many years.

He stares at the camera, an elderly, orthodox Jew. His side curls are prominent; his beard is streaked with grey, and his eyes convey a sense of sadness. His right-hand rests on the top of a book with an embossed cover, and his forefinger marks a page where the book has been partly opened; a studio pose intended to communicate his learned status. The photograph is mounted on a plain piece of brown card.

For the rabbi's descendants, this photograph is rich with significance, one that is part of the family story. The image of the rabbi represents scholarship, piety and tradition, and the award of a gold medal from the Tsar took on almost mythical status. As one of my aunts remarked with awe in the 1970s, "It was almost unheard of, for a Jew to get a medal from the Tsar."

Rabbi Meir Michael Kahan, state rabbi of Oshmiany.

Recently, more information has come to light about the medal. It was awarded in 1859, and it was one of the highest distinctions at that time – the gold medal 'for services, to be worn on the St. Stanislaus ribbon around the neck'. The medal was granted at the initiative of the municipal police, on whose behalf a request was submitted to the provincial administration to award the rabbi because he performed his duties 'honestly and diligently'. As a state rabbi, an official administrative position, Rabbi Kahan would have had a fluent knowledge of Russian, and the tone of the official citation suggests a good relationship with the local authorities.[7]

The medal was taken to America by one of Rivka's brothers and disappeared. But as a child, I felt that the story of the rabbi was a mystery or a puzzle: who was he? Finding out about the rabbi also seemed an important way of understanding more about who I was, and where my paternal family came from. I will therefore digress from telling Rivka's story, to assemble what scraps of information I have been able to find about the rabbi, with the intention of providing more background to my grandmother's family in the Pale of Settlement.

***

Rabbi Kahan was born in about 1812 (another source gives 1814), and according to the obituary that appeared in the Hebrew-language newspaper, *Ha-Melitz* ('Fine talker' or 'Advocate'), he died in 1890, aged seventy-eight. If the rabbi's date of birth was 1812, it was also the year of Napoleon's invasion of Russia and his disastrous retreat from Moscow. The remnants of La Grande Armée passed through Oshmiany in December 1812 as they fled towards Vilna, a reminder of how contested this part of Europe has been for hundreds of years.

Oshmiany was one of the oldest settlements in Lithuania, and its Jewish community developed there at the beginning of the eighteenth century. By the end of the nineteenth century, the total population was almost eight thousand, of which over half were Jews. They earned their livelihood mainly from small trade and crafts, such as tanning, shoemaking, tailoring and carpentry. By the beginning of the twentieth century, most of the Jewish workers organised themselves into trade unions or associations. At this time, there were seven synagogues in the town, three of them belonging (respectively) to the unions of the tanners, shoemakers and tailors. Prominent rabbis served the community during the nineteenth and early twentieth centuries, and a new synagogue was built in 1902, evidence that the community was flourishing.

One family story about the rabbi was remembered by my American cousin, Harris Weinstein. His grandfather, Moshe Shir (born in 1870), was one of Rivka's older brothers, and he emigrated to the USA in about 1899. Harris remembers being told that his grandfather, as a young boy, attended a *cheder* taught by the rabbi. There were over thirty pupils in the *cheder*, and most were the rabbi's grandsons; how many of the pupils were in fact the rabbi's grandsons, it is not possible to say, but the story provides a glimpse into life in the *shtetl* in the 1870s and early 1880s.

Rabbi Kahan's obituary, which appeared in *Ha-Melitz* in January 1891, describes him in glowing, saintly terms. He had been the principal rabbi of Oshmiany for fifty years, occupying the same position as his father before him. He came from a family of thirty-two generations of rabbis, and he is praised as being, like Aaron, a peacemaker between members of his own community, and also, between Jews and non-Jews. He was an early 'Lover of Zion' (*Chovevei Tsion*), a movement that started in a number of Russian cities in the early 1880s, with the aim of encouraging Jewish emigration to Palestine. It was an early form of political Zionism before Theodore Herzl and his writings achieved prominence.

According to the obituary, Rabbi Kahana urged his community to participate in the movement to 'settle the Land' [of Israel], and this wasn't just rhetoric, because he had agreed to his youngest son emigrating to Palestine. On receiving a letter saying that his son had arrived safely in Jaffa, the obituary relates, he made a blessing and pronounced:

> "Whoever has a relative in the Land of Israel, it is as if he is there himself, for he will have a name and remnant in the Land."

> He was also among those who loved the Hebrew language and he read all of our new literature and current events that were published in Hebrew. And frequently, Hebrew was the spoken language in his home, because the educated *rebbetzin* [Rabbi's wife] knows the Hebrew language as one of the living languages.

As with many Litvak families (that is, Jewish families with Lithuanian roots), we claim a connection with Elijah of Vilna (1720-97), also known as the Vilna Gaon, the foremost Talmudic scholar of his age. Both Rivka and her older brother, Moshe Shir, told their grandsons that there was a link with the family of the Vilna Gaon, and they must have heard this from their mother, Sarah Miriam. It is not clear at this distance in time what the link was.

When the subject of pedigree was discussed in our family, as it often is in Jewish families, and a famous figure from the past was claimed as an ancestor, my father would quote the Yiddish saying: *ferds fus potkeves an eynikl* - your relationship is as close as the grandchild of the shoe of the horse's hoof. My mother would make the same point by repeating the German saying: *Durch Zehn Kellerlöschen* – (you're related) through ten cellar-keyholes – though the Yiddish always seemed more expressive. Given the absence of historical records from those distant times, I can only record the stories.

According to the rabbi's obituary, his youngest son (by his second marriage), Yitzchak, settled in Jaffa, most probably around 1890. He was, therefore, part of the first wave of Jewish immigrants to Palestine, which became known as the 'First Aliyah' (from the Hebrew *aliyah*, literally 'going up', or emigration to Israel). One of his half-brothers went to Paris to study medicine, and another went to Vienna to study law.

For me, the rabbi is a fascinating figure, representative of an ancient tradition, yet on the threshold of modernity. If the family tradition is to be believed, he was the last in a line of rabbis that stretched back almost a thousand years, as none of his sons became rabbis. The fragments of information that exist about him are tantalising, and there are many times and spaces in his life and the life of his family that we simply cannot see; the torch cannot shine there.

***

As she passed the age of twenty-three, Rivka was still at home, when most of her female Jewish contemporaries were married, and already mothers. It was time to consider marriage. She had a number of introductions to suitable young men, provided by the local *shadchan* (matchmaker), with a view to arranging a marriage. The man she chose was Chaskel Taborisky (Tabrisky),

Family tree of Rivka Weinstein

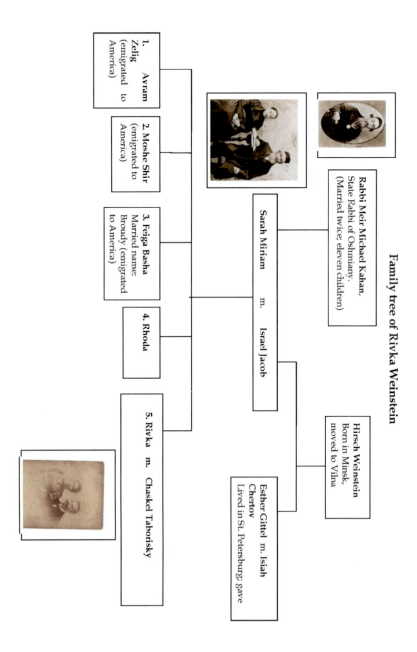

- Rabbi Meir Michael Kahan, State Rabbi of Oshmiany. (Married twice; eleven children)
  - Sarah Miriam m. Israel Jacob
    1. Avram Zelig (emigrated to America)
    2. Moshe Shir (emigrated to America)
    3. Feiga Basha Married name: Broudy (emigrated to America)
    4. Rhoda
    5. Rivka m. Chaskel Taborisky
- Hirsch Weinstein Born in Minsk, moved to Vilna
  - Esther Gittel m. Isiah Chertov Lived in St. Petersburg; gave

recently discharged as an armoury officer from the Russian army, and now setting up his own business, and Rivka chose him because he was the only suitor who could take her away from Vilna.

Chaskel and Rivka Taborisky.
Newly married, Vilna, January 1898.

They were married in Vilna within two weeks of their first meeting, on 11 January 1898. Rivka was twenty-three years old, and Chaskel was twenty-six, and after their marriage, he took her back to Kozlov in southern Russia, where he had been stationed. Rivka's choices were limited, but this was one decision she could make. It turned out to be a very successful partnership.

Immediately after her marriage, Rivka's parents left Vilna and went to live in Konotop, in present-day Ukraine. Why Rivka's elderly parents moved to Konotop, a considerable distance from Vilna, is not known for certain, though it was most probably because a sister of her mother's, Malke Braine Schapiro née Kahan (and an aunt of Rivka's), who had married Hirsch Schapiro, lived there. Their daughter, Chava, stayed in Konotop, and along with her husband, perished in the Holocaust in 1941.

***

Rivka's husband, Chaskel Taborisky (my paternal grandfather) was born in 1871 in Smorgon (Smarhon in present-day Belarus), a town not far from Oshmiany. We do not have a lot of information about his family and upbringing. His parents were Hirsch and Bessy Taborisky, and Chaskel was one of thirteen children. Although of a scholarly family (according to the family tradition), poverty meant that Chaskel and his siblings were not able to receive much of an education, except at the local *cheder*.

Hirsch Taborisky, father of Chaskel.

His hometown, Smorgon, was established in Poland in the early seventeenth century but passed from Poland to Russia in 1793 as part of the Russian Pale of Settlement. From the period shortly after the First World War to the beginning of the Second, Smorgon was part of independent Poland, though it is now part of Belarus. Smorgon's Jewish settlement probably dates from the early seventeenth century, and by the mid-nineteenth century, the community was well established; by the 1860s, a tanning industry was begun in the town as a result of Jewish initiative. In addition to this, the Jews of the town earned their livelihoods from carpentry, the knitting of socks, the baking of bagels (which were famous throughout Russia), retail trade, and peddling. By the early twentieth century, Jews comprised three-quarters of the town's population of approximately nine thousand. Photographs from the period show single-storied wooden dwellings and unpaved streets, though there were some larger brick buildings, most of which were connected to local industries, such as tanning or baking. This was the Smorgon that Chaskel would have known as a boy.

Bessie Taborisky, mother of Chaskel.

At the age of thirteen, Chaskel started work as an apprentice metal worker and at twenty-one, he entered the Imperial Russian army as a private. Soon, he was promoted to corporal and later became an armoury officer (non-commissioned) at the military barracks at Kozlov near Tambov, in southern Russia. This was an unusual achievement since the official anti-Semitism of the time barred Jews from holding any positions of rank in the army. Both Kozlov and Tambov had been founded in the early seventeenth century, to protect the southern borders of Russia from Tartar attacks, and to enable the area to be inhabited more rapidly by Russian settlers.

Chaskel enjoyed his time in the army and was respected by his commanding officer and colleagues for his skills as an armoury officer. On one occasion, he created a display of weapons in the form of the double-headed Russian eagle for a visit of the Tsar's uncle, the Grand Duke Nicholai Nicholaevich, who conducted an inspection of the regiment in 1896. The Grand Duke was a pan-Slavist, and a devout Orthodox Christian. He also had the reputation of being xenophobic and very anti-Semitic. Unlike his nephew, Tsar Nicholas II, he was tall and imposing in appearance, and when I asked Rivka in the 1960s what she thought of the Grand Duke, she immediately replied, "A fine figure of a man!"

The Grand Duke was so impressed by the armoury display that Chaskel was summoned to meet him. However, the Grand Duke immediately deduced that Chaskel was a Jew (most probably because he spoke Russian with a Yiddish accent) and told the commanding officer, a Colonel Gororev, that if Taborisky wished to stay in the Russian army, he would have to join the Russian Orthodox Church. This Chaskel declined to do. The colonel, according to what Chaskel told his children, was a decent man, and greatly embarrassed by this official order. He assured Chaskel that if he stayed in the same town, he would still turn to him for help in armoury matters.

After a brief spell working on the railways, Chaskel set up a private gunsmith and metal-working business in Kozlov. His business was rather successful because the officers from his former regiment continued to use his services. As a result, he was in a position to get married, and from Rivka's comments, they were happy in Koslov and had many non-Jewish friends. They lived in a flat in the Moscovskaya Ulitsa (one of the main thoroughfares); Rivka used to tell her children proudly that they had a maid and a telephone, and Chaskel would receive calls from the regiment to help out with the repair of guns and other armoury problems.

Chaskel Taborisky, the young officer.

Their first child, Simon, was born in 1900 in Konotop in the Ukraine, where Rivka had gone to stay with her parents during her pregnancy. She went again to stay with her parents in 1902, when the second child, Bessie, was born. Rivka was not unique in this respect; Jewish women were prepared to travel considerable distances in the Pale to be with their mothers when giving birth. Golda Zewi (another descendent of Rabbi Kahan) has described to me how her grandmother travelled hundreds of miles in the same period to be with her mother for the birth of her children.

With the following testimonial, Chaskel was able to obtain an Exit Passport, dated 29 April 1904, which also recorded that he had been discharged from his reserve infantry battalion in August 1896. As a result, he could leave Russia, thereby avoiding the possibility of a military call-up during the Russo-Japanese War of 1904–5, when the Russian Pacific fleet was sunk. It was a period of considerable political uncertainty, exacerbated by the suppression of popular protest against the Tsar in 1905, and renewed pogroms in 1903–6, which intensified the wave of Jewish emigration westwards.

The testimonial was from Colonel Gororev; Chaskel was able to obtain an exit visa in 1904 which enabled him to leave Russia. Its tone suggests something of the friendly relationship which existed between him and his former commanding officer:

> ATTESTATION
>
> This attestation concerns reserve-craftsman n.c.o. ('under-officer' corporal) Taborisky who served under me in our affairs in the 222 Shatsky Reserve Battalion (now regiment) as armoury assistant craftsman – and on completing his official military service continued voluntarily as armoury craftsman.
>
> During his service, his conduct was excellent, his application to official duties always executed neatly and conscientiously. Apart from his armoury skills, he could install and handle the working principles of telephones.
>
> All this I testify with my signature and official government stamp. Koslov, 19 April 1904.
>
> > Commander of Battalion 222 Infantry Reserve Shatsky Regiment, Lieutentant-Colonel …

Another document from this period, relating to Chaskel's decision to leave Russia, was a testimonial from the Vilna Artisan Council stating that he was accredited as a mechanic-cum-metal worker, and was allowed to travel in Vilna *gubernia* to practise his craft. It is dated 1899, that is, a few years after he had been discharged from the army.

Initially, Chaskel had planned to go to America to stay with one of Rivka's brothers, who had found them an apartment, and a job. But *en route*, he stopped in London, where two of his brothers were already living, and he decided to stay. It took him almost four years to earn enough money to pay for his wife, Rivka, and their three young children, to travel to Britain

Israel Jacob and Sarah Miriam Weinstein.
Konotop, Ukraine 1916.

During their four-year separation, Rivka returned to her parents' household in Konotop in the Ukraine, where their third child, Alfred, was born in 1904, after Chaskel had left Russia. After her arrival in London in 1908, Rivka kept in touch with her family in Russia until the First World War, but then contact stopped. The only photograph of her parents that Rivka possessed was from Konotop, dated 1916. An old couple in their eighties stare at the camera, survivors from an earlier age. Rivka's father is slight in build, with his side curls neatly bunched by his ears, and a somewhat bemused expression on his face. His wife is dressed in an ample black dress, with a full skirt, and she wears a dark wig. Her expression is a mixture of resentment and long-suffering resignation. Their clothes and appearance would not have appeared out of place in a photograph of the 1880s, though the First World War and the Russian Revolution destroyed the world with which they had been familiar. There is no record of what happened to them after 1916.

***

Rivka's and Chaskel's journeys.

This chapter has described the experience of the Russian Pale, as told to me by my grandmother Rivka, and supplemented by my own research. She had a strong sense of place, and her memories of the contrasting worlds of St Petersburg and Vilna were, as we have seen, revealing of the tensions between Jewish life and Russian culture and society in that period.

Like millions of other Jews between 1881 and 1914, Rivka and her husband Chaskel made the difficult decision to leave Russia and seek a new life in a distant country. How would their marriage survive the experience of separation? How would they establish themselves, socially and economically in London, when they didn't speak any English?

Chaskel and Rivka wondered what sort of future their children would have there. They knew that as poor Jewish immigrants, life would be hard in Britain, but it had to be better than in the world they had left behind.

Chapter 2

Home in Notting Hill

Every year, during the August Bank Holiday, the streets of West London come alive with the Notting Hill Carnival, a massive celebration of Afro-Caribbean culture. The streets are packed with steel bands, Calypso music and tempting food stalls. It's a huge street party, and around two and a half million people regularly attend over the carnival weekend. The main parade, on Bank Holiday Monday, is a sea of colour as amazing floats and costumed performers wind their way through the streets of London in what is Europe's biggest street festival.

What is less well known is that Notting Hill was also the home to a small Jewish community between the wars, yet another example of London's remarkable ability to provide a refuge for different immigrant communities over many centuries. It was here that my grandparents, Chaskel and Rivka, settled and raised a family, and where my father, David, and his siblings grew up. Their memories of family life and the Jewish community of Notting Hill were a source of nostalgia, and it was where they became British Jews.

Their story in London started in the first decade of the twentieth century. In 1908, Rivka travelled by herself with three small children from the Russian Pale to Great Britain. She travelled in steerage across the North Sea, with about two hundred other passengers, a journey which took three to four days. Rivka's eldest daughter, Bessie, a young child at the time, remembered being on the ship, and being told to keep away from the side. The conditions on board were crowded and unsanitary, and it is perhaps difficult to imagine, over a hundred years later, what conditions on board ship were like.

Rivka and Chaskel were one family among the millions of Jews who left the Russian Pale and moved westward in search of a better future. From 1882 to 1905, it is estimated that over one hundred and twenty thousand Jews emigrated to Britain. Most settled in London, but many went to other big cities such as Leeds, Manchester and Glasgow. There was considerable opposition to this 'alien invasion'. The immigrants were accused of living in unhygienic conditions, of being 'sweated labour' and of taking the jobs of the British worker – rhetoric which has a contemporary ring. This led to the passing of the Aliens Act in 1905, which severely restricted the rights of immigrants to stay in Britain. Chaskel had timed his arrival well, because by 1906, Jewish immigration to Britain had already become a trickle, and the majority of those seeking a new life in the West made the long journey to America.

The original plan had been for Chaskel to go to America in 1904, but he stopped off in London, where he had two brothers, and was persuaded by his older brother, Alter, a cabinetmaker, to stay in England. His younger brother, Joe, also a cabinetmaker, was already living with his young family off Brick Lane, so as a newly arrived immigrant speaking only Yiddish and Russian, Chaskel had a family network in London. He stayed with Alter, his wife Sonia and their children in Bethnal Green. At first, Chaskel was employed by his brother, but after a while, he was able to start his own metal-working business, making customised items to order. He lodged with his brother and sent the equivalent of twenty roubles a month to Rivka (a relatively small amount of money). It took about four years for him to send enough money to enable Rivka to make the journey to London with their three young children.

In later years, Rivka claimed that her brother-in-law, Alter, had charged Chaskel too much rent, and that was the reason why it had taken so long for him to send her enough money for the journey to England. Alter left his wife, Sonia, and their children a few years later, and disappeared from the family scene. Relations between Chaskel and his younger brother soon soured, because Joe accused Chaskel of stealing his original design for a lathe. As a result, there was little contact between the families once Rivka and Chaskel were established in London, and my father remembered meeting some of his cousins for the first time at his mother's funeral in 1970.

Chaskel's business, the Cleveland Art Metal Works, was in Cleveland Mews, Howland Street, off Tottenham Court Road. Headed notepaper for the business from before the First World War gives 'C. Tabrisky (Russian)' as the Proprietor, and the range of work undertaken described as: 'Manufacturers of Fenders,

Grates, Chandeliers, Jardiniers [sic], Overmantles, Mirrors and all other Hammered Work'.

By the time my father, David, was born, in 1913, the family had moved to the somewhat better residential area of Lancaster Road, which ran from North Kensington to Notting Hill. This was west London (W11), not the East End, where many Jewish immigrants, including Chaskel's relatives, lived. The move was possible because the business was successful; the clients included Heals, Fortnum and Masons, Harrods and well-known architects of the time. Chaskel was a good 'gov'nor' and had two or at the most, three (non-Jewish) employees, including a man called Lacross who worked with him for over thirty years.

David sometimes visited his father's workshop as a schoolboy, in the 1920s and early 1930s, and he remembered, "… The characteristic smell of hot metal, oil-soaked wooden floorboards and the display in the front ground-floor window of a wrought-iron grate." My cousin, David Lush, remembered our grandfather as "stern but kind," and sometimes visited the first site of the family business, which he described as: … A magic treasure place … relatively dark actually, an old-fashioned workshop where all the people there were skilled craftsmen in whatever they did."

***

My father, David, remembered the family home in Notting Hill:

> We lived then in 80 Lancaster Road, which was a lower-middle class residential area. We had the top half of the house, and the lower half of the house was inhabited by a non-Jewish family by the name of Moss. Our front room looked out on the street, but our back rooms and our bedrooms looked out over the infants' department of the local school – none other than Portobello Road School.

It was at this school that Rivka began to learn English, from listening to the morning singing of hymns, including *All Things Bright and Beautiful*. Chaskel and Rivka had seven children altogether, the youngest of whom, Henry, was born in 1917. They were divided into two groups: the three older children, Simon, Bessie and Alfred who had been born in Russia; and the four younger children, Esther, John, David and Henry, who were all born in England. John and Esther, with whom David had his closest attachment, formed a tight-knit group while Henry, the youngest, was a little too young to join in their games, which included desert island adventures under the dinner table fuelled by an exotic beverage termed Rumba, made of desiccated coconut and lemonade. The eldest, Simon, who helped run the family business, was thirteen years older than David and already living away from home, as was Alfred, who was training to be an accountant. Bessie, the eldest daughter, played the role of deputy mother and was a much-loved figure in the family.

80 Lancaster Road, Notting Hill, August 2013

The central figure was their formidable mother, Rivka, who oversaw and made all the decisions about virtually every aspect of family life and, in particular, the education of the children. Their father Chaskel worked six days a week to support his wife and children. He would leave home early in the morning and return in the evening in time for dinner.

Rivka and Chaskel with their children, c. 1916. Older ones (L. to R.): Simon, Alfred and Bessie. Younger ones (L.to R.): John, David and Esther. Henry had not yet been born.

My father, David, recalled a routine of coming home from school, sharing a high tea at five o'clock in the afternoon with his brothers and sisters, and then sitting around the dinner table doing homework with a radio playing band music in the background. Their father would return around 7pm and they would then have a cooked family dinner together. A favourite dish was their mother's luscious potato pudding, known in the family as 'Wait and See', Rivka's response to her son John when he asked what was for dessert. The name stuck. Most probably this happened in 1936, because the phrase gained popular currency after being used by the then Prime Minister, Stanley Baldwin, during a debate in the House of Commons.

The Tabor family, growing up in London

- **Alter**
  - **Joe**
    - **Chaskel (1871-1943)** and **Rivka Tabor (1875-1970)**
      - **Simon (1898/9-1980)** m. Jeanette Isaacs
      - **Bessie (1902-1989)** m. Hymie Lush
        - David Lush
      - **Alfred (1904-1991)** m. Renee Panner
        - Betty
      - **Esther (1909-1993)**
      - **John (1911-1991)** m. Lena Silverston
        - Judith
        - Ilana
        - Meira
      - **David (1913-2005)** m. Hannalena Stillschweig
        - Daniel
        - Michael
      - **Henry (1917-2015)** m. Vivienne Landau
        - Sharona
        - Dahlia

NOTE: John and Henry's children grew up in Israel, David's sons grew up in Cambridge, while Bessie's and Alfred's children stayed in London.

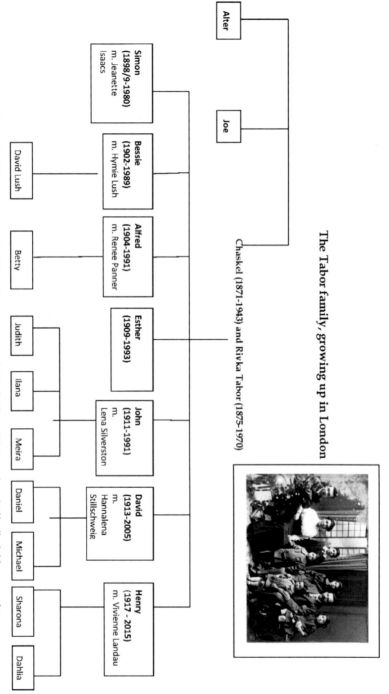

David's younger brother, Henry, recalled that their father was an avid reader in Hebrew, Yiddish and English. By the time Henry was born in 1917, his father was already remarkably well-educated in history and other subjects. Only years later did Henry realise that his father was almost entirely self-educated. Esther Tabor, the younger of the two sisters, wrote a memoir of her father in 1966, when she was fifty-seven years old, and living with her widowed mother. The following extracts show the respect and affection with which he was regarded by his children:

> [Father] was an honest, hard-working craftsman and I never heard him complain once that he was tired, although the physical and mental energy he used up were enormous. He was inventive and original in his work and two of his designs [were] made for architects, I remember. I was very young at the time but recall the chandelier made to resemble the emperor's crown to hang in [the] Viceregal house in Delhi and also some complicated light designs for one of the exhibitions at Olympia or the White City …
>
> He had a great affection for his wife and children but never interfered in their upbringing. He was quite happy to leave everything in my mother's hands. She was much more strict. We obviously benefitted from this for our parents never argued about our upbringing or discipline. Dad was imaginative and inventive, and many glorious hours were spent by us listening agog to his never-ending serial involving his hero, with one foot as long as Tottenham Court Road and one the size of a matchstick. We never realised at the time that he made it up as he went along. At the beginning of every instalment, he would ask where he had left off and of course, we would always tell him. …
>
> He astounded us frequently with tales of wars, intrigues and dates. It was through him, I think, that I first became interested in politics. He was strongly in favour of better conditions for workers and public ownership. I'm sure we got our political leanings from him.

The Tabor siblings grew up in a tightly knit community of eastern European Jewish immigrants. Jewish family life in this community was much more about tradition than religious practice, though Chaskel and Rivka were typical of Jews from their background, in that they were both deeply religious, but not orthodox in terms of strict adherence to religious practice. My father, David, wrote the following account about his father's religious outlook:

> Father was Jewish to his bones. For example, he would have found it impossible to eat non-kosher food [kosher: food prepared according to Jewish dietary laws]. But although he supported the local synagogue and the rabbi, it was not out of orthodoxy but out of his sense of belonging. He was not strongly attracted to Jewish religious ceremonial. The real exception was on *Pesach* [Passover] when he conducted both *Sedarim* [ceremonial meals at which the Exodus from Egypt is recounted] with great gusto, with all the family round the table …
>
> I remember the only occasion when I tried to discuss Judaism with him. I had come home from Cambridge over the Christmas break [in 1939] … He remarked that he didn't care for the whole business of rabbinic ritual but firmly believed in the *Hashgocho,* which is best translated as 'Providence'. He certainly had faith.

I never knew my paternal grandfather as he died four years before I was born, so I cherish these recollections of him and family life in Notting Hill. The language around the home was a bilingual mix of English and Yiddish. Initially, only Yiddish was spoken, until the teachers advised Chaskel and Rivka that their children's grasp of English, and hence their education, might suffer. English was then spoken more frequently at home, but they would lapse into Yiddish if a word or phrase would seem more appropriate or expressive.

Their parents reserved Russian for use as a secret language, which spurred David into learning Russian when he was in Australia during the Second World War. The family joke was that when David returned to England, his mother was shocked that a son of hers should speak such bad Russian, and with such a strong English accent. However, after the war, his weekly letters to his mother were sometimes written in Russian, and this gave her great pleasure. Rivka spoke better English than Chaskel, or at least was less self-conscious about her accent, and she would be the parent to visit the schools and interview the teachers (the word 'interview' here being well chosen).

David had a few early memories of their neighbours and neighbourhood. He recalled the milkman who would deliver the milk which in those days, meant ladling the milk out of a big bucket into the bottles of his customers:

> He was a man with a little goatee beard, and he used to look like a goat himself, and we all knew him because he used to help out in our synagogue as a sort of second *chazan* [cantor], and he had a sort of piping voice, but he was … an essential figure in the community.

In about 1921, he also remembered his parents pointing out a Mr Boluk or Bolam, a tall, slim, upright man in his eighties, walking along the Lancaster Road near the Upper School. Mr Boluk was a 'Nikolai soldat': these were Jewish soldiers who had been press-ganged in the tsarist army at the age of twelve or thirteen. This practice was ended in 1853, suggesting that Mr Boluk had been born around 1840.

David's sister, Esther, wrote an evocative description of family life in Notting Hill in the 1920s and 1930s, with a strong sense of place, as these extracts show:

> We didn't mind running errands, for the shops were almost literally on the doorstep. We had no such thing as a fridge and bought dairy produce daily … Portobello Road Market, a turning from our street, was a very busy one selling all varieties of food. There was no particular time in those days to cease trading, so people could go out late in the evening if they wanted to buy anything. The barrows were lit by flares, paraffin I expect, as they were very smelly, and these lit up the whole road. At the other end of the street was our local picture palace. At this fleapit, we could follow for a few pence every week the adventures of an intrepid heroine like Pearl White and each instalment left her in imminent peril of her life, miraculously escaping at next week's instalment. With one bound she was free …

> Further along [Lancaster Road] was the children's library, most patronised by us. I used to go in and read bound copies of the *Boys Own* paper, so I was able to read a serial from start to finish. Going beyond Ladbroke Grove were the swimming baths and public baths where we went whenever our geyser played up. I remember having to call out to the attendant, "More hot water for number seven, please."

One end of Portobello Road led towards the poshest parts of the neighbourhood, while the other direction led first to our school, and opposite was a sweet shop that sold our childhood delights of liquorice comfits, tiger nuts or delectable bars of liquorice called hard sticks. Further on, I can remember that Dad told us, and at that time we of course believed him, that he had seen Edward VII going into a shop to buy a pair of kippers …

***

The Jewish community in Notting Hill was mainly composed of working-class Lithuanian Jews; most of the immigrants were of limited education and their first language was Yiddish. They were shopkeepers and tradesman although some, in their past lives, had been scholars and now performed menial jobs to support their families. A few, like David's father, were craftsmen such as metalworkers and watch-smiths.

There was also something of an ideological divide in the community between those whose activities centred around the life of the local Notting Hill Synagogue in Kensington Park Road, and those with left-wing leanings who formed a friendly society, the Jewish Workers Circle. This was concerned with the social and political issues of the day and helping Jewish families in need. However, the community as a whole was, and felt itself to be, separate from the Anglo-Jewish establishment, which consisted of families that had come to Britain in the preceding two or three centuries, and had become highly anglicised.

After the First World War, the children all had Hebrew lessons, which tended to have a secular, as opposed to a religious, flavour. Chaskel took the initiative with some other families in organising these lessons. They were not particularly keen on the classes organised through the synagogue, which imparted a basic Jewish religious education.

The idea of Hebrew as a spoken language was stimulated by the then current interest in Zionism, following the publication of the Balfour Declaration of 2 November 1917. The Foreign Secretary, Arthur Balfour, stated in a letter to Lord Rothschild (the leader of Anglo-Jewry), that the government viewed 'with favour' the establishment in Palestine of 'a national home for the Jewish people.' This declaration represented an extraordinary achievement for the Zionist Movement, when Britain was about to take control of Palestine after the defeat of the Ottoman Empire.

The first Hebrew lessons in Notting Hill were given by two Palestinian Jews who had served in the Jewish Brigade in the First World War and had settled in England. David particularly, recalled one of the teachers, a Mr Razilly. The focus of the lessons was on Hebrew as a living language, and the classes were called (in the Ashkenazi, eastern European pronounciation) *Ivris b' Ivris*: 'Hebrew in/through Hebrew'. *Ivrit* (modern Hebrew) had not yet arrived. There were thirty to forty children, aged between six and twelve, who participated in the classes, which were held in a disused grocery shop, almost opposite the synagogue.

After a few years, Mr Razilly returned to Palestine (and subsequently became a senior figure in the national bus company Egged) and a new Hebrew teacher had to be found for David and his siblings. After much discussion, the family chose a family friend, Israel Herman, on the advice of Mr Razilly. Mr Herman was a considerable scholar, who supported his family with a small cigarette-rolling business. Mr Herman's son, Abe, was one of David's closest childhood friends. In later life, as Avraham Harman, he became Israeli ambassador to the USA (1960–67) and then President of the Hebrew University of Jerusalem. Other close childhood friends included Kopul Rosen, who founded Carmel College, Sydney Black, the son of the local grocer, who became a rabbi, and Nathan Goldenberg who became the chief food chemist of Marks & Spencer.

Religious observance and regular synagogue attendance became important for David at an early age, perhaps more so than for other members of his family, and this lasted for the rest of his life. The Notting Hill Synagogue was traditional, with a gallery upstairs for the ladies and the men seated downstairs. It was adequately filled on the Sabbath, but on the festivals, it was crowded out and it became noisy and hot. Many of the congregants only came to the synagogue on the festivals, and it was an opportunity to exchange all sorts of anecdotes and family history while they were there, or to talk about business or the political situation.

The courtyard at the back of the synagogue in Notting Hill was where the men had their toilets and that was the only place where you could buy the Irish sweepstake lottery tickets on *Yom*

Kippur (Day of Atonement), because you were sure the police wouldn't raid it. At that time, it was illegal to sell those lottery tickets in Britain. On the other side, there was an adjoining room which was especially for the overflow crowd at services, and that room also became the meeting place of the Young Zionist Movement.

Notting Hill Synagogue, August 2013, now a fitness and wellbeing centre.

In 1930, David and some of his teenage friends started a Young Zionist Society, though girls were initially excluded because he and his friends thought they were too frivolous for such a serious undertaking! Around 1934, David merged his interests with *Habonim* (a Zionist youth movement founded in 1929), and became the leader of West London *Habonim*, helping to organise functions for affiliated groups.

A strong influence on him at this time was *The Ethics of the Fathers*, a compilation of ethical and moral maxims of the rabbis from approximately 200BCE–200CE. This work, in David's mind, epitomised the religious humanism of Judaism which he embraced for the rest of his life. He was also much impressed by the personality and contribution to Anglo-Jewish life of Chief Rabbi Joseph Hertz (1872–1946), who was also a strong supporter of Zionism.

***

Bessie Tabor's shop in Notting Hill, 1920s most probably.

Education was highly valued in the Tabor family, but the two eldest children, Simon and Bessie, had to help support the family: Simon went into the family business with his father at the age of fourteen, which eventually he took over and ran until he retired. Simon was a self-educated intellectual, widely read, fluent in several languages and with a good knowledge of Hebrew.

His sister, Bessie, was an attractive, outward-going woman, and after attending the Jewish Free School, she took a secretarial course and was offered a job in an office at the age of sixteen. When Chaskel saw the letter from the firm, he tore it up and told her that her job was to help in bringing up the children. After the siblings had grown up, her parents helped her to open a hat shop, but she was not a businesswoman, and the shop was not a success.

It was only in her late twenties that Bessie married and was able to leave home. Her husband, Hymie Lush, had served with distinction in the Royal Army Medical Corps during the First World War. In civilian life he made a living as a tailor, and selling women's coats.

Their son, David Lush, remembered the modest circumstances in which his parents lived in the 1930s, and his father's commitment to charitable causes, describing him as the family's "poor philanthropist."

The third child, Alfred, studied accountancy and in due course, opened his own practice, Alfred Tabor and Company, though once he left home, he did not have a lot of contact with his siblings. The two older brothers fell out at an early stage; no one knows why, but they were not on speaking terms for the rest of their lives.

As the economic circumstances of the family improved, the four younger children, all born in London, were able to gain a secondary education, even though most Jewish children in the inter-war years left school at fourteen. Unlike her older sister, Bessie, Esther had a good secondary school education and trained as a dispenser in a pharmacy. After the Second World War, she retrained as a primary school teacher, and eventually, became head of biology at John Kelly School in north-west London. Her brother, John, trained as an electrical engineer, and the youngest sibling, Henry, became a physicist. Both John and Henry emigrated to Israel after the Second World War; their stories are told below in Chapter 13.

***

Portobello Road School, 1923-24.

My father, David, the sixth of the siblings, attended the Portobello Road School from the age of five. As a small child, he collected magnifying glasses and liked making models of things that worked, such as a cardboard house with a door that opened. He believed that this early predilection for the simple and practical influenced his approach to scientific research in later life. He also recalled on one occasion hiding in the basement at home because there was an alert that German Zeppelins were going to bomb London; he couldn't have been more than five at the time.

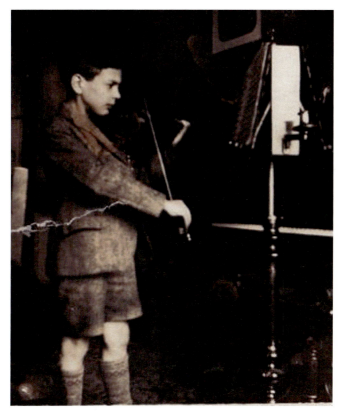

David practising the violin, aged 7 or 8, c. 1920.

Despite their very limited means, his parents spared no effort in bettering the education of their children and Rivka made sure that they all had music lessons. David's brother, Henry, remembered that even if there wasn't enough money to buy groceries or to pay the wages of Chaskel's employees at the end of the week, money was always found for music lessons. David had violin lessons with Sascha Lasserson, formerly of the Imperial Conservatory in St. Petersburg, who lived in a modest flat nearby in Ladbrook Grove. Lasserson had studied with Leopold Auer at the Conservatory; he was a brilliant violinist and an outstanding teacher. After a while, he told David's parents that their son was not destined to be a violinist and that it was not worth continuing with the lessons. Rivka enjoyed the visits to Mr Lasserson, as it was a rare opportunity for her to converse with a native Russian speaker, but, even so, the lessons came to an end. The eldest brother, Simon, was an accomplished amateur clarinetist, and for a number of years, he played in a jazz band.

At the age of eleven, David gained a place at the Regents Street Polytechnic, where his older brother John was already a student, but two years later, David was struck down with osteomyelitis. This resulted in his having to spend almost a year in hospital, and in an age before antibiotics, he was lucky to survive. His parents visited him every day. Major surgery saved his leg but resulted in arresting its growth with the consequence that, as he continued to grow, one leg ended up slightly shorter than the other. This necessitated the use of a surgical boot and walking stick for the rest of his life.

In 1985, David wrote an account of his time in hospital:

A Taste of Honey

During the years approaching my *Bar-Mitzvah*, I became very pious, and this phase extended well beyond my adolescence. It left its mark on me for the rest of my life. In my fourteenth year, I contracted a severe bone disease in my left leg at a time when antibiotics were unknown. I have since learned that the mortality rate, at that period, was over thirty per cent. My G.P. was a Catholic and recommended a small semi-private hospital run by nuns about ten miles away from our home where, he assured my parents, I would be well looked after and where the consultant staff was first-rate. I remember that soon after I arrived, I was examined by a giant of a man in company with the resident house doctor. I heard him say, "There is only one diagnosis – get his father over at once to sign for an operation." They operated that very afternoon.

Young boys are only aware of pain, of headaches, of fevers, not of illness as such, but I think that at that time, I must have been perilously ill. One of the ward-maids, a cheerful Irish lass with the unremarkable name of Mary, told me a couple of months later that she was sure I would never survive. The nursing staff must have had similar worries because they spoke to my parents about my not eating the food given me. I must have been one of the first Jewish patients they had, and they could not quite make it out though they knew that Jews did not eat pig. They also spoke to the visiting rabbi and must have convinced him of the urgency of the situation. He came and spoke to me and explained that the saving of human life is a greater religious duty (*mitzvah*) than observing the dietary laws – I was to eat everything.

I do not remember the whole list of forbidden foods that I consumed. There remains in my memory, only my encounters with bacon, served on several mornings a week for breakfast. At first, I approached it with repugnance, then with resignation and very soon, with relish. I really enjoyed it. I still recall, sixty years after the event, an embarrassing occasion when the kitchen had not sent enough rashers to go round. The serving nurse apologised and said she thought I should be the one to go without since "in any case, you are not supposed to eat it." I was indignant and I believe another portion was finally ordered from the kitchen. I do not know if the bacon saved my life but in fact, I survived, and in my childish piety, persuaded myself that I was performing a religious duty by eating everything …

I left the hospital after nearly ten months with a left leg that was shorter than the other, weaker and would always be at risk. But I was young and vigorous, and it seemed the most natural thing in the world to wear a surgical boot and to walk with a stick. Nowadays, when I watch professional athletes run the mile in four minutes, engage in ski-ing at supersonic speeds, climb mountains, and perform gymnastics, I am lost in wonder at the excellence that the human body can achieve. But I am not really envious. For me, simply to be able to walk around the block is miracle enough. Yet I would be less honest if I did not confess that, if I had the choice, I would rather have two sound legs than rabbinic permission (*hechsher*), at a time of mortal illness, to eat bacon.

I have never touched the stuff since.

***

After matriculation, David was awarded a scholarship to study physics at Imperial College. He really wanted to study medicine, but the headmaster saw David's future as that of a brilliant academic. He thought that physics was a purer or more intellectual subject than medicine, and he persuaded David to study physics. He enjoyed the physics course and came top of his year on graduation in 1936 and started to study for a PhD under the supervision of the Nobel Laureate, G.C. Thompson, on some problems in electron diffraction. When he expressed a desire to pursue further studies in mathematics, Thompson discouraged him from doing so. David described this as one of the worst pieces of academic advice he ever received.

David was very politically aware, and his time at Imperial College coincided with Hitler coming to power in 1933. German Jews were soon expelled from the professions, the civil service and universities, and David acted as a steward at a unique public meeting at the Royal Albert Hall in 1933, at which Albert Einstein made a powerful and memorable plea for those forced to flee from Hitler's rule.

***

This section of the chapter describes the wider family network that the Notting Hill Tabors were part of; relatives who were also immigrants, or the first-generation to be born in Britain. Like my father's family, they were poor, hard-working (in most cases), and often with limited opportunities for higher or further education in the period before and after the First World War. The memories I have drawn on convey stories of poverty, hardship and thwarted aspirations.

The women played a crucial role in maintaining these family relationships. Thus, while Chaskel had virtually no contact with his two brothers after moving to Notting Hill, Rivka remained in touch with her two sisters-in-law, Sonia and Millie, and she was very supportive of them.

Sonia had been married to Chaskel's brother, Alter, who had left her, and she had had to bring up her family single-handed. Sonia seemed to thrive on adversity, and David's eldest sister, Bessie Lush, remembered her vividly:

> She used to stand with one foot on the cradle, rocking the cradle and reading an English book. She wouldn't waste any time ... In those days in the East End [before the First World War], everybody used to have a barrow and they started making blouses ... and

from those blouses arose the business that they had. Bessie Feldman [Sonia's eldest married daughter] used to sew the blouses; Tabby [Sonia's second son] used to go out and travel with them. That is how they lived. But she gave the younger children a very good education … Aunty Sonia was strong … She had to learn and learn … They didn't have pennies for the meter, [so] she used to read by candlelight … I thought my mother was, you know, a cut above, but Aunty Sonia was wonderful …

My father, David, recalled his Aunt Sonia as a well-educated, strong-willed woman who had an opinion on all matters great and small, and with a thirst for knowledge. David remembered a visit from her in the 1950s, with her eldest daughter, Bessie (Feldman):

Sonia and her daughter made a tempestuous couple because they were both identical in temperament. It used to be a standard joke that they would have a discussion as to whether King George V slept with his beard above the sheet or under the sheet. They could discuss this all evening with tremendous gusto and enthusiasm and fire. I think they were great fun, but they must have exhausted one another; [yet] they seemed to thrive on it.

One of Sonia's sons affected an exaggerated English heritage and styled himself as Denis Charques. He became a successful literary critic and minor author, writing a well-regarded history of Russia and a book about England called *In This Other Eden*, which reflected his admiration for all things English. Denis Charques worked for many years on the *Times* as a writer of special articles, an assistant drama critic, and as a reviewer of fiction for the *Times Literary Supplement*. He turned himself into an English literary gentleman, and in later years, denied his Jewish origins.

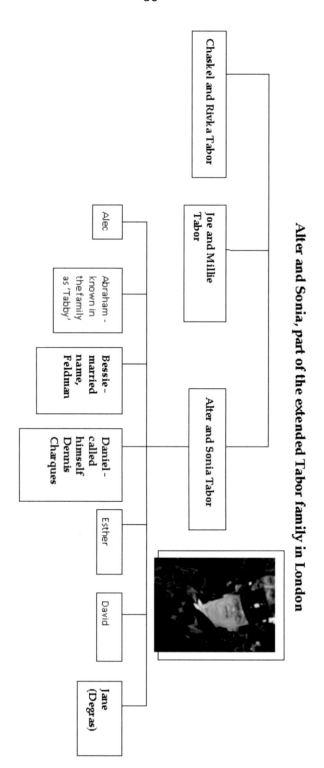

Alter and Sonia, part of the extended Tabor family in London

His younger sister, Jane Degras, was a specialist in modern Russian history, and as a young woman, worked in Moscow for three years at the Marx-Engels Institute. She became completely disillusioned with Communism as a result, and later, from 1942, worked at the Royal Institute of International Affairs at Chatham House in London. She collaborated with E. H. Carr on his monumental *History of the Bolshevik Revolution*, as well as translating and editing Soviet policy documents from 1917 to the early 1940s, and after her retirement, she was one of the editors of *The Journal of Contemporary History*. I never met Jane Degras; she must have been a remarkable woman.

Other members of the extended family did not have the same opportunities as Sonia's younger children. For example, David's cousin, Jack (one of the sons of his uncle, Joe Tabor), married a very artistic woman, Min Wachter. Her story says much about the limited choices open to Jewish women from working-class backgrounds between the two World Wars.

At the age of thirteen, Min had been awarded a scholarship to study at St Martin's School of Art, but her father objected to it, as she remembered when I interviewed her in 2012. "He couldn't bear it. He said, 'How can a Yiddisher girl study art?'"

After she had studied for about eighteen months, her father took her out of art school and put her in his clothing workshop, and she had to become a pattern cutter. Reflecting on those years, Min said, "It is only in recent years that I've forgiven him. I realised that he didn't understand … What did they [men] know about artists then? They knew nothing about it."

Though the 1930s saw a gradual improvement in living standards after the Great Depression, it was also the period of the rise of Fascism on the Continent and in Britain. Min remembered the fascist marches in the East End in the 1930s, and described the Battle of Cable Street in 1936, when she saw thousands of people (Jews and non-Jews) at the corner of Commercial Road and Whitechapel, determined to stop the fascists marching through the East End.

Min met her husband, Jack Tabor, through a mutual friend at a musical event, and they were engaged for five years. The declaration of war in 1939 was the jolt that made them get married. She commented, "I wouldn't have been married till today if it wasn't for the war. Everybody got married then."

Jack and Min Tabor as a young couple.

Joe Tabor with the twins, Jack (next to Joe) and Harry, and an unknown family friend, c. 1930.

Jack wasn't called up on health grounds, but joined the Land Army, and Min was evacuated to Derbyshire, where her eldest child was born.

Min had fond, though rather sad memories of her father-in-law, Joe, Chaskel's younger brother:

> He was lovely, really lovely. I got on well [with him] … He was a bright, clever man, but he didn't have any ambition or *joie de vivre*. So consequently, they were always on the poverty line, and that's why my husband was so restricted … it did something to him. There was no money, ever. I don't know how his wife, Millie, managed … She would take a chicken liver and make a meal out of it, she was so careful. She used to love to bring it round to me as a gift, like before *Shabbos* [Sabbath]. She was so proud of being able to make a thing like that into a meal …

Min Tabor at age 92, with her daughter, Jane.

Min Tabor – part of the extended Tabor family in London

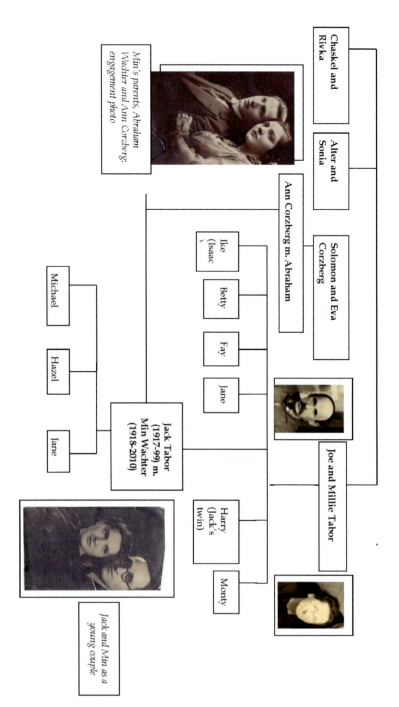

Min's parents, Abraham Wachter and Ann Corzberg: engagement photo

Jack and Min as a young couple

In later life, Min attended evening art classes, and at the age of forty-five (after raising a family), she went back to St Martin's for half a day a week. She became a successful amateur artist, depicting scenes of traditional Jewish life, as well as portraits and landscapes. She exhibited her work at a number of galleries and other venues, including the Royal Festival Hall.

These brief accounts reflect the varieties of Jewish working-class experiences within one family, as remembered by the first generation born in Britain. The immigrant generation had what was often a desperate struggle to make a living. Their children (usually the boys), if they were fortunate to have parental support and educational opportunities, were eventually able to flourish and to transform their lives. In the process, they integrated into the wider British society.

***

Rivka thought that she didn't have any family in England, but she did discover quite by chance that she had a distant relative in London, as her eldest daughter, Bessie (Lush), recalled:

> In the East End in those days [before the First World War], there used to be corset makers, and you used to go and be fitted for a corset, and you would wait there until the corsetière fitted you. [In the waiting room] they had photograph albums on the table, not magazines. My mother was looking through [an album] and she saw a photo of a man there … and Mrs Molinsky was there too, though she didn't know her, and my mother said, "I think that's an uncle of mine," and Mrs Molinsky said, "That's my father." And that is how they found out that they were related. It was a coincidence that they were in the waiting room at the same time …

Mrs Molinsky's father and Rivka's father were half-brothers, because Hirsch Weinstein (Rivka's paternal grandfather) had been married twice. After this unexpected meeting, a very friendly relationship was established between the two families. Mr Molinsky made walking-sticks and umbrella handles and ran a barber's shop in Commercial Road. He also ran a bookie's business from his barber's shop, which was illegal at that time. Bessie remembered him as a very good-looking man with the 'gift of the gab'.

The family story was that when Chaskel applied for naturalisation, it went through smoothly, while Mr Molinsky's took rather longer. When an official from the Home Office came to interview Mr Molinsky at work, as part of the naturalisation process, he was invited into Mr Molinsky's office at the back of the shop, where he saw half a dozen telephones. It was apparent that his business wasn't exactly legal, and his naturalisation took several more years to come through. David remembered being sent to Mr Molinsky to borrow money so that his father could pay his employees at the end of the week.

***

The family name in Russia was Taborisky and when they arrived in England the 'o' got lost and became Tabrisky. When Chaskel's and Rivka's second son, Abraham (Alfred) Tabrisky, tried to get a job in an accounting firm or an insurance company, all his applications were turned down. A friend told him it was due to his name; he changed it by deed poll to Alfred Tabor, and his next job application was successful. It was this experience that prompted Chaskel to change the name for the whole family. The deed poll is dated the thirty-first of August 1927, and in it, he is identified as 'Charles Tabrisky a Naturalised British Subject', who is going to adopt, henceforth, the surname of 'Tabor'. At an early stage, he had adopted the first name, Charles, perhaps because it sounded closest to Chaskel. In this context, Henry Tabor (Chaskel's youngest son) remembered his father telling him of a quarrel he once had with a local supplier, who called him "a bloody foreigner" who should go back to his own country.

Chaskel replied, "Shut up! You are an Englishman by accident; I am one by qualification!"

***

There was already a tendency before the First World War for the immigrants to move out of east London to the north parts of the city, and in the 1930s, there a was considerable spread of the Jewish population to suburban areas in north-west London. This movement was made possible by the development of public transport, the improvement in family incomes, and the boom in private house building in the middle and late 1930s. A new house with a garden, outside the congested inner areas of the city, was now available on relatively easy terms.

The Tabor family was able to take advantage of these changes, and move to north-west London (NW2), as the older siblings were already married and had left home. The new house was registered in John's name, because as an employed engineer, it was easier to get a mortgage, though all the family chipped in. The house had a front and back garden, which Chaskel loved. He planted fruit trees and created metal garden ornaments in the shape of elegant cranes.

By this stage, the Tabor children had all become British Jews as a result of their education, qualifications and occupations, and how they spoke and dressed. Though very aware of their Jewishness, they were in many respects similar to their non-Jewish contemporaries. For my father, David, his commitment to political Zionism became a core expression of his Jewish identity. In the next chapter, I will explore what this commitment meant for David in the context of the rise of Nazism and the resurgence of anti-Semitism.

Chapter 3

A Rarity in Cambridge

The late 1930s in Britain were dominated by the growing threat from Nazi Germany, the Spanish Civil War, the Munich crisis, and the eventual declaration of war in September 1939. It was against this backdrop of crisis and international tension that David left home in Notting Hill and moved to Cambridge in 1936 to complete his PhD in Physics. David's memories of Cambridge around this time were vivid, and his sense of place comes across clearly in his diaries, articles and interviews. At the same time, he was very politically engaged, as this chapter describes.

How unusual was it in the 1930s for a Jew from a working-class immigrant family to do research at Cambridge, and how did David adapt to this new environment? How did it affect his relationships with family and friends in London?

In the late 1930s, a relatively small proportion of the British population attended university. In general, many or most of those attending were from wealthy backgrounds, though there were more scholarships and grants available in the inter-war years than had existed before 1914. Though Jews were less than one per cent of the population as a whole, they constituted about two per cent of the student population at Oxford and Cambridge, and a higher proportion at some provincial universities, such as Manchester or Leeds.

Nationally, postgraduates like David were a rarity, and he was one of only two students in his year at Imperial College to receive a grant for scientific research in 1936. Within the Jewish community of Notting Hill, he was most probably unique, even though some of his peers had very successful careers in other fields. I remember David telling me of an occasion in the mid-1960s when he went into Mappin and Webb's, near Piccadilly Circus in central London, to have a watch repaired. The man serving him was an elderly Jew who recognised David's name and asked if he was the David Tabor who had gone to Cambridge University in the 1930s to do research. It transpired that the man was originally from Notting Hill, and David's achievement was remembered with pride by members of his community, even thirty years later.

In 1936–37, there were one hundred and twenty-five Jewish students (undergraduates) at Cambridge, out of a total student population of just over six thousand. Of the Jewish students, ninety-six were 'native born' (British) and of these, fifty-six were 'assisted', in other words, receiving some form of grant. The majority of overseas Jewish students were from Germany, from families that had the financial resources to support them. Though medicine was the most popular subject among Jewish students nationally, at Cambridge, a range of arts subjects, such as economics, history, English, and law were also popular. In practice, fifty to sixty of the Jewish students at Cambridge at this time, identified with the Jewish life of the university, and they provided the social circle in which David moved, through participation in synagogue services and the membership of different Jewish or Zionist groups.[8]

David's experience was markedly different from non-Jewish working-class students at Oxford and Cambridge between the wars, and also in the years immediately after the Second World War. Many autobiographical accounts describe feelings of extreme loneliness, of being a fish out of water socially, and being embarrassed by or alienated from one's working-class roots.

In contrast to these accounts of 'not fitting in', David was confident intellectually, and proud of being the non-conflictive product of his Jewish heritage and English education. Socially, he inhabited what one could describe as a Jewish bubble, though this is not to say that he was, in some sense, sealed off from the rest of the university. His interest in people and his intellectual curiosity meant that this never happened, but he had more in common with his Jewish contemporaries than with other students, particularly as he was heavily involved in the Zionist youth movement. The majority of Jewish students at Cambridge (and Oxford) at this time, came from more bourgeois backgrounds than David, with family members already established in the professions or business. As my brother Michael put it, their families had arrived on the earlier boats.

***

The Jewish community in Britain had undergone huge changes in the previous sixty years. In 1880, the Jewish population of Great

Britain was approximately sixty thousand, centred on the major cities. The oldest Jewish families in England were Sephardim, that is of Spanish and Portuguese origin, who came to Britain via Holland in the late seventeenth century. They were followed in the eighteenth and early nineteenth centuries by Jews of Dutch or German origin, mainly Ashkenazim, and many achieved prominence in business, banking and, in the second half of the nineteenth century, in politics and the professions.

These grandees formed a closely-knit group which Chaim Bermant has called 'the Cousinhood', 'a compact union of exclusive brethren with blood and money flowing in a small circle'.[9] They represented the Anglo-Jewish community to the wider society through the Board of Deputies of British Jews, and the aristocratic Anglo-Jewish Association, which emphasised the loyalty of its members to the British Empire. They regarded Zionism as not only irrelevant, but also harmful, because they believed (to quote Walter Lacqueur, in *A History of Zionism*), '… that it jeopardised the legal rights won by Jews over many decades, and that Jewish patriotism was incompatible with their loyalties as British subjects.'[10]

Lucien Wolf, the President of the Anglo-Jewish Association before the First World War, was representative of this view when he described Zionism as a form of 'treason'. He argued that there was no specifically 'Jewish interest' that distinguished British Jews from the rest of the King's subjects. Zionism would only serve to provoke anti-Semitism, and it was doomed to failure. However, the influx of approximately one hundred and fifty thousand working-class, predominantly Yiddish-speaking Jewish immigrants from Eastern Europe between 1881 and 1914 totally changed the composition of Anglo-Jewry. This relatively large influx of Jews contributed to an increase in anti-Semitism before and after the First World War, which was often expressed in terms of 'anti-alien' legislation. This was not only reflected in curbs on immigration but also (for example) in limiting access to educational scholarships or discrimination in the allocation of housing by the London County Council (LCC) in the 1920s.

When David went to university in the 1930s, the Jewish population of Britain was over three hundred thousand, and the main ideological divide in the community then was between pro- and anti-Zionists; a divide which was more significant than any differences between orthodox and reform Jews. The more established families felt that their position as loyal Britons had been threatened by the Balfour Declaration of 1917, which had supported the establishment of a National Home for the Jewish people in Palestine, though it was not clear what this meant, in practice. Since Anglo-Jewish grandees dominated the Board of Deputies until the mid-1930s, they promoted a non- or anti-Zionist line. In spite of this, by the late 1920s, most of the other leading Jewish communal organisations had adopted, to a greater or lesser extent, a pro-Zionist position. This often consisted of little more than social events or fund-raising to support Jewish settlements in Palestine, rather than agitating for a Jewish Homeland, which would have raised the spectre of dual loyalties.

The Zionist movement grew in appeal in the late 1920s and 1930s and attracted a younger generation of Jews. The more militant forms of political Zionism enabled young Jews like David to express their Jewish identity in activist rather than the apologetic terms associated with the Board of Deputies or the Anglo-Jewish Association. Political Zionism regarded its goal as the creation of a national home for the Jewish people, preferably in Palestine. Jewish youth movements, in particular *Habonim*, provided a range of common activities linked to this aim, such as discussions, camps, sports meetings and so on, through which a sense of community was developed.

The rise of the British Union of Fascists in the 1930s, and Hitler's leadership of Germany from 1933, soon changed the nature of the debate about Zionism within Anglo-Jewry. As the situation of Jews in Germany became dire, the need to find a refuge for Jews from the Continent became more pressing, even though the Board of Deputies was initially reluctant to confront the dangers of fascism head-on. In the East End of London in the 1930s, the Communist Party was seen as being the one organisation that was prepared to oppose Mosley and the Blackshirts directly, particularly when contrasted with what was widely perceived as the ineffective response of the Board of Deputies. It was only in the late 1930s, when the composition and leadership of the Board of Deputies changed, that it took a more assertive role in opposing British fascism and supporting Zionist aspirations.

***

After London, Cambridge appeared to David 'like a dream city'; he noted that 'there was a sense of elegant solidity, antiquity and beauty, particularly in those parts near Gonville and Caius College, to which I was affiliated'. In his first two weeks in October 1936, he walked everywhere. The new university library had recently been opened by King George V, and undergraduates were still tittering over the royal reference to 'this magnificent erection', but it made an outstanding impression on David. It was a turbulent time politically, and Cambridge students were very much involved in the Spanish struggle for democracy against Franco's fascist army. David recalled a passionate public meeting in 1936 on this issue in the Corn Exchange, and some students, such as the poet John Cornford, volunteered and died in the International Brigade.

David started a diary during 1937, and kept it, with some gaps, until 1943. I retrieved his diaries from a dustbin in the nineteen-nineties when my parents were downsizing. Many of David's diary entries convey the excitement and energy of his postgraduate years in Cambridge. The opening page was written on 14 January 1937, in which David describes why he had decided to keep a diary:

> Today begins a new adventure and a new experience. I had intended keeping a diary as soon as I came up to Cambridge last October, but an inherent lethargy and a latent fear of writing foolish thoughts … somehow prevented me … At the same time, my enforced stay in hospital [for a minor operation] seemed the culmination of unhappy events, and the appointment I received simultaneously for this position in Cambridge seemed a heaven-sent opportunity … The new surroundings pleased me very much, and I found the general atmosphere conducive to study. For the first time for nearly two years, I found it possible to sit down of an evening and do three or four hours of solid work – and enjoy it, too.

At that time, there was only a handful of Jewish residents living in the city, and a small number of Jewish academics, such as Charles Fox (an expert on child education), and the economist Richard Kahn, later Lord Kahn. But the two most important figures in life of the small Cambridge Hebrew Congregation were

Herbert Loewe and Harry Dagut, as David remembered many years later:

> Loewe was the reader in Rabbinics, a saintly rather unworldly man, punctilious in his observance of orthodox practice – he was the grandson of Moses Montefiore's private secretary – but very liberal in outlook ... [He] combined orthodoxy and liberalism with an opposition to political as distinct from cultural Zionism, [and] occupied a unique place in the spectrum of Cambridge Jewish opinion of the time.
>
> Harry Dagut (the son of a Manchester rabbi) was Master of the Jewish [Hillel] House at the Perse School. His wife May was a sister of Leon and Maurice Simon. On Saturday mornings, if the weather was fine, Dagut and his boys would traipse from Glebe Road into the centre of Cambridge for the morning service ...[11]

Dagut and his wife May were very hospitable, and David felt great respect for them both. As an older couple, they were, in some respects, like substitute parents.

***

There was no synagogue when David went up to Cambridge, but this changed in April 1937, when David attended a function in Thompson's Lane, where the foundation stone of the new synagogue was laid by Sir Robert Waley-Cohen. Waley-Cohen was a pillar of the Anglo-Jewish establishment, a highly successful businessman, and a generous supporter of Jewish causes. Before the stone-laying, a lunch was held at the Red Lion Hotel, at which Waley-Cohen gave a speech about the spiritual values of Judaism and the greatness of its traditions.

The building of the new synagogue proceeded rapidly, and in October 1937, David attended the formal opening by Mr Lionel de Rothschild. Chief Rabbi Hertz gave a very moving address in which he emphasised the role of the synagogue as a place of study. The vice-chancellor of the university attended, and distinguished members of the Anglo-Jewish community (former Cambridge men) were also present. Students filled those seats unoccupied by more illustrious personalities. The new synagogue provided the

Cambridge Hebrew Congregation, residents and students alike, with a centre, both for services and social events.

David remembered:

> The services on Saturdays were attended by all – orthodox, reform and traditional – wearing their gowns and squares as well as their *tallitot* [prayer shawls]. The service began at ten thirty … and finished before noon, reputedly so that students could attend their twelve o'clock lectures. Saturday lectures were very common in those hardworking days.

***

The shared commitment to political Zionism underpinned David's close friendship at Cambridge with Aubrey (Abba) Eban (1915–2002), later Foreign Minister and Deputy Prime Minister of Israel. Eban had a brilliant mind and was reputed to have obtained the highest marks ever awarded in the Hebrew Tripos.

David recalled their friendship many years later:

> We knew one another from the Young Zionist movement [in London] and he encouraged me to read modern Hebrew literature … Whenever the Government published an important paper on the future of Palestine and/or Zionism, public discussion would be held in Cambridge at which Eban would be the star speaker and the defender of Zionist interests. He was already considered as a serious thinker in British Zionism …

At about this time, David recorded meeting Eban's parents in Cambridge with Mrs Blanche Dugdale (1880–1948), the niece of Arthur Balfour, and a convinced Zionist. After attending her talk on Zionism, David wrote in his diary (2 May 1937):

> What a woman – to know our Jews as well and yet to be such a philosemite. Her general treatment was refreshingly interesting although her one conclusion that we should join the O.T.C. [Officer Training Corps] so as to be prepared to defend Palestine was the one thing on which we agreed to oppose her. The discussion was extremely good … All told, one of the most successful meetings we have had.

Eban's mother worked in the Zionist Office in London, where she met the leading Zionists of the day, and she had got to know Mrs Dugdale, who worked in the Political Department. Their boss, and the dominant figure in the Zionist Movement between the wars was Chaim Weizmann (1874–1952), later to become the first President of Israel. Weizmann, originally born in Motal, near Pinsk (in present-day Belarus), qualified as a chemist, and came to Britain in 1904 to take up the post of senior lecturer in chemistry at Manchester University. He was an enthusiastic Zionist, and in 1917, he became President of the British Zionist Federation; he played a crucial role in persuading the British government to issue the Balfour Declaration. In 1920, he assumed the leadership of the World Zionist Movement, a position he held for most of the inter-war period. Weizmann was based in London, and Eban has described the impact of his personality:

> One of his devices for promoting a Jewish state was to behave as if it already existed ... all his mannerisms, his air of tranquil superiority and social ease ... were those of a chief of state engaged in a permanent summit conference. He addressed foreign statesmen as though his status were equal to their own. They and he knew that this was not strictly true, but something in his bearing and in their own historic imagination forbade them to break the spell. With Jewish audiences, he was at his best when addressing recent immigrants in Yiddish, which he commanded to the full scope of its irony, pathos and self-deprecation.[12]

David heard Weizmann speak on a number of occasions, and when I interviewed him in 1985, he remembered the way Weizmann could establish a rapport with his audience:

> Weizmann had tremendous charisma and personality; he was extremely impressive. I heard him speak on a couple of occasions. On one of them, he talked [in Yiddish] ... about the problems he had as head of the Jewish Agency, trying to allocate the funds [in Palestine], which were very limited, for a variety of purposes ... In a typical Weizmann way, he explained the difficulties in a rather humorous but meaningful way ... There was not enough money to go around, and he had to decide between one and another. He told the story about his grandmother (so-called), who had two sons. One of the sons made his living by selling fur coats, and the other one made his living by selling ice cream. The grandmother, being

a very pious lady, was very anxious that both her sons should prosper. Every night when she went to bed, she used to pray to God that he should send 'a warm frost', so they could both make a living.

The World Zionist Movement was not a monolithic organisation, and it was often riven by ideological differences, and the conflicts between strong personalities, both from the *yishuv* (the Jewish community in Palestine), and the different Zionist organisations across the world. Weizmann advocated a gradualist approach to realising the goal of a Jewish state, by working closely with the British government, particularly as Palestine was administered under the British mandate. He represented what might be termed the 'General Zionist' position, a sort of middle ground between left- and right-wing currents, but without any real ideological cohesion. The majority of young Zionists in Britain followed the 'Weizmann line' of moderation and co-operation with the British authorities.

***

Recurrent violence in Palestine in the late 1920s and 1930s between Jews and Arabs was, in part, triggered by the increase in Jewish immigration from Europe. Palestinian Arabs felt threatened by what they perceived as the 'taking over' of Palestine by the new arrivals. After the Arab revolt in 1936, the British government commissioned what became known as the Peel Report, to examine the situation in Palestine and to come up with recommendations. The report, published in July 1937, was a thorough examination of the issues, and recommended the partition of Palestine between Jews and Arabs.

The recommendations of the Peel Report were strongly opposed by Arab representatives, and they were subsequently rejected by the British Government in 1938. The report was widely discussed by David and his friends, and in particular, with Aubrey Eban, whose powers of analysis David admired. He greatly valued Eban's friendship, and after they had met up during the Long Vacation, he wrote in his diary (22 July 1937):

> It was like a breath of fresh air having him near again: like coming back from the wilderness into touch with civilization ... He is clearheaded, lucid, brilliant, possessed of a very rich humour (which I so envy) and above all, he remains unconceited. He has a great future ahead of him ...

The ideological differences between young Zionists like David on the one hand, and the members of the Anglo-Jewish establishment who emphasised their loyalty to Britain and the Empire on the other, now seem rather remote. Yet for David and his contemporaries, how they negotiated their sense of 'Jewishness' and 'Englishness' could not be separated from their engagement with the political issues of the day, in particular, the future of Palestine and the fate of European Jewry. In this context, David remembered one friend in particular:

> One of my student contemporaries was taking his Tripos in Chemistry. His name was John [...]. His family had been living in England for so many generations that he used to say that he was more British than King George V. He was a reserved, quiet man, but sometime in 1937 or 1938, he came to me and said [that] he wanted to go and settle in Palestine. He felt he wanted to revert and become a fully Jewish Jew. He asked me to show him how to lay *tefillin* [phylacteries] and he began learning modern basic Hebrew.
>
> His family could not understand what had happened. His father had been a member of the League of British Jews which had established itself during World War I in order to fight against the issuance of the Balfour Declaration in 1917. But John could not be deflected. I met his parents in Cambridge shortly before he left for Palestine, I think in mid-1939. They were gentle, kind people completely mystified and a little sad. To some extent, I shared their anguish and their sense of wonder. But John could only move forward. Eventually, he became a Professor in the Physical Chemistry Department of the Hebrew University and in this sense, was completely fulfilled.[13]

David did not keep a diary during 1938; it was the year when he completed and submitted his PhD thesis on areas of contact between surfaces. He then had his first job at the Britannia Laboratories in East Road in Cambridge, a small laboratory started by David's PhD supervisor, Philip Bowden, specialising in the study of wear and lubrication.

By this stage, David had moved into digs in Collier Road, where Mrs Searle was his landlady. Her son was a young student studying at art school in Cambridge, and he became famous as the cartoonist Ronald Searle. Mrs Searle became very pro-Jewish and pro-Zionist, and David remembered receiving a note after he had left Cambridge in 1940, from someone who recorded that he came to Cambridge on a visit. He thought he'd call on David, didn't find him in and received a lecture from Mrs Searle on the virtues of Zionism.

***

The situation of Jews in Germany deteriorated markedly in 1938. It was an increasingly desperate situation since the Jews of central and Eastern Europe were also under pressure to leave their countries of origin but had nowhere to turn. In response to this situation, President Roosevelt had called the Evian Conference in July 1938 to discuss the plight of Jewish refugees, and representatives of thirty-two governments attended. The British government insisted that Palestine should not be discussed. One delegate after another reported, some with expressions of regret, that there was no territory in their country suitable for Jewish settlers. In reality, the western democracies were afflicted by a paralysis of will in dealing with Hitler and his anti-Jewish policies.

To quote Laqueur:

> In a more tolerant age, nations and governments had been willing to extend help to the homeless stranger. Britain had taken in one hundred and twenty thousand French Protestants in 1685 after the revocation of the Edict of Nantes. By 1939, in contrast, Britain had given entry permits to barely nineteen thousand Jewish refugees from the Continent. It could be argued that the country was no longer capable of absorbing immigrants on a massive scale, but what of the less densely populated countries overseas? 'Give me your tired, your poor, your huddled masses, yearning to be free'; but since Emma Lazarus' poem had been inscribed on the Statue of Liberty attitudes had changed. The United States in 1935 accepted 6,252 immigrants ...[14]

What these statistics do not convey are the heart-breaking stories of the individuals and families concerned. I cite one example. Rosa Weinstein is married to my American cousin Harris, a grandson of one of Rivka's older brothers, Moshe Shir, who had emigrated to the USA at the end of the nineteenth century. Rosa was born in Vienna, where her parents ran a grocery shop. They were in Vienna during the *Anschluss* in March 1938, when Austria became part of Germany, to scenes of delirious rejoicing by most of the populace.

After the *Anschluss,* Rosa's parents were put out of business, and they were desperate to leave. They were destitute, and could only get food from a soup kitchen, though they were helped by non-Jewish friends who brought them food and gave them some of their rations. Rosa and her parents were only able to leave Austria after war broke out because an uncle in America had nominated them for three visas.

As Rosa remembered, when I interviewed her in 1991:

> We were one of the very few. Terribly lucky. And it was also a terribly difficult decision for the uncle in Taunton [USA] to make – which member of the family he should sponsor for visas, because he could bring only one family out of Europe. How do you choose? … And so, because my father and mother were first cousins, he decided that this would be saving the greatest remnant of the family at once, so he sent the three visas to us and that is how we escaped. Our visas arrived on the same day that we received a deportation notice.
>
> The Holocaust Museum's papers show that my uncle obtained the $429 for our tickets to America through a private act of charity by a well-known philanthropist, Dewey Stone. Stone was a great man – an unsung hero – who used his money and his connections to save Jews and to provide a homeland in Israel for thousands of Holocaust survivors … After the war, we learned that the rest of the family had been murdered in Treblinka and Auschwitz.

Other avenues for Jewish emigration were also being closed, and there was a steady reduction in the number of permits issued to refugees seeking to emigrate to Palestine, from 1935 onwards. The reasons were political, not economic – in fact Jewish immigration had stimulated economic development in the 1930s in Palestine. The pressure from Arab governments made itself felt, and in the White Paper of 1939, in effect, the government tore up the Balfour Declaration, limiting Jewish immigration to seventy-five thousand over the next five years. After that, it would stop altogether (unless the Palestinian Arabs gave their permission), and an Arab state would be created in Palestine.

Anglo-Jewish notables were ambivalent about allowing Britain to become a haven for Jewish refugees from Germany and Austria. To some extent, they shared the view of government officials and ministers that this would only fuel anti-Semitism and create a British 'Jewish problem'. Those refugees who were admitted were looked after by a host of refugee organisations and supported with funds raised by British Jewry. They were dispersed to different parts of the country, to avoid concentrations of 'foreign' Jews in large cities.

Up until November 1938, approximately eleven thousand refugees had been admitted, but after *Kristallnacht* (on 9/10 November) and the Nazi take-over of Austria and Czechoslovakia, the government admitted a further forty-four thousand refugees, including almost ten thousand children (unaccompanied by their parents) on the *Kindertransporte*. There was little social contact between the newcomers and the established members of the Jewish community, and what contact there was, often left the refugees feeling patronised and resented. In the wider society, the reception given to the refugees, in particular, the children of the *Kindertransporte* became part of the national myth in the 1940s. The widespread conviction that genuine refugees were treated fairly and decently became essential to notions of Britishness and the belief in an innate tolerance.

***

David's diary started again in August 1939, when it was clear to everyone that war was imminent. In mid-August, he attended the conference of the World Union of Jewish Students in Geneva, which overlapped with the World Zionist Congress. Most of the diary entries describe the social activities, excursions and flirtations that David and his friends enjoyed. At one outing to the cinema, they saw part of a French film, which David noted in his diary (24 August 1939) was 'a terrific piece of propaganda for

French Rearmament. It was pretty impressive, particularly the scenes from the Maginot Line'.

David outside the Senate House in Cambridge, after receiving his PhD degree, June 1939.

David with John, Esther, Henry and his parents at St John's College, after he had received his PhD degree, June 1939.

David with Aubrey Eban, travelling to Geneva for the Congress of the World Union of Jewish Students, August 1939.

On 25 August, the news of the Russo-German agreement was announced. Many years later, David still remembered a conversation with a left-wing friend, who had claimed that the Molotov-Ribbentrop Pact was 'the greatest blow for peace'. David had replied that he completely agreed on condition that his friend changed 'for' to 'to'.

The World Zionist Congress was held in Geneva during the same week, and David attended some of the sessions. With war about to break out at any moment, the mood among the delegates was very apprehensive, as David recalled:

> When at the closing session, Weizmann said farewell to all the European delegates, he added amid great emotion that he did not know when they would meet again. He spoke more truly than he knew.

War was declared on 3 September 1939, and a few days later in his diary (12 September 1939), David began with a review of his personal development. After several paragraphs of self-analysis, he returned to the declaration of war:

> … I still somehow could not believe it, and even today, ten days after it has started, I feel that it is all so surreal. This is partly due to the fact that except for gas masks (which we are supposed to carry with us wherever we go) and darkened windows in case of air raids, the War has so far hardly affected me; and also partly by the fact that my parents are staying with me [in Cambridge] and my father's health worries me more than the War… as far as the War is concerned, the outstanding fact is I think that nobody has any illusions about War, nobody likes it, yet everyone thinks it was unavoidable and must be fought to the bitter end, however long it lasts.

A few days later, the unexpected arrival of refugee children presented a challenge for the Jewish community in Cambridge. David described in his diary (16 September 1939) how on that Saturday afternoon he went,

> … to [Herbert] Loewe's for tea (only tea & biscuits – they call it a War Tea). There heard that there were 90 Jewish children in Ely sent there from the German-Polish No-Man's-Land a day before

War began. The wife of the local vicar explained to Loewe that they were fanatically [sic] *frum* [orthodox]. They had been fixed up in a large house but a very *frum* rabbi from London was making things difficult. Loewe was very upset. Gershom [a friend of David's] offered to go with him tomorrow and if necessary, to try and organise the place. Hope he has success …

The Russian de facto annexation of part of Poland in September 1939 prompted much discussion among David's contemporaries. One evening, David returned to his digs and found Aubrey Eban waiting for him, as he recorded in his diary (19 September 1939):

… He explains the Russian entry into Poland quite simply: an occupation to prevent Hitler taking Ukraine and starting on Russia. Certainly, Russia's action can only be explained in terms of power politics and the desire to safeguard the USSR. But ideologically, its stand is quite confused …

There are a few references to the international situation in the diary for the last months of 1939, and most of the time, daily life continued as before. David recorded the sinking of the *Ark Royal*, and the first news of an air raid on ships in British waters. Of greater significance for David's future was the news that Philip Bowden, his former supervisor, who was visiting Australia, had decided to stay there.

***

Anti-Semitism was widespread in Britain between the wars and could be encountered in restrictions on membership to social and sports clubs, in the professions (such as medicine, law and education), and in popular culture. Many well-known writers of the period used negative stereotypes of Jews in their writing. Alienated from, and often despising, main-stream liberal culture, writers such as D.H. Lawrence, T.S. Eliot, Ezra Pound and Wyndham Lewis often described the Jew as embodying the evils of modern-day capitalism and liberal democracy.

For example, in his early poetry, such as *Burbank with a Baedeker: Bleistein with a Cigar* (1920), Eliot represents the Jew as a symbol of decaying European civilisation:

... On the Rialto once.
The rats are underneath the piles.
The jew is underneath the lot.
Money in furs.

Eliot was much influenced by the Judeophobic language used by the rabidly anti-Semitic Action Française of Charles Maurras. Some popular writers in Britain, such as John Buchan, Dorothy Sayers and Agatha Christie, while not as extreme in their language as Eliot, often populated their work with mythic, offensive Jews in the Shylock tradition. Yet, at the time, few people made any effort to understand the deep-seated origins of anti-Semitism. One person who struggled to understand anti-Semitism and to change attitudes towards it was an Anglican clergyman, James Parkes, with whom David became friends towards the end of 1939.

With the publication of *The Jew and His Neighbour* (1929), Parkes started the Christian re-evaluation of Judaism. Influenced by first-hand exposure to the brutality of anti-Semitism on the Continent, Parkes traced its animus to the deeply rooted antagonism of Christianity to the Jewish people and their faith. For twenty years, his was a lone clerical voice against attempts to convert the Jews, and he became the driving force in the founding of the Council of Christians and Jews.

On 26 November 1939, David records that he attended an afternoon meeting at the synagogue in Cambridge to hear Parkes give a talk about Zionism and the situation of the Jews in Europe. A few days later, he typed a long letter to Parkes, dealing with some of the points raised in the talk. The upshot of their subsequent correspondence was that David was invited to visit Parkes at his rectory at Barley, near Royston. David described their discussions in his diary (19 December 1939):

> ... General Jewish gossip till nine. Then on subjects of Future of Poland and settlement of refugees & Palestine till 11. His ideas were not so much new as presented in a form that made me think for the first time clearly about all the problems. He also spoke about Judaism and Christianity with an obvious depth of understanding and spiritual feeling. Bed at 11.45 in his bed – he slept on a settee in his study. My sleep was rather disturbed. Up at

seven. Parkes brought me some tea & bread & butter. He gave me a lift to Barley. Then caught 7.50 bus.

Parkes's sincerity made a deep impression on David, as is evident from his recollection of their meeting, written over forty years later:

> I remember Parkes' marvellous understanding of various Jewish organisations and personalities and the humanity and saneness [sanity] which he embodied. I stayed overnight and recall in the morning laying *tefillin* [putting on phylacteries] in the bedroom (those were my more pious days) under the image of a striking crucifix.

The Reverend James Parkes.
Photographer: Edward Leigh, Cambridge 1962.

***

1940 proved to be a momentous year for David. Unexpectedly, on the 2 January, he received a letter from Philip Bowden offering him a job in Australia at the University of Melbourne. He noted in his diary, 'It completely knocked me over'. Initially, he decided not to accept, because of concerns about his parents, but his brother John, an academic colleague, and Mr and Mrs Dagut encouraged him to go. By mid-January, he had decided to accept Bowden's offer, knowing that it was a unique opportunity, and that his siblings would be on hand to care for their parents. Home for the weekend to celebrate his parents' forty-second wedding anniversary on 13 January, David informed his family of his decision, though he noted that his mother was 'visibly upset', and his father was rather confused and unwell.

On 5 February, he received the letter confirming his appointment in Australia and commented in his diary that this was 'a very important day for me.' He was to receive an annual salary of £426 (Australian pounds) and £75 (sterling) for his fare, good money for the time.

David spent one week in early March in Cambridge, packing up and making his farewells. Concern about his father's health and ensuring that his parents had sufficient income to live on, remained sources of anxiety and were frequently mentioned in his diaries for 1940–43. At the end of his last week in London, he was seen off at Waterloo Station by his parents, other family members, and a group of friends.

We shall find out about David's journey to Australia, and what his life was like there, a bit later.

Chapter 4

Germans of the Mosaic Persuasion

Before we pick up David's story again, we need to go back in time to Germany at the start of the twentieth century, to find out about another important member of the family and her early life.

While Chaskel and Rivka Tabrisky were celebrating their first year of marriage in 1899 in Kazlov, in Tsarist Russia, a baby girl, soon to be named Melita, was born into the bourgeois Rosenbaum family in Giessen, a historic town north of Frankfurt, in the state of Hesse (German: Hessen). Melita Rosenbaum was my maternal grandmother, and though the lives of Rivka and Melita could not have been more different, they were to become intertwined in ways that neither of them could have anticipated.

Melita was born into a world of prosperity and optimism. Indeed, at the turn of the twentieth century, German Jews could look back on an extraordinary century of social and economic progress. Middle- and upper-class Jews prospered, and were often remarkably successful in industry, banking, science and the arts. Grand Synagogues rose in the main cities, statements of the confidence and achievements of German Jewry. Though oriental motifs and styles were widespread in a range of secular and religious buildings in the nineteenth century, for many Jewish communities the pseudo-Moorish style of the largest synagogues recalled the 'golden age' of tolerance in Muslim Spain, and perhaps symbolised the hope of a similar symbiosis with German culture.

As Amos Elon observed, in his study of German Jewry, *The Pity of it All,* by the end of the first decade of the twentieth century, with an expanding economy and powerful army, Germany:

> … also boasted an unrivalled educational system, excellent scientific and research facilities, and a rich cultural life. The combination of material strength with cultural wealth was unparalleled on the Continent … German universities surpassed those of other European countries. The contribution of the Jews to this pre-eminence was enormous; in some fields it was overwhelming.[15]

The reasons for such an outburst of creativity has long been a matter for speculation, though it is also worth remembering that the majority of German Jews were perfectly ordinary shopkeepers, businessmen and professionals – hardworking, but no more so than others. The vast majority saw themselves as ardent German patriots, as Germans of the Mosaic persuasion, and opposition to the nascent Zionist movement (Herzl held the first Zionist Congress in Basle in 1897) seemed more vehement among German Jews than anywhere else in Europe. Herzl's vision of the Jewish state in Palestine seemed to threaten German Jews to their very core, and in the first decade of the twentieth century, fewer than two per cent of Germany's half a million Jews had registered as Zionists. The attractions of integration and eventual assimilation into German culture seemed irresistible for many German Jews.

The emphasis on secular education among German Jews had its origins in the Enlightenment, and the ideas of Moses Mendelssohn. He urged his co-religionists to master the German language and German culture. By the last quarter of the eighteenth century, the key to integration in the eyes of young Jews was through the passionately held ideal of *Bildung*, the refinement of the individual self and character in keeping with the ideals of the Enlightenment. Even though they remained Jews, *Bildung* and *Kultur* would make them one hundred percent German.

By the second half of the nineteenth century, three generations after Moses Mendelssohn, Jews were indistinguishable in language, dress and national sentiment from their German compatriots. The journey that many Jews made, within several decades, and certainly within two or three generations, from a relatively restricted, religious way of life, to membership of an emancipated, largely secular culture, was remarkable. The use of German first names, rather than biblical names, was part of this process, to such an extent that by the second half of the nineteenth century, Siegfried and Sigismund were such common names among Jews that non-Jews began to shy away from them. We can see this change from biblical to German first names, over several generations, in Melita's family.

***

Melita's hometown, Giessen, was well-known in Germany for its four-hundred-year-old university. Records of Jews living in Giessen go back to the fourteenth century, though the Jewish community did not become established until the mid-eighteenth century, when the Jews living in Giessen started to meet in a converted dwelling and use it as a synagogue. The Jewish community grew and flourished during the nineteenth and early twentieth centuries, and by the 1920s, there were about one thousand one hundred Jews, out of a total population of thirty-three thousand five hundred – just over three per cent.

My maternal grandmother, Melita, was the seventh of eight children, the eldest two having died in infancy or early childhood. Her parents were Siegmund and Fanny Rosenbaum. Siegmund Rosenbaum was born in 1859 in Rodheim, a small village outside Giessen. His father, Isaak Rosenbaum, traded in agricultural produce; he owned a country store and some farmland. He was considered by his family to be an educated man, as he received his newspapers regularly from Frankfurt.

Isaak and Rosette (née Rosenstein) Rosenbaum.

Siegmund attended school in Giessen, and when he settled there as an adult he started a business with his younger brother, Samuel. They ran the family business, Gebrüder [Brothers] Rosenbaum, which dealt in corn and agricultural produce. Siegmund became a respected and successful businessman, and an active participant in the Jewish community, though his core business kept him close to the land, and he spoke with a strong Hessian accent all his life.

Siegmund Rosenbaum and Fanny Geis.
Engagement photo, Cassel, November 1883.

Siegmund married Fanny née Geis, a talented woman with a strong personality. She was born in 1859 in Rhina but as a small child, moved to Cassel with her parents and three brothers. Her father, Moses Geis, ran a highly successful business in hide and animal skins and was described by my great-aunt Rosy as 'a really beautiful man'.

Most of the information I have about the Geis family comes from the correspondence I had with my great-aunt Rosy, which started in 1966, and continued, with gaps, until 1987, and this enables us to see something of Jewish life in Germany in the early and mid-nineteenth century. In one letter, Rosy explained that Moses Geis, her maternal grandfather married Elise née Nussbaum, who was educated at a convent in Fulda, where she learned French, how to play the piano and how to sew. For a young Jewish woman at this time, such a level of education was unusual.

Moses and Elise Geis (née Nussbaum),
the parents of Fanny Rosenbaum.

Rosy and Melita's mother, my great-grandmother Fanny Rosenbaum, was the daughter of Moses and Elise Geis. She was brought up in Cassel, which was famous for its cultural life. In the early nineteenth century, it had been the seat of King Jerome, the brother of Napoleon, and the capital of the short-lived Kingdom of Westphalia (1807–13). Fanny received an excellent general education for a Jewish woman in the 1860s and 1870s, studying with her three brothers, who had a private tutor. She also went to two English teachers who had classes for young ladies, and she spoke an elegant 'King's English', as well as speaking and writing French. For my grandmother and great-aunt, the Geis side of the family (their mother's family) was regarded as more cultured and educated than the Rosenbaums.

Fanny Geis and siblings, early 1880s. Back row (L. to R.):
Isi and Max Geis; sitting (centre): Diego Geis.

In the early 1960s, my maternal grandmother, Melita, wrote a memoir, entitled *My Childhood.* She described what it was like to grow up in a bourgeois Jewish family before the First World War, and how they negotiated their identity as both Germans and Jews. Her sense of place, and the affection she felt for her hometown, Giessen, permeate her narrative. The memoir starts with Melita setting the scene:

> I would like to tell you something about my early childhood, but my thoughts are running ahead of my pen and everything in my mind is in a jumble. I had better start with the city I was born in. Giessen in Hessen was a fortress. The castle in the middle of the town [was] surrounded by beautiful gardens. Round the city was a moat, which in my time had very little water running through. The gardens were open to the public and called the Botanical Gardens. Our Archduke of Hessen was from time to time in residence, and then the gardens were kept closed to the general public. Beautiful avenues were planted around the moat and called

South, East, West [and North] Avenues. I still remember the Octroi houses where heavy transports were weighed and a toll imposed. Slowly, the city spread out behind the moats and one part was called the Neustadt, the New City. ...

Melita went on to describe the first house where the family lived, in which she shared a room with her sister:

My father built our first house in the West Avenue [Westanlage]. It consisted of three stories, a garden in the front and a large courtyard in the back. The ground floor was used for offices; the first floor had sitting rooms, kitchen and two bedrooms. One was occupied by my parents and the other by the youngest member of the family. The second floor had the bedrooms of the elder children and my sister Sidonie who was ten years older than myself had her own sitting room with the most beautiful cherry wood furniture, part of which is still in use in her family. I used to sleep with Siddy in the same bed, upstairs, and when I went up, it was dark. I was not allowed a light and I was always frightened till she came. From this day on, I was always a bit frightened of the dark. Siddy really brought me up …

The house had no bathroom, the toilet no running water, but there was a tap in the kitchen. We did our own cooking; there was help, maybe with the cleaning of vegetables, but my mother did the cooking because of *kashrut*. You didn't have tins in those days; everything was fresh. In the courtyard was a pump to draw water. We had great fun playing in our courtyard where there were the stables with horses, the wagons and huge buildings for the produce like flour, grain, fodder, etc.

My parents seemed rather remote and removed from us, and I can only remember a dutiful goodnight kiss, never any display of affection. My father was a stern patriarch in the German mould, rather Victorian. He was never a Zionist – he was a German. He was in the army and his wedding had to be postponed because of his call-up for manoeuvres as a new recruit. He was too young for the [Franco-Prussian] War (1870), but my mother remembered that Napoleon the Third was in Cassel. He stayed as a prisoner in the Orangerie, and we were told that he bathed in red wine!

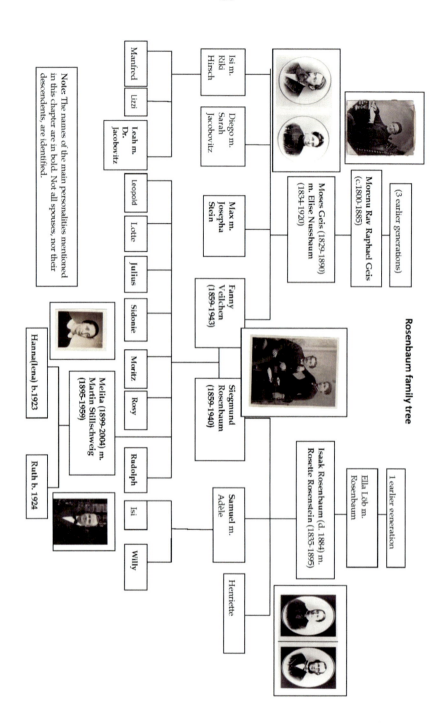

A highlight for the people of the town was the annual visit of Kaiser Wilhelm. One visit in particular, just before the First World War, with Tsar Nicholas, stood out in her memory. It symbolised the old political order in Europe, soon to be irrevocably shattered. Melita also emphasised the significance of the university and the importance of education for her family:

> Giessen had a large university and a regiment which was called [the] Kaiser Wilhelm Regiment. The Kaiser came every year to take the salute, it was a great event with a holiday for the whole city, the school children flanking the streets and a glittering ball at night. Our Archduke also came on that occasion and once shortly before the First World War, Tsar Nicholas joined in. I can still see these three men driving through the streets sitting in an open carriage. It was a huge parade, and the school children had to stand in rows and rows, all the way to the regimental barracks.
>
> The university was founded in 1607 and has seen many famous men. Liebig was born in Darmstadt; [he was] the great chemist, who had his own laboratory [in Giessen], now a museum. A Liebig monument is standing in one of the parks in [East] Avenue…
>
> My father had a good education, but my mother's knowledge was outstanding. She had learned French and English, played the piano, had a tremendous Jewish knowledge, did beautiful embroidery, and learned with her sons Latin and Greek.

Melita was proud that her father was one of the founders of the orthodox synagogue:

> There were two synagogues in Giessen; one was strictly orthodox, and one was a bit more liberal. My father, together with some of his contemporaries, founded our first (orthodox) synagogue which stood in the North Avenue…. My father did not quite agree with something in the first synagogue and left it. Later, my father was elected president of our second synagogue and was a member of many organisations. He also was a judge of the Arbitration Court for produce merchants and (was) greatly respected. He was a wealthy man, but money was never mentioned in our house. It was always there when needed and no lesson was too expensive if we wanted to learn. We all played a musical instrument; my sister Rosy having singing lessons besides her piano lessons.

For Melita and her family, religious observance was very important:

> Religion in our home was taken for granted. My mother was a very religious woman with a great knowledge and brought up in the orthodox way which she never changed. A *Shabbos* was a *Shabbos*, a day of rest, a *Jontef* [High Holy Day] was a *Jontef*, everything done with strict observance. We had private religious lessons apart from scripture lessons at school and Sunday morning teaching. It was unthought of to miss a lesson. …
>
> From an early age my mother made me accompany her to the hospitals visiting the sick and taking kosher food. Later, I was sent visiting families and taking food parcels to them. We always had strangers to our table whom my father brought home from the synagogue …
>
> In our teens, we were members of an *Agudat Yisrael* [an orthodox anti-Zionist organisation] youth group, which met on *Shabbos* afternoons. We received small presents on *Simchat Torah* [Rejoicing of the Law] and *Channukah* [Festival of Lights] and on our birthdays, which were properly celebrated. We were allowed to choose our birthday cake, my brother Rudolph the finest petit-fours and I, a huckleberry [blueberry] cake because my birthday was in July and I could eat off the cake to my heart's content, getting a very blue mouth and discoloured teeth.

Melita described how stylish clothes were worn by the children at the different seasons of the year:

> Our dresses and all the boys' suits were bought in Frankfurt am Main because there was a special children's shop [there]. We wore summer and winter sailor suits, in summer white or blue and white striped, in winter navy, and sailor coats with shining gold buttons, sailor caps on our heads. I remember that once my mother had some hats made for my sister and myself out of black taffeta with white lace ruffles inside the brim and small red rosebuds around the crown. I thought it the most beautiful and elegant hat I ever wore.

When Melita was a youngster, her parents decided to move:

Our first house became too small, and we moved further away from the city into a lovely district. The new house had four floors. We occupied the ground floor, the other three being leased. The flat had rooms as big as ballrooms, two entrance halls, a proper bathroom and toilet. …

The new house had a front garden with flowers, a vegetable garden and drying lawn at the back and through a door in the wall, one came to an office building, the stables with a flat over them and the hayloft, and an open garage for the carriages. When my father married, Giessen did not have a tramway. We used a coach in summer and a horse-drawn sledge in winter. In 1912, when we moved to Wilhelmstr. 12, Papa also bought our first auto, an open car where one had to turn a handle in front to make it start, a 'Brenabor', and I think the second car in the whole town.

Melita described the unchanging pattern of daily life, and she also reflected on her family's attitude to others:

We were snobs in our way, which I didn't realise at the time. My parents' friends were the rabbi, doctor, the bank director and business associates. We didn't mix with the shop keepers and only visited them on special occasions. … We didn't consciously look down on the Jewish shopkeepers, but we did. Today, looking back, I would like to know what they thought of us, if there was a feeling of envy or disdain …

There was anti-Semitism, but it was not open … I mean, people met. For example, every year, there was a celebration which was called the 'Fifty Years Celebration', to celebrate every man who turned fifty. Jew or non-Jew, Catholic or Protestant, they all came together and there was a big fête for everyone. It was a whole day. I remember my father's fiftieth; we all went there…

For Melita, graduation and going to university were priorities:

I was ambitious to learn and when I was twelve years of age had made up my mind to do my 'leaving' [*Abitur* – graduation from high school] and go to university. With hard work and perseverance, I succeeded, and studied Chemistry until I married. My father was proud of my being the only one of his children to do her 'leaving', and my parents gave me a lovely ring for my achievement which unfortunately was later lost.

Melita's parents in middle age: Siegmund and Fanny Rosenbaum, pillars of the community.

Melita's memoir paints a picture of the settled existence that she experienced before the First World War. Walter Benjamin, the German-Jewish philosopher, cultural critic and essayist, evoked a similar sense of solidity in *A Berlin Chronicle*, where he described growing up in the prosperous suburb of Grunewald in Berlin, in the early twentieth century. In his description of his grandmother's large flat, with its many rooms, walls lined with books, fine paintings and precious objects, Benjamin noted '… the almost immemorial feeling of bourgeois security that emanated from these rooms.' For my grandmother, as a young girl in Giessen before 1914, daily life had a pattern or rhythm that was predetermined and unchanging.

My great-aunt Rosy was a beautiful young woman, very popular and with a lot of admirers. Melita wrote in one of her last letters to me that the boys were 'mad' about her sister. It must have been difficult for my grandmother, growing up in the shadow of the glamorous older sister whom everyone admired, and who was also her mother's favourite.

Rosy's letters to me created a detailed picture of family life before the First World War, which complements Melita's memoir. The following extracts evoke a delightful sense of place, with happy memories of family life in the summer. The description of her brothers, on the other hand, suggests the conflicts that took place between her father and his sons. Each son wanted, in different ways, to establish his own identity, and to break free of paternal control:

> In the summer, [our mother] went with us on long walks in the forests. During the school holidays, we went every morning picnicking. As our father had through his business (grain crops and fodder) so many connections with farmers, millers and peasants, we were always highly welcome in the surroundings of Giessen. We travelled there (into the countryside) with a little train which travelled from Giessen (not from a station, but from about one kilometre from our house) only into the countryside to small villages or mills – I think all in all [a journey of] about one hour. The locomotive had a little bell, and as the bell was ringing all the time, and as everybody called the train 'Lieschen', which means 'Little Elizabeth', we called the train 'Bieberlieschen' [Bieber was the terminus]. It went generally by this name. Packed with baskets with food, we went during the long holidays nearly every morning into the country, spent the day in wonderful forests, and came home tired and happy.
>
> … My oldest brother Julius was eight years older than I. He was a very beautiful boy, a very good horseman already when he was young, a bit wild and used to take in the absence of my father a horse from the stable and ride with the officers of our Regiment outside town. Of course, when your great-grandfather (my father) heard of this, there was always an unpleasant scene in the house. We children disappeared and trembled when we heard our father shouting. When Julius was sixteen years old, he had an argument with his teacher in school, and in front of the whole class, he threatened his teacher with a hiding. There was great excitement, but of course, he had to leave the school. I remember well that my father offered him much what he could do then, but Julius wanted to go to America. He had already decided for himself that he wanted to go. … My father tried everything to keep Julius at home, but without success.
>
> About my brother, Moritz, later Maurice Pena, I know little. He was five years older than me, and he had a gift for languages. My father sent him to a firm in Frankfurt to learn our business, but he did not do well there and also, he wanted to leave Germany. He

went via America to the Argentine where he worked in Tucuman and became a sugar expert. He never married and I think he was a homosexual. He died in Palm Beach, USA, where he had a beautiful villa. … Rudolph (the youngest of the children) started dog-breeding when he was still a schoolboy and breeders from far away came to see his dogs. This was the start of his later career, when he became a superintendent of the police [in Israel], and in the last years of his life worked in Ethiopia for [the Israeli] Foreign Office. You can see that none of my brothers was an intellectual as a profession. …

We also have a well-known rabbi in the family, Dr. Robert Geis. He was a reform rabbi, and after World War II, he was sent to Germany to take care of the remnants of Jews from the camps in Baden. He heard of me and sent me a nice letter and a book about Judaism which he had written.

***

On 28 June 1914, the Archduke Ferdinand (heir to the Austrian throne) and his wife were murdered in Sarajevo. The resultant crisis led to the start of the First World War in early August, after Germany declared war on Russia and France, and attacked Belgium. So began what George F. Kennan, the American diplomat and historian, has called 'the great seminal catastrophe of this [twentieth] century.'[16]. Millions of people died, and the established political order was destroyed. For Germany, it was a national disaster, and defeat in 1918 unleashed extremist forces on the Right and the Left that were to have terrible consequences.

Many years later, in her ninetieth year, Melita wrote an account of how the First World War affected her as a teenager:

When war broke out, I had just turned fourteen years. I was a pupil of our girls' high school. In my school, addresses of soldiers without family or relatives were distributed and I started writing and receiving letters with some soldier I didn't know. I sent him parcels with sweets, biscuits, warm socks and knee-warmers, soap, etc. I never heard what happened to him or if he returned. … We all had ration cards for food and general goods. Everything became very scarce with time passing. Imports were completely blocked. My sister (Rosy) went sometimes to the surrounding villages to buy some butter or eggs, which was not permitted. War materials were so scarce that iron fencing and gates were confiscated to use for melting down and making weapons. The war went on.

As a vegetable, we ate sugar beet which normally was not used for human consumption; it was also made into very sweet red jam. There were no fresh eggs, only egg powder, no real coffee but chicory, roasted and powdered, and milk powder. I can still taste the jacket potatoes with a brown onion sauce for our supper. My mother made me a dress from hessian, normally used for grain or flour bags; she dyed it into a nice lilac colour and embroidered the front with small flowers.

I was keen to matriculate and go to university. My girls' school had only ten classes, and I had to enter and go the last three years to a boys' school [*Oberrealschule*, which focused on the study of mathematics and the sciences]. I think we were five or six girls who went together at the same time. I was only an average pupil but determined to succeed, and I worked hard. The boys were offered a choice to enlist to go to war and get matriculation certificates without sitting for an examination. A number of students took advantage of it but not all of them returned home. I enjoyed my schooldays and at the end of them, I passed my exam [*Abitur*].

I have one story of a lighter note. I had nice, long hair and wore it in two long plaits. One day in the courtyard of the school, a young boy pulled my plaits. I chased him all over the court, caught him and walloped him. When we returned to our class, all the boys stood up and clapped their hands for me. The War didn't affect me too much personally. I was submerged in my studies and probably too young to realise the horrors and the losses. A peace treaty was signed on 29 June 1919 in Versailles between Germany and the Entente. All the aristocrats had to abdicate. Kaiser Wilhelm II fled to Holland and lived in Doorn. Germany became a republic.

***

After the War, Melita fulfilled her ambition to study chemistry. She matriculated at the University of Giessen on 14 May 1919, though she continued to live at home, and went daily to the university.

Women had been allowed to attend lectures at the University of Giessen from 1900 and they could become full members of the student body after 1908. In 1919, when Melita matriculated, two thousand three hundred and seventy students enrolled at the university, of whom one hundred and thirty-six were women (5.7 per cent). Of the total intake, there were sixty-one Jewish students, including eight women. Melita was one of two Jewish students in her year to study chemistry, and from the Jewish community, only one (male) student completed the chemistry course in the inter-war period. Melita was a hard-working, conscientious student, as she remembered at the age of eighty-seven:

> We started very early in the morning in the laboratory, and in the afternoon, there were lectures: chemistry, physics, and I (also) took geology. I knew from an early age that I wanted to go to university. I went very often to bookshops, buying books if I had pocket money. I was always interested in learning, which I am still today. It will never stop as long as my mind works. That was my interest. I couldn't do sports. I was very anaemic, and I was not allowed to go swimming [in case] I got flu; I had to get out of the water. I couldn't go skating, because I got chilblains ... so my interest was learning.

As a student, Melita took advantage of the cultural life of Giessen, as she recalled:

> When I was a student, we had special seats (at the Stadttheater) near the podium that only cost us one mark. We had the most famous musicians. We heard Wilhelm Backhaus, the Beethoven player; during World War I, he was in Giessen, and we heard him several times. There was Klemperer; there was Klinger, a cello player. They were special visitors. We also had authors who read from their own writing, such as Wassermann, and other writers. These people come because Giessen was a big centre at that time.

She had an admirer at the university, a medical student who had fallen in love with her. On one occasion, when they were alone, he went down on his knees, smothered her hand in wet kisses, and proposed marriage. As my mother (Hanna) told it, Melita was appalled by the sight of a man humiliating himself in this way, and she said that she never wanted to have anything to do with him again. In later years, he had a very successful medical career in Israel, and as my mother recounted this story, she sighed.

It was a sigh that said, in effect, if only Melita had married the doctor, her life would have been so different. But it was not to be.

Sometime in 1920 (or possibly early 1921), Melita went to Berlin to stay with her sister Rosy, who had moved there in 1919 after her marriage to Bernard Schragenheim, a businessman. Bernard was friendly with Alfred Peltesohn, a dealer in precious metals, who was married to Greta née Stillschweig. While Melita was staying with her sister, the Schragenheims were invited to supper at the Peltesohns, and took her, too. One of the other guests was Greta's cousin, Martin Stillschweig, a handsome young man in his mid-twenties.

My mother, Hanna, gave me the following account of how her parents met, based on what her mother had told her:

> It was a typical continental evening meal, a supper where you have bread and butter and various things to put on your bread ... a *smorgasbord* ... On the table, there was smoked salmon and my mother, who was always very shy and modest, helped herself but only took a little bit. My father sat opposite her and said, "Why don't you take a bit more?" or "Why do you take so little?" Anyway, he made some comment that she was being too modest.
>
> My mother blazed at him saying, "This is none of your business." My father jumped up and went into the kitchen where Aunty Greta was, and said to her, "This is the girl I am going to marry."

The next day, a bunch of red roses arrived for Melita at Rosy's apartment. Martin called and took her out for a walk in the Tiergarten, a large park in Berlin, near where Rosy and her husband lived. Shortly after that, he travelled to Giessen and asked Siegmund Rosenbaum for the hand of his daughter. And so, they got engaged.

Melita's view was that their meeting was due to fate, pre-ordained, and completely unexpected. For Martin, it was love at first sight, and Melita was swept off her feet by this extrovert, very handsome young man with blonde hair and blue eyes. She left the University of Giessen to get married (the marriage took place in November 1921), and then moved to Berlin with Martin to start her new life as a married woman.

By this stage, the only Rosenbaum siblings still living in Giessen were Siddy (with her husband, Isi) and Rudolph, the youngest son. He was a keen Zionist and had gone to Palestine in 1922 as a pioneer, in the face of his father's opposition. Rudolph had participated in the draining of the Hula swamp in Galilee, where he caught malaria. At the time, he realised that the task of reclaiming the land would be easier if there were sufficient machines for the task, as most of the drainage and other reclamation work was done by hand. He wrote to his parents about the need for machinery, and his father, Siegmund, said that he would supply the machinery, if Rudolph came back to Giessen to collect it.

Melita as a young woman.

Siegmund Rosenbaum, man of substance, 1928 or 1929.

Sacks of flour being delivered to Siegmund Rosenbaum's office, behind the apartment at Wilhelmstrasse 12, late 1920s.

When Rudolph returned to Giessen, there was no machinery. It was a trick to get him home, because Siegmund was worried that his son's Zionism would undermine the family's standing as loyal Germans. Rudolph married his wife Rivka (born in Kaunas, Lithuania) after his return to Germany; they had one son, Ilya, and lived for a time in Giessen, where Rudolph may have worked in the family business.

In spite of the political and economic turbulence of the Weimar years, the daily pattern of life in Siegmund and Fanny Rosenbaum's household continued in Giessen in the 1920s, much as it had done before the war. My mother, Hanna, interviewed in 1983, remembered visiting her grandparents in Giessen as a small, pre-school child in the late 1920s:

> My sister Ruth and I used to be sent to stay with my grandparents when my mother [Melita] was ill with TB, or something like that, when she had to spend time in a sanatorium.
>
> There was always a rather large number of people round the table, particularly on Friday night and *Shabbat* [Sabbath, Saturday], because my Uncle Rudolph lived close by with his wife and his son (my cousin Ilya), my Aunty Siddy and her husband and their two sons, my cousins Irvin and Hans. They all lived in Giessen, and they used to come to the grandparents' home.
>
> My grandfather would sit at the head of the table and when we children were a bit difficult about food, didn't want to eat or played around, he would take his knife and fork and bang it on the table and he would say, "Nicht auf andere Teller gucken," which means, 'Don't look on other people's plates' ... I also remember the large soup tureen which would stand in front of my grandfather. He would ladle out the soup and at the end, he would always put the bones on his plate because he was very fond of the bone marrow and the little bits of meat that would cling to the bone ...

***

In 1985, Melita sent me some old family photos. One of them showed three rows of elderly men, formally dressed, photographed against a background of trees and shrubs in the Botanical Gardens. In the bottom left-hand corner was written '1859–1929'. In the bottom right-hand corner was the date of the photo: 19.VI.29. In her memoir, Melita described the 'Fifty-Year Celebration' in 1909, which her father attended. This is the same group of men (or those that survived) who celebrated their seventieth birthdays in 1929. My great-grandfather is in the back row, second from the right, with the other worthies of Giessen. He could look back on a successful life in business, respected in the wider community, and as a leader of the local Jewish community. As a loyal German citizen of the Mosaic persuasion, he was undoubtedly the most successful member of the Rosenbaum family in Giessen. In his lifetime, he had seen the improvement in the condition of Jews in German society, and the abolition of many restrictions which his father's generation would have experienced. I think of him posing for the photo in the company of his peers, and looking forward to a peaceful, honourable old age.

The 70-year olds' celebration in Giessen, 1929.

The year of the photo is ominous. Barely four months after it was taken, on 24 October 1929, the Wall Street Crash occurred. By 1932, industrial production in Germany had halved since 1929, and unemployment had trebled from two to six million. After the elections of 5 March 1933, the Nazis were in government, and Hitler proceeded to consolidate his power.

In December 1933, Siegmund Rosenbaum was arrested and sent to a concentration camp, where he was kept for five or six weeks. A local historian in Giessen thought that it was most likely to have been Osthofen, about one hundred kilometres from Giessen. This was one of a network of concentration camps set up in 1933 for the imprisonment of opponents of the Nazi regime, and selected Jews. These camps were used to help the regime stamp out opposition during 1933–34, and as the Nazi regime became more firmly established, most of them, like Osthofen, were closed in 1934 (or soon after). No one was killed in Osthofen, though prisoners were badly treated, and Jews were singled out for particularly humiliating and brutal treatment. Osthofen was also used as the model for the fictional concentration camp 'Westhofen' in Anna Segher's novel *The Seventh Cross*.

The entrance to Osthofen concentration camp, 1933-34.

Rosy described what happened:

> In 1933, twelve prominent citizens in Giessen were arrested, in an attempt by the Nazis to intimidate the local population. Those arrested were not all Jews. Our parents were so well-known and respected in our town, and that night a Nazi knocked on the door of our house to say to my mother how sorry he was that he could not do anything to get my father out. He was the son of former neighbours when we lived still in our old house in Westanlager. In those days, the Nazis were not [as bad] as they were afterwards. Your grandmother [Melita] went to Giessen to stay with your great-grandmother … He did get out after five or six weeks and went with my mother straight to Wiesbaden for recuperation where I went to see them.

Melita went with her mother to visit Siegmund in the concentration camp and to bring him food parcels. She remembered that he was wearing striped pyjamas and had been set to peel potatoes. The conditions were those of a harsh military barracks, unpleasant enough for anyone, and especially so for a man of seventy-four years.

Rosy's account continued:

> He was arrested because not only was he supposed to have said, "Hitler konne ihm mal," which means he could lick him somewhere, but also his secretary, an old spinster, said he had made her some certain proposals: "and that a German virgin could not accept." The latter, having known my father, I think not quite impossible. Your great-uncle Rudolph still lived at that time in Giessen and whenever the Nazis made a *razzia* [German: police raid] someone amongst them came to warn Rudolf, and he and my cousin, Willy Rosenbaum, took their car and went to Frankfurt, where they stayed overnight in the railway station. Later, Rudolph came to me in Berlin and then went on to Palestine.

Siegmund Rosenbaum was completely broken, physically and mentally, by his experiences in the concentration camp. The anti-Semitism in Giessen grew worse, and the family felt they could not stay, because they were too well-known. In 1934, Siegmund and Fanny moved to Berlin, where they felt they would be less conspicuous, though his brother, Samuel stayed in Giessen, where he died in 1937.

Siegmund was forced to sell his business and his property. This was part of the 'coercive liquidation' or sale of Jewish businesses, which began in 1933 and was virtually complete by 1937–8.

To summarise, in 1933 there were 1,266 Jews in Giessen, less than four per cent of the population. Many left Giessen in the 1930s; there is evidence that about five hundred and twenty emigrated to the USA, Canada, South Africa, South America and the UK, and about fifty to other European countries. The two synagogues in Giessen were burnt down during the officially organised pogrom of *Kristallnacht,* 1938. At least seven of the Jews who stayed behind committed suicide in the late 1930s or early 1940s, and a further one hundred and seven died before the deportations began. By September 1942, the last one hundred and fifty Jews were deported and killed, and the Jewish community in Giessen, which had grown and flourished for two hundred years, had been destroyed.

Chapter 5

Weimar and After

In 1921, the year Melita and Martin were married, the Weimar Republic had been in existence for two years. Jews were among its most ardent supporters. In the new Germany, fifty years after their official emancipation, Jews were finally equal, not only in theory but also in practice. Politically, Jews were no longer outsiders, and most of the remaining barriers in the universities, upper ranks of the judiciary and public administration now fell. There was an extraordinary flowering of the arts and sciences, as nowhere else in modern Europe. The excitement and (by 1933) the fear of living in Berlin were reflected in my mother's memories of those years.

However, in the 1920s, Berlin was a city vibrant with sex and culture, and the crucible for every conceivable innovation. German Jews made a remarkable contribution to this explosion of creativity, out of all proportion to their numbers. It was to this dynamic cultural environment, combined with the economic and political instability that marked the Weimar years, that Martin brought his young wife.

Martin Stillschweig's grandparents had settled in Berlin during the last quarter of the nineteenth century. They were part of an influx of Jews from the then-Prussian province of Posen (now Poznan, in Poland) that trebled the Jewish population of Berlin from thirty-six thousand to approximately one hundred thousand between 1870 and 1914. The proud Germanised Jews of Berlin tended to look down on these newcomers, but fifty years after their arrival in Berlin, the extended Stillschweig family was well established. Many of its members were in the clothes trade, mainly on the manufacturing side.

Martin used to tease Melita that he was really an *Ostjude* (an 'Eastern Jew'). She would get very upset at this and answer indignantly, "My husband isn't an *Ostjude*." Her response reflected a widespread prejudice about the supposedly backward nature of Jews from the Eastern Europe *shtetls* in Poland or Russia, that was so unsettling for Jews like the Rosenbaums, who considered themselves to be cultured German patriots 'of the Mosaic persuasion'.

Martin, the eldest of four children, was born in 1895; he had two brothers, Dagobert and Sigismund, and a sister, Johanna. Martin's parents were cousins, and his father, Hermann, had been a furrier and a tailor. He had died from a heart attack in 1914, when Martin was nineteen years old, and the younger children were brought up by their mother, Fanny. They lived in the family apartment near the Rykestrasse Synagogue in Prenzlauer Berg, a predominantly residential district to the north-east of central Berlin.

Martin served in the German army in the First World War on the Western Front, near the border with France, and according to the family story, he was awarded the Iron Cross, though it may in fact have been a service medal. After the war, he worked in different branches of the clothing industry, and had a wide social circle that included his cousins, the Peltesohns and the Hepners (related to him on his father's side), who were successful in different lines of business. Some family members entered the professions, and one of his uncles (Sigismund) was an attorney.

Fanny and Hermann Stillschweig.

Melita also had relations in Berlin, and her sister Rosy, married in 1919 to Bernard Schragenheim, lived in considerable splendour in a flat near the Tiergarten, with a fountain in the dining room as the main feature. Members of the Geis family (relatives of Melita's mother, Fanny) lived in Berlin, and there was social contact with that side of the family, particularly on special occasions such as weddings.

In the early 1920s, when Melita and Martin set up home in Berlin, there was a severe housing shortage, but fortunately Melita's uncle, Max Geis (her mother's brother) owned an apartment block in the Kreuzberg district, in which there was an empty first-floor flat, and he rented it to the young couple. It was also a time of economic turbulence, and at the height of hyperinflation in 1923, money lost its value almost completely, and the most dramatic and serious effects were on the price of food. Melita remembered needing a suitcase of banknotes to buy a loaf of bread at that time.

My mother, Hanna, was born in April 1923; her sister Ruth was born eighteen months later. Though Martin and Melita took advantage of the cultural life of Berlin – for example, they attended the first production of *The Threepenny Opera*, directed by Max Reinhardt in 1928 – their priorities were to raise a family and to maintain a good standard of living.

Martin and Melita had very different personalities. Martin was extrovert, competitive, good-hearted and non-intellectual. He spent his professional life in the world of fashion, and one of Hanna's cousins described him as "loving beautiful dresses and beautiful women." He prided himself on being a man of the world, of knowing his way around, and being able to impress the head waiter when in a top restaurant. He was devoted to his family, and very proud of his two beautiful daughters. Melita was shy, introverted, intellectual, deeply religious, with great dignity and motivated by a strong sense of duty. In some ways, it was an attraction of opposites.

In the 1920s, Martin worked for a firm that specialised in fine dresses. He was involved with both the design and the wholesale sides, and as a result, he travelled at least four times a year with the new collections for several weeks at a time, so Hanna and her sister were often alone with their mother. In spite of the economic volatility of the period, they managed, and my mother had happy childhood memories. Her full name was Hannalene (sometimes Hannahelene), after an aunt, Johanna (Martin's sister) and Great-Aunt Helene. Combining the two names was a way of not offending either relative. In later years, she shortened her name to Hanna.

Her earliest memory, from the age of four or five, was of a holiday with her parents and her younger sister, Ruth, in Heringsdorf on the Baltic Sea coast, a favourite resort for the well-to-do from Berlin. She remembered mornings on the beach, followed by afternoon walks in the nearby woods, where they would pick wild strawberries, but "If we went walking in the forest on *Shabbat* we weren't allowed to pick the strawberries, so my sister and I lay on our tummies to eat them!"

Another one of Hanna's early memories was when she and Ruth were bridesmaids at the wedding of Leah Geis and a Dr Jacobovitz in Berlin. Leah Geis was Melita's first cousin, and Dr Jacobovitz, a medical man, was the uncle of Immanuel Jacobovitz, who later became Chief Rabbi of the British Commonwealth. The family was, in Melita's words: "black orthodox," and Melita remembered her cousin Leah saying, "[Religious] concession is your Satan!"

Often on Sunday afternoons, Melita would take her daughters to visit their paternal grandmother, Fanny Stillschweig, in Prenzlauer Berg. It was a long journey by tram, past the Weissensee Jewish cemetery. After her husband's death, Fanny had taken over the coat-making business to support her family and was an out-worker. Hanna had fond memories of visiting this grandmother, who (as a treat) would make them toast on an old-fashioned, black coal stove. Her apartment contained several sewing machines, and Hanna and Ruth enjoyed playing with the buttons and coloured chalks. Later in life, Fanny Stillschweig suffered from senile dementia, and Martin and Melita found a small private nursing home quite near to where they lived, where she spent her last years until her death in 1934.

Hanna's uncle on her mother's side, Max Geis, and his wife Josepha, lived in the same block in Kreuzberg as her family. Max and Josepha were members of the *Adass Yisroel*, the small, ultra-orthodox community in Berlin, and they had their own *shtiebel* (prayer room) in a courtyard at the back of the building. It was a small room, but it was divided by a curtain, which separated the men and the women, and that was where Hanna and her sister, with her mother and aunt, would sit when they attended a service. They would quite often visit their uncle and aunt on *Shabbat*, but the visits were rarely reciprocated, because though Melita kept a strictly kosher home, Martin had to work on Saturdays, and therefore, didn't observe the Sabbath. As a result, Uncle Max would not eat in their flat, and he was so orthodox that he even refused to shake hands with Hanna and her sister while they were little girls of only four and five years old.

My mother, Hanna, c. 1927

Martin and Melita had two live-in maids; one helped with the housework, and the other looked after the children. This was the usual pattern for middle-class families at the time and they were treated as part of the family.

Hanna remembered:

> Every Christmas, my mother used to lay two tables for the two helps, with Christmas presents and a tree ... I remember the tables full of presents, and oranges and nuts, and then after that, they had the evening [Christmas Eve] and day off and could join their families ...

Another pre-school memory was of visits to Great-Uncle Sigismund and Great-Aunt Helene Stillschweig. He had been a very successful 'Justizrat' – equivalent to an attorney. They had no children, and the two little girls were frequently taken to visit them at their large apartment behind the large department store *KaDeWe* [*Kaufhaus des Westens*].

Hanna recalled:

> They often took us out in their car, which was chauffeur-driven. I still remember one outing to Tempelhof Airport and we sat in the restaurant there, watching the aeroplanes. One feature of all these outings was that every time on the way back, in the dashboard, there used to be a present for Ruth and me. I remember one present was a kaleidoscope. When you shook it and looked through it, there were always the most gorgeous, coloured patterns.

> It was a very friendly and warm relationship between us children and this elderly, childless couple ... I still remember where their apartment was. If I ever went to Berlin, I would go to the *KaDeWe*, and I think I could find where they lived, even though I don't remember the name of the street ...

***

School started at the age of six. Hanna and her sister went to a small Zionist primary school, which was located in the Fasanenstrasse Synagogue, off the Kurfustendamm, a street famous for its luxury shops. The synagogue had been opened in 1912, and its imposing exterior represented a public statement about the advanced nature of Jewish emancipation in Imperial Germany. Kaiser Wilhelm II had donated tiles for its highly decorated portico, and Rabbi Leo Baeck, one of the most outstanding leaders of the Reform Movement in Germany, officiated at this synagogue.

Hanna's cousins, the children of the Peltesohns and the Hepners, also attended the same school, and as they were also great friends, it seemed natural for Hanna and Ruth to go there too. They learned to speak, read and write in Hebrew at the same time as they learned to read and write in German. While Melita and her two daughters attended the Geis *stiebel* for orthodox services on *Shabbat* and the Festivals, the children's education took place in the more progressive environment of a Zionist primary school organised under the auspices of a major Reform synagogue.

The family felt there was no real conflict, and it reflected the growing support that Zionism enjoyed among German Jews during the inter-war years. Martin also belonged to the Zionist 'Blue-White' rowing club in the 1920s.

Hanna had decorated her first school report with a couple of flowers and a border, and her teacher had written:

> Hannalene is very industrious, a good, dear girl and tidy. She does arithmetic and drawing particularly well.

Hanna attended the primary school until 1933, when she was ten. Traditional religious instruction was not neglected either, and Hanna and her sister studied the *siddur* (the Hebrew prayerbook) at home with Manfred Geis, an orthodox nephew of their uncle.

The comfortable pattern of life that the young family enjoyed in Berlin changed very quickly after March 1933, when Hitler came to power. In the days leading up to the boycott of Jewish shops and businesses on the first of April, the atmosphere of violence and intimidation intensified. Writing in his diary on 30 March, Victor Klemperer, an assimilated Jewish writer and academic living in Berlin, noted at the time that the atmosphere was,

> … like the run-up to a pogrom in the depths of the Middle Ages or in deepest Tsarist Russia … We are hostages … 'We' – threatened Jewry. In fact, I feel shame more than fear, shame for Germany. I have always truly felt a German. I have always imagined: the twentieth century and *Mitteleuropa* were different from the fourteenth century and Romania. Mistake.[17]

Hanna, as a sensitive ten-year old, quickly became aware that something frightening was happening. She and her sister had returned home after school, and in the afternoon were taken for a walk-in a nearby park by their nanny. They passed a well-known local chocolate shop, and saw a crowd of people throwing bricks through the window, as Hanna remembered:

> They were shouting things we didn't understand, something that sounded like ''*Jude*'' or ''*Juden*'' [''Jew'' or ''Jews''] and having pots of paint and brushes and painting stars of David all over the wall by the side of the shop. Smashing in the door, smashing in the window and throwing all the stuff on the street and shouting …

That was my first experience of the Nazis coming to power and I will never forget it.

Round about that time, one of our live-in helps, who was the nanny, made a terrible confession to my parents, in floods of tears. She said that she was so happy with us, but she had to leave our employment because her brother forbade her to go on working for Jews. He was in a high-up position in the Hitler Youth. She confessed that she herself was a member of the Hitler Youth, and that she had the brown uniform and the badge which she kept always hidden in her room, and on her day off, she took it out of the house with her in a little parcel. As soon as she was a certain distance from our apartment, she changed into it, so that on her day out with her family she was in the uniform of the Hitler Youth. Before she came back to us, she changed back into ordinary clothes … She was a very nice young woman …

Soon after this, in 1933, the family moved to an apartment in Grunewald, a beautiful residential district in the west of Berlin, with a relatively high proportion of Jewish residents. By the end of the year, the Peltesohn and the Hepner families, cousins and friends of Hanna's family, had emigrated to Palestine, and the Peltesohn's maid, Illi, came to my grandparents as a live-in housekeeper. Illi (Ella Hannasky) came from a poor Berlin family and had gone into service with the Peltesohn family in 1917 at the age of nineteen. By the time she came to work with my grandparents in 1933, her father was no longer alive, though Illi used to visit her widowed mother on her days off. In the 1930s, Illi became Melita's closest friend and confidante, and Hanna doubted whether her mother could have coped without Illi's support.

Other family members were also affected by Hitler's rise to power. Melita's older sister, Rosy, was working at this time as a secretary to Professor Oskar Vogt, at the Kaiser Wilhelm Institute for Brain Research (Kaiser-Wilhelm-Institut für Hirnforschung) which was opened in 1931 in Berlin-Buch, a suburb of Berlin. Vogt was a very distinguished neurologist, as was his French- born wife, Cécile, and they had examined Lenin's brain, at the request of the government of the Soviet Union.

The Institute was raided twice in 1933 by members of the local SA (Brownshirts), searching for communists and other subversives. The Institute was under attack, as the Nazis tried to control the way it was run, and the personnel who were employed there. The legislation passed in April 1933, 'The Law for the Restoration of the Professional Civil Service', resulted in the dismissal of Jews and those whose political views were suspect, such as Communists or Social Democrats, from government employment. The decrees of 1933, particularly those aimed at Jews, set off a wave of denunciations, often personally as well as politically motivated; most of the denouncers were voicing grudges or personal resentments, and were not Nazi enthusiasts.

In late 1933, Rosy received a letter telling her to report to Gestapo Headquarters (at the Prinz-Albrecht-Palais) for questioning. She received ten days' notice of her impending interview, but at the time, her husband, Bernard, was in Brussels, trying to get a permit to move his factory there. Bernard's efforts were unsuccessful, but he returned to Berlin on the day before Rosy's interview at Gestapo Headquarters. The next day, he accompanied Rosy to the Prinz-Albrecht-Palais, and waited for her in the road outside, while Vogt and his wife waited at the Institute to learn the outcome.

Rosy recalled:

At Gestapo Headquarters, I went upstairs, and that was also so typical in those days, on the sixth floor, because you had to go upstairs and yet more stairs, walking with one of those horrible people in their black uniform. You went upstairs without knowing what was going to happen.

On the stairs coming down, and we didn't know about this beforehand, was Dr Tenenbaum [another Jewish employee at the Institute]. She had also had a letter and hadn't talked about it and when she passed me, she said, "It isn't so bad." … I went in, I was examined about what work I was doing at the Institute, and [asked] where my husband was. I was what was called in those days a *Doppelverdiener*. That was forbidden. It was not allowed that two people in one family had a profession or job …

A *Doppelverdiener* was a person with two incomes; in the plural it referred to a couple with two incomes, or a 'double-income' family. The idea was to reduce unemployment by taking women out of the labour market, though the dismissal of *Doppelverdiener* started during the financial crisis in the 1920s, to ensure that one family member (usually the man) had a job. From 1933, it became official policy and, as a result, married women who augmented their husband's income by engaging in waged or salaried labour were fired from the civil service and were also under pressure in the private sector.[18]

Rosy defended herself robustly from these accusations:

> I said my husband did not work; he was in Brussels. I didn't say he was standing in the street downstairs. They said I could go and that I would hear from them. I went down and went with my husband immediately back to the Institute … to the room where we knew Professor Vogt and his wife were sitting. He said, "You have been lucky. Somebody denounced you, probably a jealous colleague of yours. This can happen to you again …"

Vogt advised Rosy and her husband to leave Germany as quickly as possible, but without telling anyone about their plans. Subsequently, they asked Bernard's brother, an architect, to look after their affairs in Berlin, and early in 1934, they emigrated to South Africa. Rosy maintained a cordial correspondence with Oscar Vogt from South Africa until 1939, and after the war they continued to exchange letters until his death in 1959. Rosy and Bernard were in a relatively privileged position: they were wealthy, well-connected and they knew that they had to leave Germany as soon as possible.

It became increasingly difficult in the 1930s for German Jews (and Jews in countries under Nazi domination) to find a country that would take them. For many people, it was impossible to leave, either because they did not have the financial means, or they could not find someone to sponsor them, or the quota for Jewish immigration was filled already. This was quite apart from the emotional difficulty of wrenching oneself away from a familiar and loved social setting, with the networks of family and friendship ties that defined one's sense of identity. The priority of the German Reich, on the other hand, up till the declaration of war, was to eject the Jews at no cost to the state, stripping them of their assets before they left, while knowing full well that foreign countries would not welcome would-be immigrants who were penniless.

***

Martin and Melita on holiday in Merano, Italy, in 1934.

In 1934, Siegmund Rosenbaum and his wife Fanny (Hanna's maternal grandparents) left Giessen after his incarceration in a concentration camp. They moved to Berlin, where they hoped they would be less conspicuous, and lived within walking distance of Martin and Melita's new apartment in Grunwald, and the local synagogue in Franzensbader Strasse.

    Siegmund attended the local synagogue frequently, and every Friday evening and *Shabbat* lunch, the grandparents would come to Melita and Martin's flat for a meal. However, Siegmund's imprisonment in the concentration camp had taken a terrible physical and mental toll on him. Whenever he was out for a walk and saw men in the brown uniform of the SA, he would lose his self-control and start shouting abuse, so he was often accompanied by a family member or Illi when he was outside.

Julian Schragenheim, one of Siegmund's grandsons, was interviewed in Cape Town in 2012, and remembered his grandfather in those years:

> His life was completely broken up ... all of a sudden, with the concentration camp and the forced sale of his property and having to move to Berlin and live in a small flat there, his whole world was destroyed ...

Aunt Josepha's birthday, 1934, Berlin. Back row (L. to R.): Rosy Schragenheim, sister Melita and husband Martin Stillschweig, an unknown man, Siegmund Rosenbaum. Front row (L. to R.): Unknown woman, Fanny Rosenbaum, Josepha Geis, Max Geis.

In 1935, Hanna was sent to a Gymnasium (High School), the Goethe-Lyzeum, so that eventually, she would be able to matriculate and go to university, since after 1933, matriculation was not possible at Jewish schools. At the same time, her sister Ruth was sent to a non-Jewish primary school, from which she could have progressed to the Gymnasium. For Hanna, it was an awful experience, as there was considerable anti-Semitism from some of the teachers:

> ... Though I was never physically abused in any way, it was unpleasant, and I felt very isolated. I was the only Jewish girl in my class; I had no friends there and I was very unhappy. It turned out to be a terrible mistake, so after that one year our parents sent us back to the Jewish school.

During Hanna's year at the Goethe-Lyzeum, it had become increasingly difficult for Jewish children to attend state schools, and the situation continued to worsen. Jewish children were gradually excluded from state schools, until they were all expelled at the end of 1938. Hanna found that her old school had changed during her year at the Gymnasium, as she remembered:

> Meanwhile, because it had become virtually impossible for Jewish children to go to non-Jewish schools, the school had increased in its roll enormously. During the year I was away, the school had moved to a new building on the Kaiserdamm, near a busy junction with Adolph-Hitler-Platz, so named because Hitler had an apartment in the vicinity.
>
> The school occupied a fairly modern building, and it was renamed Theodor Herzl School. It was Zionist in approach, with pupils right up to seventeen or eighteen years old. It was run on progressive lines, and the headmistress was a wonderful woman called Paula Fürst. We were taught different languages and of course, we had the best possible teachers, because we had all the academics who were thrown out of their jobs in the higher educational institutes [in 1933], so most of our teachers were a doctor or a professor. My favourite subject was art, and I received a lot of encouragement from my art teacher, Adele Reifenstein.

The headmistress, Paula Fürst, became the head of the Theodor Herzl School (which had about six hundred students) in 1933. Following the pogrom of *Kristallnacht*, Leo Baeck offered Paula Fürst the position of head of all Jewish schools in Germany, which she accepted. She also accompanied many children on the *Kindertransporte* to London but refused to stay abroad, even when life for Jews in Germany had become unbearable and the beginning of the Second World War was imminent. Paula Fürst was arrested on 19 June 1942 and deported to Minsk on 24 June 1942, together with two hundred and one other people. It is thought that she died in a death camp, possibly Auschwitz, later that year.

As the Nazi party tightened its grip on all aspects of German life, more restrictions against Jews were introduced. The ban on the production of kosher meat resulted in Melita running a vegetarian household, though for a time, they could buy imported kosher sausages from Holland. Once a month, all German families had to cook a 'one-pot meal', using ingredients that cost no more than fifty pfennigs, and in the evening storm-troupers, SS men or representatives of the Nazi People's Welfare would appear at the door to demand the difference between fifty pfennigs and the normal cost of a family meal. Jewish families were not exempt, and Melita remembered members of the local Nazi party coming to their apartment to collect this monthly 'donation'.

In 1936 or 1937, Hanna and her sister were taken by their mother for a short holiday in Heringsdorf, on the Baltic coast. They stayed at a 'Foundation', which had originally been a private mansion owned by a couple of Jewish academics. They left it as a holiday resort for other Jewish academics and their families, and Melita was entitled to stay there because she had studied at university. There were beautiful grounds, and lots of places for children to play. One day, Hanna remembered that there was an 'eerie atmosphere' on the beach, and people had been seen pushing wheelbarrows full of rocks. Rumours went round the hotel that it might be attacked, though the management tried to calm the guests down by saying that nothing would happen.

Hanna described what happened next:

> My mother shared a room with us, so the three of us were together … We were not in the main building, but in the annexe across the road, not by the seafront, but a little bit further back. We were woken by noise and shouts, and somebody from the main house came running over to us and knocked on the door. We were already all in bed, but this person said, "They are shouting for all the men to come out, and they are throwing stones." My mother said, "Children, get dressed. We have to get out of here."
>
> I remember getting out of bed and my legs were trembling, they hardly supported me as I put my little white socks on, and some sandals. I could barely stand with fright. I quickly got dressed, it was very dark, and my mother led us out of the building at the back and we made our way to the forest. We walked through the forest in the dark, all night, passing a few other people, while this pogrom was going on. Early in the morning, when my mother thought things had quietened down, we went back to the annexe, and we packed …

The annexe had not been attacked or looted, but all the windows of the main building, which was a huge mansion, had been smashed … We got a *droshky* [a horse-drawn carriage] to take us to the station and we returned to Berlin that morning. When we got back, my father was already [home] and he said, "I knew something was wrong, because I tried to phone you and I couldn't get through. I tried all night to get through. The phone was cut off and I realised something had happened." … I think my grandparents must have heard something on the wireless, and they were terribly worried about us. The first thing we did was to go to the grandparents …

A major event at about this time was the Berlin Olympic Games. They were held during the first two weeks of August 1936 and were a propaganda coup for Hitler and the Nazi Party. The Games are often remembered for Hitler's refusal to shake hands with the black American athlete, Jesse Owens, who won four gold medals. However, it should also be remembered that Jesse Owens was never invited to the White House, nor were honours bestowed upon him by President Franklin D. Roosevelt (FDR) or his successor, Harry S. Truman, during their terms of office.

Hanna was taken by her father to see Owens compete:

Everyone was pointing and saying that that was Jesse Owens running. There were huge numbers of people in this enormous stadium … I don't know how we got tickets, but my father could get anything he wanted because he looked like a typical Aryan, he was so tall with blue eyes. Whenever people saw him; they would raise an arm and say, "Heil Hitler." In response, he would just say "Heil." He didn't make the Nazi salute and he didn't wear uniform, obviously, just ordinary clothes.

Hanna remembered feeling very frightened. She often saw lorries full of Nazis driving through the streets shouting, "*Juden raus, Juden raus*" ['Jews out']. At the time, the Nazis were collecting money for rearmament, and she recalled an occasion near an underground station, when one of them was shaking a collecting box and shouting, "One-way tickets to Palestina, one-way tickets to Palestina. *Juden raus, Juden raus.*"

The main thing that gave Hanna's life a sense of purpose was her commitment to Zionism and her desire to emigrate to

Palestine. She lived for the meetings of her *Habonim* group, and preparing for *aliyah*, as she recalled:

> Nearly every week groups left from the Anhalter Bahnhof [a major railway station] to Palestine. Most people travelled to Marseilles and then got the ship. This was 'Youth Aliyah': young people leaving for Palestine without their parents. It was customary to see the comrades of your group or the children from your form off at the station. I remember one occasion when Miriam and Joachim Sternberg left. They were twins, both in my form, and some of us went to the Anhalter Bahnhof, parents and children, to see the train leave. Children were waving and singing Hebrew songs, while their parents cried. I remember Mrs Sternberg breaking down and crying, "Children, children, don't leave me." She cried and cried, and ran after the departing train ...
>
> We all realised that we had no future in Germany. Everybody was going somewhere ... One of my best friends, poor thing, went back with her parents to Poland, because her father came originally from Poland. He was an invalid from the [First World] War, and he received a pension there; the pension would have been stopped unless he went back. So they went back to Poland, and I never knew what happened, but she most probably perished ...

Martin and Melita considered going to Palestine, but after discussion with relatives already established there, it was agreed that this was not a favourable environment for Martin's plan of starting his own *haute couture* business. One of Hanna's uncles, Moritz Hepner, on a visit to Berlin in 1936 or 1937 from Palestine, saw that she was serious about going on *aliyah*, and told her parents that he would look after her. The upshot of these discussions was that Martin and Melita gave Hanna permission to apply for a permit through the Youth Aliyah authorities in Berlin to go to Palestine, then under the British Mandate, while they started to make preparations to emigrate to Australia with their younger daughter, Ruth. Though there were only a limited number of permits available, eventually Hanna's permit to go on *aliyah* to Palestine came through, along with a list of things she would need to take with her.

She remembered preparing for her departure:

> ... I remember going shopping with my mother to buy these items, and how distressed she was at the prospect of my departure. As I got ready for leave, I took it for granted that I would go to Palestine with my group ... we were idealistically motivated by the dream of having a homeland for the Jewish people, [and] we wanted to go there and help build up the land with our own hands.

Looking back many years later, Hanna acknowledged that this sounded naïve and idealistic, but given the fact that things were getting worse for the Jews in Germany almost day by day, the Zionist ideal was something she and her contemporaries in *Habonim* really wanted to do. It took on a reality for them, because by the late 1930s, virtually every Jewish family they knew was trying to make plans to leave Germany, and there were not many countries that were prepared to take Jews.

The increasingly difficult situation in Germany, coupled with the prospect of Hanna leaving for Palestine, proved too much for Melita, and she had a complete breakdown in health. At one stage, she was so ill that even her own mother was not allowed to see her. Martin blamed Hanna's decision to go to Palestine as the trigger for Melita's breakdown, and for Hanna, the atmosphere at home became unbearable.

A few weeks later, on her return from school, Hanna was told by Illi that the doctor had visited Melita and had asked to see Hanna later that afternoon. When she got to the doctor's, he tried to persuade her to go to Australia with her parents and talked about the wonderful opportunities that would await her there.

However, Hanna was not to be swayed:

> He soon saw that he was making no progress, and that I was determined to go to Palestine. At that point, he looked at me directly and said, "If you persist with your plan, I cannot guarantee the life of your mother in her present critical condition." This was an immense shock to me. I just didn't know what had hit me, and I replied, "All right. Of course, I won't go to Palestine, I'll go with my parents to Australia if that's how it is." You must realise I was only barely fifteen years old, I was really a child, although we were all grown up beyond our years. Somehow, it was all very dramatic ... and a terrible shock.
>
> I ran home, and I went into my mother's room, and I said, "Of course, mummy, I'll come with you to Australia, I won't go to

Palestine." My father straight away phoned the Youth Aliyah office and said, "You can use her certificate for somebody else, she's going with us to Australia." I was so terribly upset that even my father felt sorry for me. He phoned our headmistress, Mrs Fürst, because he knew that I liked and respected her enormously, and he asked her if she would come and comfort me.

She came that very afternoon and we sat in the living room together, and she talked to me, and tried her best to comfort me, because there was really nobody else to talk to … Whether [my mother] really would have died if I hadn't changed my mind, of course I don't know. I think maybe that was put rather strongly to me, but I don't think it is fair to speculate on what precipitated the visit to the doctor.

Martin and Melita applied to the Australian government for a fourth permit for Hanna, but without success, and it looked as if Hanna was going to be left behind, though they did not tell her this until after they had left Germany. Martin went to the Zionist Office, and begged the woman in charge, Gisela Warburg, to reinstate Hanna's permit, but to no avail – it had already gone to somebody else. In desperation, Martin and Melita asked Illi if she could hide Hanna, because there was nobody else they could have left her with, and Illi had become Melita's closest friend and confidante. Martin then appealed to his relative, Alfred Peltesohn, living in Palestine, to intercede if he could. He wrote back, requesting a photo, and Hanna remembered that her parents sent a charming 'sporty' photo of her, sitting on a wall and holding a tennis racket. Her Uncle Alfred sent the photo with an accompanying letter to the Australian authorities. It was as a result of this letter that a fourth permit was granted, but it didn't arrive until very near the time that Hanna's parents had planned to leave.

Hanna remembered their traumatic visit to Gestapo Headquarters:

By 1938, you weren't allowed to take any money out, and when we went to Gestapo Headquarters to get our passports, they asked us, "What are you going to do about the landing money?" The Australian government expected you to have the equivalent of £100 with you, so that they could be sure that you wouldn't be a liability on the state and could support yourself. In 1938, it was quite a lot of money, and of course, it was a trick question. My father said, "My relatives in Palestine are making it available to me."

My father already had a passport, because he travelled a lot with his work, so it was creased, maybe even slightly torn. The official shouted at him, "Is this how you treat the Führer's property?" My father said, "Perhaps I could repair it and stick it together again." This made the official even more angry, and he replied, "Interfering with the property of the Reich – don't you know what a crime that is?" But maybe he was a father himself with children, because he issued us with passports, stamped with a large 'J'. Afterwards, my parents said they thought we would never come out of there alive.

The regulation for all Jews to have their passports stamped with a 'J' had been introduced in August 1938, along with the requirement for Jews to add the name 'Israel' or 'Sara' to their existing names, as part of the Nazi programme to denigrate and humiliate the Jewish population.

***

Martin's early attempt to set himself up in business, soon after his marriage, had ended in bankruptcy, and Hanna's uncles, Alfred Peltesohn and Bernard Schragenheim, had come to the rescue and bailed him out. During the time that Martin lived in Berlin, his income went on the family's living expenses, helping the grandparents and paying off his debts. But he did not want to arrive in Australia as a pauper, so he delayed his departure until he had accumulated some savings.

Martin had a very good job with a firm of clothing manufacturers, and he travelled a lot with the model, who modelled the clothes for potential customers. She was married to a member of the Cossack Choir, which travelled all over Europe to perform; it had some sort of immunity, and its members were not searched. Martin arranged for this mannequin's husband to take his (Martin's) savings out of Germany and to deposit the money in Amsterdam. Martin and Melita packed a shoe box with banknotes, and late at night, Melita went by tram to the other end of Berlin, to the apartment of this couple and left the money there, never knowing whether they would ever see any of it again. The arrangement was that the couple would smuggle the money out of Germany but would take half as their fee. Melita said with a half-smile, during one of her visits to Britain in the 1960s, "If I had been caught, I would have been shot."

At the end of September, Chamberlain flew to Munich to negotiate with Hitler about the future of Czechoslovakia. Hanna sat up late with her father, listening to the radio broadcast of Chamberlain's return to Downing Street, and his declaration that he had brought back "peace with honour". The agreement was a shameful betrayal of Czechoslovakia, but Hanna remembered her father's relief at the news. If an agreement had not been reached, and war had broken out at that point, many Jewish families in Germany would never have been able to leave.

During the course of 1938, Martin and Melita took English lessons from a Quaker called Dr Zenker. He was a highly qualified teacher who had been thrown out of his job because of his anti-Nazi views. He and his wife had had some contact with the British Quaker, Corder Catchpool, when he was based in Berlin during the years 1931–36. Hanna remembered the help he gave her family very clearly:

> Dr Zenker gave English lessons to Jewish people who were about to emigrate to English-speaking countries. He came to our apartment, and he gave lessons to my parents, and Ruth and I also had lessons after school, and he became quite a friend of my parents ... Once, just as he was leaving, my father pulled one of his own overcoats off the hall stand and pressed it in his arm and just didn't give him time to say anything and closed the door behind him. He didn't want to embarrass the man, he didn't want thanks, and he didn't want to be refused because he knew the man needed an overcoat and wouldn't have the money to buy one ...

> Dr Zenker must have been a remarkable man, and he also helped many Jews to get out of Germany. How, I have no idea. We heard later that he was taken to a concentration camp. I don't know when I first heard that he had survived. I was already living in England when we got a letter from him, telling us that he was still living in Germany. He asked us if we could send him a certain type of English book, for teaching, and of course we did so with the greatest of pleasure ...

Martin and Melita had arranged to leave Germany in December 1938, but their plans were changed by *Kristallnacht* and its aftermath. It is likely that over one thousand synagogues were destroyed, and many Jewish cemeteries were desecrated. In the aftermath of the pogrom, twenty to thirty thousand Jewish males were arrested and sent to concentration camps. The local synagogue and Hanna's school were burned down as well, but it was the aftermath of the pogrom that left an indelible mark on her memory.

As she recounted many years later:

> It was the next morning that they came to our apartment and took my father away. It was really the most traumatic experience of my life … It was early Friday afternoon, and we were having lunch. There was a ring at the door, and Illi, our friend and housekeeper opened the door, and there was someone in Nazi uniform. Just one man, and he said he had come to collect my father, to take him to the local police station, which was the collecting point for transportation. He didn't say, but we knew it would be a collecting point for shipping people off to concentration camp.
>
> It was a terrible shock for all of us, but my father was amazingly calm, and the first thing he said to my mother was, "Melitchen, pack me some warm underwear." Then he said to the man, to the Nazi, "Is it all right if I change into some warmer clothes? And would you like to come with me into the bedroom?" because, presumably, the Nazi might have thought that my father would jump out of the window or find some way of escaping …
>
> Before my father left, he said to my mother, "I'm just going to take a big gamble; I'm going to take our passports and our permits for entry into Australia with me," because four weeks after that was actually the date when we had planned to leave Berlin and catch the ship from England to go to Australia. So, my father, with tremendous presence of mind, with his warm underwear on and all our documents, which was a tremendous risk, went off with this man. I think the Nazi official was the caretaker of the block of flats where we lived.
>
> My mother burst into tears, saying, "I shall never see my husband again," and broke down completely, and I suppose we cried, too. She then phoned one of my uncles, one of my father's brothers who was still in Berlin, she got in touch with a solicitor, and she went

off to the solicitor to see if anything could be done. We children were obviously at home with Illi, in a terrible state, not knowing what would happen …

We spent the afternoon in the apartment, and as it was Friday, we gathered as usual for the Friday evening meal. It was November, and *Shabbat* came in early. My mother lit the candles, my grandparents were there, and we sat down together at the table, but nobody felt like eating anything. Suddenly, the door opened, and who should walk in but my father. I can't tell you this without bursting into tears after all these years. He walked in just in time to make the *kiddush* [Hebrew: blessing over wine and bread]. There he was, making the *kiddush*, and we were all in tears about it, and after we all pulled ourselves together, he told us what had happened.

When he got to the local police station he said, "I want to see the person in charge." The man who took him, the caretaker of our block of flats, knew and liked my father, so he said he would see what he could do … My father was well-known as 'a good Jew', because he was very tall, with fair hair and blue eyes, and no-one ever took him for a Jew. He was liked and respected.
The caretaker was successful in arranging for my father to see somebody in charge, and my father told us that as he walked into this room the man barked at him, "What do you want, you bloody Jew?" My father took all the documents that he had on him and threw them on the table, on the desk behind which this Nazi official sat, said, "All I want is to emigrate." I suppose there must have been something about my father's manner that impressed this man, because he said, "All right, but you must be out of the country within twenty-four hours. You can go." That's how my father came back, as he told us on that Friday evening.

During that night, by candlelight so that it shouldn't be too obvious that something was going on, and with Illi's help, we packed a few suitcases. Just what we needed, or what we could carry … Early in the morning, the taxi came to take us to the airport, and Illi said she would pack everything up, and arrange as best she could for our furniture to be sent on. As we were about to leave the flat, my father said, while we were still inside, "Illi, I can't take the risk of giving you a kiss when we are on the street because someone may see me as a Jew kissing you as a non-Jew, but I want to thank you for all did for us." And so, we all kissed Illi goodbye.

At the Templehof airfield, Hanna and Martin were chosen at random for a body search, but Hanna was at the end of a long queue of women waiting to be searched. Eventually, she reached the front of the queue, and even though her body search was over quickly, there had been a delay. She was taken back to the gate through which one left for a flight, and she ran to the plane. The propellers were whizzing round, ready for departure.

Her parents and Ruth were already in their seats, white-faced, not knowing where Hanna was. She got to her seat, the last person on the flight, and the plane took off. They did not feel safe until they had left German airspace and the plane had touched down at Amsterdam airport. This was the first leg of a long journey that eventually took Hanna and her family to Australia.

Other family members were still in Berlin, including her grandparents, Siegmund and Fanny Rosenbaum, then in their eightieth year. Their daughter Rosy, and her husband Bernard Schragenheim, had invited them to live with them in South Africa, and early in 1939, Siegmund and Fanny left Germany. They had been helped by members of Bernard's family to obtain the necessary documents in Berlin. Siegmund and Fanny went to Hamburg accompanied by Bernard's sister, Elsbeth Schragenheim, to board the ship to South Africa, and were searched before departure.

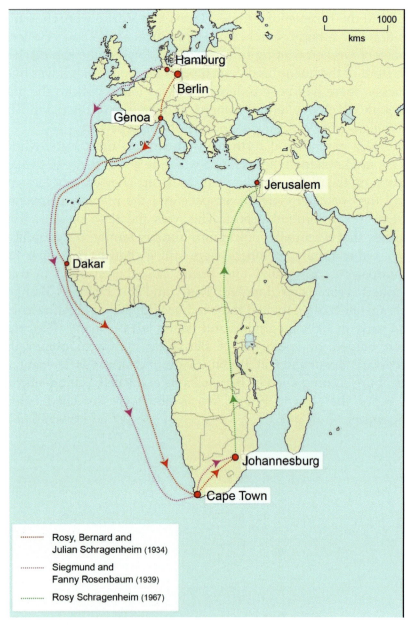

Schragenheim and Rosenbaum journeys.

According to the version of events that my mother heard from Melita, Siegmund became so incensed as a result, that he had to be physically restrained from throwing himself off the quayside into the water. A different (though not incompatible) account is provided in the letter that Elsbeth wrote to Rosy and Bernard, and it is possible that she was trying to allay the understandable anxieties of the family in South Africa:

15 February 1939

My dear ones,

Last night, I returned happily from Hamburg [to Berlin]. I had really very lovely days with parents R[osenbaum]. We got along so very well, as never in the previous years. I was allowed to board the ship and was glad to see their lovely cabin and bathroom. I also still met their stewardess who made a very nice impression.

Unfortunately, they could not take the permitted jewellery with them, as Papa had mislaid the certificate. The jewellery has been put into deposit and we will try to fix this matter as soon as possible. In Hamburg, we still had to get a doctor for Papa as he got a serious nosebleed. But on the day of departure, everything was in best order and that [news] I had actually cabled you. There still was news from Lotte that she would visit the parents in Rotterdam. Also, from Melita, there still was a letter on the last day in Hamburg, which brought the good news that Martin already has a good job. This morning, I got in touch with the tax-advisor of the parents about the jewellery and on Sunday, I will see Uncle Max [Geis] who has their power of attorney and will discuss it all with him. I also hope you have my letter from Hamburg.

At home all as usual, but Pa is a little better …

A thousand greetings, your Hanschen (Hansi)

As the boat started leaving and the band played 'Muss i' denn, muss i' denn' ['Then I must (go) …', a popular German folksong] I had thick tears running down my face.

Elsbeth Schragenheim was the dutiful, unmarried daughter who stayed at home to look after her elderly parents, Moses and Zerline. They were not well off and in poor health, and Bernard had not succeeded in obtaining the visas that would have enabled them (and their daughter) to leave Germany. They died of natural causes, exacerbated by malnutrition, as Jews were not issued with ration cards, and they were dependent on food parcels sent by family members outside Germany, via Sweden, or by a family friend in London, though these stopped once war had been declared. Moses Schragenheim died in 1940 and his wife died the following year. When Elsbeth received deportation papers in 1942, she committed suicide, and she is buried in the Weissensee cemetery in Berlin.

Moses Schragenheim and his daughter, Elsbeth, Berlin, c. 1930.

The photograph above was found in a copy of the *Judisches Liederbuch, Makkabi*. This Jewish song book was published by the German branch of the International Maccabi Association in 1930. In 1942, realizing her probable fate, Elsbeth packed her few belongings and sent them to Sweden via the International Red Cross before taking her own life on 16 November 1942. This songbook was left to her nephew Julian Schragenheim, as the handwritten words 'für Julian' indicate.

Siegmund and Fanny Rosenbaum with Rosy and Bernard Schragenheim, and their son Julian, in Johannesburg, 1939/40.

Siegmund and Fanny Rosenbaum arrived safely in South Africa, having travelled there on a ship of the German East Africa Line. Their grandson, Julian Schragenheim, by then living in South Africa with his parents, remembered being told that once on-board ship, where international maritime regulations still applied, his grandparents were treated with the same courtesy as

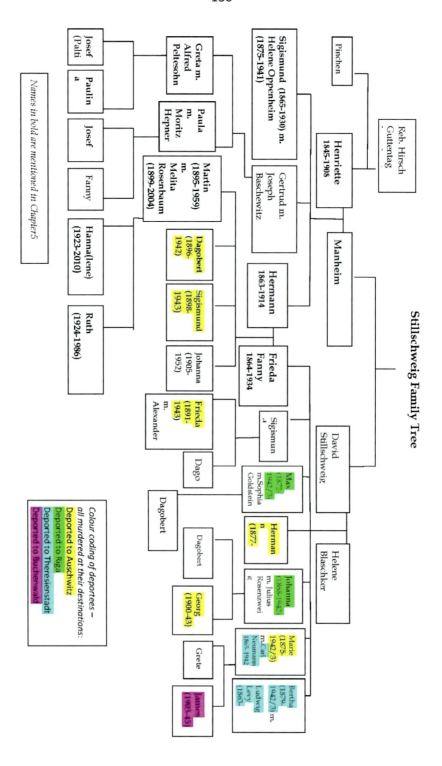

the non-Jewish passengers. They lived with Rosy and her husband in Johannesburg, though Siegmund needed regular nursing and he died within a year; Fanny died in 1943.

***

Martin's two brothers, Dagobert and Sigismund, were deported in 1942 and 1943 respectively, and killed in Auschwitz. Martin's mother (who had died in 1934) was one of seven children, and of her siblings, four were sent (two with their spouses), to Auschwitz, the Riga Ghetto or Theresienstadt, where they were killed in 1942 or 1943, as were some of their children. Hanna's great-uncle and great-aunt, Max and Josepha Geis, were deported and killed at Treblinka in 1942. These relatives were either too old, or too poor, or without the necessary contacts, to organise their emigration from Germany.

***

Why did Germans like Dr Zenker and Illi help their Jewish compatriots during the Nazi period, often at great personal risk, while the majority did not? We should also remember the small, everyday gestures of helpfulness by other Germans, that Hanna and her family sometimes experienced.

The attitude of the German population to the persecution of the Jews from 1933 onwards has been much discussed by scholars. Ian Kershaw has argued that the indifference of most of the population provided the climate within which 'spiralling Nazi aggression towards Jews could take place unchallenged'.[19]

In her book *The Other Schindlers*, Agnes Grunwald-Spier documents the lives of thirty individuals who helped or rescued Jews during the war. She notes that the most common reasons why people helped Jews were '… religious beliefs or perceiving that it was one's duty to help another who was in trouble. Other reasons are the sanctity of life, obeying one's conscience or shame at not helping a neighbour'.[20] British Quakers were very active in helping Jews to escape from Germany before the war. However, Grunwald-Spier's book does not describe in detail the part played by German Quakers, though many of them lost their jobs in 1933 because they would not sign the loyalty oath to the new regime.

From my mother's account, it is clear that Dr Zenker was motivated by deeply held religious and humanitarian beliefs.

Melita's maid and confidante, Illi, was described by my mother's cousin, Paulina, as "a very good woman." She was loved by the members of the Stillschweig and Peltesohn families who she worked for, and she behaved with great integrity and loyalty. In a chapter that has described such sombre events, it is appropriate to remember the lives of these two remarkable people.

Chapter 6

Newcomers Down-Under

By the beginning of 1939, it was clear to everyone that Europe was heading inexorably towards war, and it is against this background that Hanna's story unfolds. Her journey was that of a teenage refugee, fifteen years old, fleeing with her family from Nazi Germany, and this traumatic experience left its mark on Hanna for the rest of her life. It was so different from the journey she had dreamt about: of going on *aliya* to Palestine with her group from *Habonim* to a new life and a fulfilling identity as a pioneer, helping to redeem the land and build the Jewish state.

This chapter describes the journey to Australia, and the struggles Hanna and her family faced when eventually they reached Sydney. They were regarded with hostility as Germans and were initially classified as 'enemy aliens'. Furthermore, they were not made welcome by the local Jewish community. Hanna's memories of where her family lived in Sydney, where she worked, and where she met other young people, are inseparable from the unhappiness and difficulties the whole family experienced as refugees.

***

On arrival in Amsterdam, Hanna and her family were looked after by relatives living there, and Hanna remembered them as being very kind. After about two weeks, Hanna and her family flew to London; the plan was to go from there to Liverpool to board the ship to Canada. Her father, Martin, had all the necessary travel documents for the journey to Australia, but (as Hanna remembered it) refugees in transit also needed a letter of invitation from a British family to be allowed into the country, and the Stillschweigs possessed such a letter.

Interviewed in Cambridge in 1987, Hanna remembered their initial reception in London very clearly:

> We arrived in London, in the evening, in November. It was raining, and we got a taxi, and we showed the driver the envelope which

had the address on it. I don't remember what area it was, but it was one of those streets in North London which had a row of identical semi-detached houses. Finally, we drew up, in the dark with the rain falling, in front of this house. We rang the bell, and the woman came to the door and said, "What do you want?" My father had the letter, and he said, "Well, you invited us to come and stay with you, and we had to leave rather earlier than expected." And she said, "But that was only a formality. I didn't really invite you. You can't come and stay with me. I'm sorry. It's just not possible." She closed the door, and there we were all in the rain, with the taxi driver and our luggage. There we stood; what were we going to do? The taxi driver felt, I think, very sorry for us. I suppose he was a human being after all.

The taxi driver took them to a phone box, and Martin, ever resourceful, had the telephone number of two former school friends of his daughters, whose families were already living in London, in the Hendon area. He made phone calls to these two families, and explained what had happened, and they offered to put Ruth and Hanna up, one daughter with each family. Martin and Melita stayed in a small hotel off the Edgware Road until it was time to catch the train to Liverpool. From there, they embarked on the ship to Halifax, as part of the long journey which eventually took them to Australia.

There were two ships which set sail for Canada from Liverpool, each containing a large contingent of German and Austrian Jewish refugees: the *Duchess of Atholl*, on which Hanna and her family travelled, and the *Duchess of Richmond*. The sea crossing took seven days, and it was an ordeal, as the sea was very rough, and most of the passengers were seasick. Everybody stayed in their cabins, except Martin and a few hardy souls. Hanna remembered clutching the wooden edges of her bunk sides to stop herself rolling from side to side.

After they arrived in Halifax, they caught the Pullman train that would take them across Canada via Montreal to Vancouver, from where they would travel by ship across the Pacific to Sydney. In Montreal, there was a stop-over of several days, and the refugees were met by members of the local Jewish community, put up in hotels and entertained in their homes. The Stillschweigs were invited by one family to share a lavish Friday night meal. The conversation was somewhat halting, as the Stillschweigs did not have much English. Their hosts invited Hanna to stay overnight, as their daughter was the same age, and that night, just before going to sleep, the girl asked Hanna what a concentration camp was:

> I said, "Well, I don't know exactly, but I think they do terrible things to people there, they sort of beat them up and then kill them and things, but I don't really know exactly." I was only fifteen, and we had got out before the worst excesses happened. Of course, I didn't know much English, so I was limited in what I could tell her.

Hanna spent an enjoyable morning with this family and, in the afternoon, after lunch, she was taken back to her hotel. Being treated as a 'normal human being' became an important part of Hanna's account of the journey; in retrospect this was influenced by the unfriendly reception her family received later in Australia. Apart from the hospitality in private homes and hotels in Montreal, there was a programme of activities. Looking back on those few days in Montreal, what Hanna remembered was the kindness of the Jewish community towards the refugees.

The gratitude of the refugees was reflected in an article which appeared in the *Canadian Jewish Review* on 23 December 1938, with the following headline: 'Refugees Return Thanks to Montrealers: They Will Never Forget Warm-Hearted Help.' The article describes how the refugees were 'deeply moved by the wonderful reception and kindness … We shall never forget … the warm-hearted and loving way in which the most precious help and assistance has been bestowed on us.' Perhaps the most revealing sentence is: 'After a hard life of humiliation the wonder of humanity has dawned upon us.'[21] The article reflects the refugees' appreciation that they had been treated as fellow human beings by the Jews of Montreal, and that was what Hanna remembered forty-five years later.

Hanna remembered the journey from Montreal across Canada to Vancouver by train:

> This whole train was full of refugees who were making the same journey and we spent seven days in this train. It was December, and … it was approaching *Chanukah*, and at every station that the train stopped, members of the local Jewish community would come to the train. They brought us little tin *chanukiahs* [candelabra],

and candles and food, and sweets and little gifts, because the communities of Canada knew that refugees were travelling through. I think they had this well organised [so] that each train that came through would be welcomed by the Jews of the town and be given supplies.

It was the most moving *Chanukah* I have ever spent, because we were on the move. It got dark early because it was winter, and the people in the train lit those *chanukiahs*, lit those candles, and you could hear the sounds of 'Ma'oz Tzur' ['Mighty Rock of my salvation'] being sung by all these people up and down these carriages. It was terribly moving on the train, looking out of the window, getting glimpses in the dark of these very high snow-clad mountains ... I kept thinking, 'My God, this makes Switzerland (where I had been) look like a little toy country', because they were so enormous, these Rocky Mountains ...

There was one instance where the train stopped, and members of the Jewish community met us. There was snow outside, and we went out to stretch our legs, and we were given presents, which included tins of food and other foodstuffs. I remember one man, furiously emptying one of his suitcases, throwing all the clothes in it out of the window, and packing it full of food, as many tins and other edibles that he could get hold of. I think that man must have been in a camp and have been terribly hungry at one time. I could never forget the sight of him, opening that suitcase, wildly rummaging around, throwing clothes out, and packing it chock-a-block full of tinned food and stuff that the Jews of Canada had given us as presents.

Hanna's *chanukiah*: December 1938, Canada.

The tin *chanukiah* (eight-branched candelabrum) was given to my brother Michael by Hanna many years later, and it is one of his most treasured possessions.

Hanna and her family arrived at Vancouver, on the Pacific coast, and embarked for Australia. They sailed across the Pacific, and on the way, stopped at Suva, the Fiji Islands, Honolulu and New Zealand, until finally, they arrived in Sydney. For Martin, it was important to appear as 'somebody', as a man of substance, not as a refugee pauper, and travelling first-class gave him greater opportunities for making contacts that might be useful later on. They were befriended by one elderly couple on board; the husband was the editor of the *Sydney Morning Herald*, one of the top-quality newspapers in Australia. Hanna remembered them as a very nice couple, and the friendship continued for many years in Sydney. For Hanna and her sister, Ruth, there were plenty of young people to socialize with, though most of them (with their families) were travelling second class.

The issue of kosher food on board the ship presented problems, particularly for Melita, so she stuck to a vegetarian or fish diet, though Martin did not worry about it. Drinking tomato juice was a novelty which they encountered for the first time on-board ship. Hanna remembered their initial revulsion when it was served as a drink, but they quickly discovered that they enjoyed it.

New experiences followed as they travelled across the Pacific. The ship made a number of stops: at Hawaii, where they visited the Royal Hawaiian Hotel at Waikiki Beach; Fiji and Auckland. The Stillschweigs had never been out of Europe before, and Hanna recalled how 'exotic' these places appeared.

Eventually, they arrived in Sydney on the 14 January 1939; it was over two months since they had left Germany. As they got off the ship, Hanna felt it was like walking into a furnace. It went down in Australian meteorological history as 'Black Saturday' because of the extreme temperature, combined with a sandstorm. They were met by a couple who Martin used to know in Berlin, through his contacts in the clothing industry, and they had found the Stillschweigs an apartment. Hanna remembered that "… as we crossed Sydney Harbour Bridge, my father took his Iron Cross out of his jacket pocket and flicked it into the waters below."

***

When Hanna and her family arrived in Sydney in January 1939, Australia had a Jewish community that dated back to the earliest British settlements in the late eighteenth century. In the nineteenth century, the community, though small, became well established, and proud of its loyalty to Britain and the British Empire.

With the rise of Zionism in the early twentieth century and increased immigration from Eastern Europe, Germany and Austria in the 1920s and 1930s, the character of Australian Jewry changed. The arrival of immigrants from Poland and Eastern Europe, and the pressure on the Australian government to admit more refugees from Nazi Germany and Austria in the 1930s, created feelings of unease and insecurity among the more established 'English' members of the Australian Jewish establishment. In the event, due to the outbreak of war, less than eight thousand Jewish refugees from Nazi Germany and Austria were admitted to Australia in 1938–39.

The procedures for entry into Australia were bureaucratic and difficult. For example, refugees had to demonstrate that they had a minimum amount of savings ('landing money' to the value of £50) before they could purchase a ticket to Australia, so that they would not be a drain on Australian society. Jews from Poland and Eastern Europe (who were more traditional in their Jewish observance) tended to go to Melbourne; those from Germany or Austria preferred to settle in Sydney. Once they arrived, they were often greeted with hostility by the established Jewish community, and by anti-Semitic prejudice in the wider society, and were often referred to as 'reffos' or 'refujews'. Refugees were routinely accused by politicians and in the popular press of (for example) dishonesty, running sweatshops or forcing up property prices.

***

Hanna and her family arrived in January 1939, knowing little English and with none of the networks and contacts they had had in Berlin. except for the couple whom Martin used to know through business. The apartment they had found for Martin and his family was not a particularly salubrious home for the new arrivals, as Hanna recalled:

> It was a tiny little flat which had just a sort of living room and two bedrooms which were separated by a bathroom and a tiny little kitchen, and it was rather dark and looked out at the courtyard. There was no sort of lovely vista or anything like that … There were all these young ladies running around in the minimum of clothes and telephoning from the public telephones on the staircases. Only later, did we realise that it was part of the red-light district …
>
> It only transpired later that these people [Martin's business associates] had never even inspected the apartment; they had just rented it by means of a telephone call. However, it was an absolute Godsend to us, to be met by somebody who spoke German … there was a furnished apartment and there we went. Ruth and I were just kids, we took it in our stride. I mean, we thought nothing of it. But what my poor parents must have thought of that place, I shudder to think …

Initially, Martin started looking for a job rather than starting his own business. He had sketches with him from dress designs which he had used in Germany. He went round the fashion departments of the big department stores looking for work, without success, and would come home very dispirited. Though he got a job at one of the large department stores in Sydney, it only lasted a week, and he decided to set up in business on his own. At the same time, to increase the family's income, Melita provided cooked lunches for the young men Martin had befriended on the ship, and she charged 9d each (less than 3p in decimal currency) for two or sometimes three courses. But this was a limited success, because, as Hanna recalled:

> … Mrs Hillier said she could do it for less because the Hilliers weren't kosher and kosher meat was more expensive. So, then those chaps left us and went and ate at Mrs Hillier's, who was able to do it for less. But it just gives you a sense of the sort of life we had at the start in Sydney … To tell the truth, it was no joke.

On arrival in Australia in January 1939, Hanna was fifteen, and Ruth was fourteen. They were young teenagers who had had to grow up very fast, and adjust to traumatic changes, though at one level, they just accepted what happened. After a short while, their parents started to look round for a new apartment, and eventually, found quite a spacious one, in a building with a garden in Double Bay, and they were there when war broke out later that year, in September 1939.

Most of their friends were also refugees; the majority were people they had got to know on the ship journey from Vancouver to Sydney. For a long time, Hanna's parents held an 'open house' once a week for all the other refugees who were together with them on the ship, and many of them had children of the same ages as Hanna and Ruth. Most of them went to school, but Martin insisted that his daughters had to learn a trade, and Hanna had to work in her father's business.

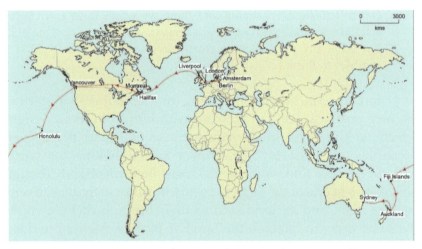

Hannah's journey from Berlin to Sydney: 1938/39.

***

The struggle Hanna's family had in getting established has to be seen in the context of the prevalent attitudes to refugees in Australian society at the time, and the way these predominantly negative attitudes were mirrored by the Australian-Jewish community. In the late 1930s, the Australian-Jewish community, based mainly in Sydney and Melbourne, was keen to establish its loyalty to Britain and the Empire, and its leaders at the time failed to support European Jewry.

Refugees were referred to the Australian Jewish Welfare Board, which advised them to be inconspicuous, to change the way they dressed and to avoid speaking German in public. Many refugees found it difficult to get jobs, and were often treated with hostility as 'enemies', though they were, on the whole, educated people who regarded Australia as something of a cultural desert, and still felt attachment to their German cultural heritage.

Soon after war had been declared in September 1939, stricter regulations were introduced for the registration and internment of those classified as 'subversive' or 'enemy aliens', even though the registration of refugees had already been introduced in 1938. Several thousand Jewish male refugees were interned, and the remainder were subject to humiliating restrictions, such as having to report to a police station once a week, not being allowed to move from a 'police district' without permission from the military authorities, as well as restrictions on owning property, cameras, motor vehicles, and so on. As 'enemy aliens', the Stillschweigs had to register every week at the local police station and carry identity papers. For Hanna, this process was traumatic; to start with she dissolved into tears when lining up outside the police station because it reminded her of going to Gestapo Headquarters in Berlin.

Refugees from Germany and Austria bitterly resented being classified as 'enemy aliens' (which put them in the same category as Nazi sympathisers from Europe or prisoners of war) because their countries of origin were at war with Britain and Australia. They suspected that the Australian Jewish Welfare Society was pleased with the restrictive legislation aimed at refugees, and as a result, the refugees turned increasingly to the Australian Council for Civil Liberties (ACCL) for assistance. Early in 1942, the refugees, with help from the ACCL, were able to secure the change in their status to 'refugee aliens'. Other restrictions were reviewed and gradually loosened, and by 1942 'refugee aliens' were permitted to serve in the Armed Forces.

The hostility to the refugees, and the difficulties they experienced in getting jobs, started to ease in late 1941, when the cessation of imports created a demand for the goods and services offered by refugee businesses. Though the refugees were relatively small in numbers, they made a significant contribution to the war effort, and to the social and economic development of Australia, by starting new industries. They moved into the cottage production of cosmetics, leatherwear and other luxury items, meeting a demand created by wartime shortages. It was by responding to the demand for luxury clothing that eventually enabled Martin's business to flourish during the war years.

Martin was determined to start his own business, and initially, he set up together with a partner, a Mr P., who Hanna remembered as being very difficult, though his wife (who had been the head designer of a firm in Berlin), was quite nice and a very good dress designer. Martin and Mr P. decided on the range of dresses, using continental designs, which they planned to show to the buyers of the fashion departments of various department stores in Sydney and later on, it was hoped, in other cities in Australia. Mr P.'s role was to handle the money and office work, while Mrs P. was the cutter and in charge of the workroom. Martin's main role was that of salesman.

Hanna went with her father to inspect premises, and they found a suitable place in the Strand Arcade, near George Street, in the centre of Sydney's business district. At that time, it was a very dilapidated area, though it is now part of a protected Victorian heritage site. The premises consisted of two rooms on the second floor; one was the office where clients would be received, and the other was the workroom. The building consisted of three or four stories with an old-fashioned lift. The lavatories were one or two floors up from the workshop, and the conditions were very primitive.

Hanna remembered how they set up in business:

> Once we found premises, my father went round with me to wholesalers of cloth, looking for materials. Finally, we moved into these premises and Mrs P. was the cutter, some machinists and hem finishers were engaged, and I was there to do everything, picking up the pins from the floor, running all the messages. They [also] used me as a clothes horse to try on the clothes and they fiddled around on me which I hated, pushing pins here, a bit tighter here, a bit looser there, pleat there and a dart there or whatever, which meant they had their hands on me, and I simply loathed that.

> Mr P. would hand out the wages at the end of the week, and I started work at six shillings a week. I had to do everything and when I was running messages, I literally ran instead of taking a tram because a tram fare would be one penny or a penny ha'penny, probably a penny ... so I literally ran to wherever I had to go to

match up material with buttons or material with cottons … and Mr P. would ask me how much the tram fare was. I would say a penny, or whatever it would have amounted to if I had really taken the tram, and he would give me the penny or tuppence or whatever it was. Then one day, he said to me, "Well next time, Fraulein Stillschweig, please bring me the ticket so that I have it for the record for my bookkeeping." He caught on to the fact that I ran and pocketed the extra penny or penny ha' penny, so that was the end of that.

Out of the six shillings a week that Hanna was paid, her father insisted that she gave her mother two shillings and sixpence towards the housekeeping expenses. Acting as a model, she needed to wear stockings, and she and Ruth were allowed to wear lipstick, but they had to pay for these items out of their wages as well. As a result, she could save very little. Her younger sister, Ruth, earned four shillings a week to start with and she too had to give her mother some money for housekeeping.

Hanna remembered vividly her sister's first day at work:

I [was] looking out the window one afternoon or early evening, when Ruth came home from the first day of her work at Sachs, probably named after Sachs Fifth Avenue [in New York]. She got a fantastic grounding there and she really learned the basics of the dressmaking trade, which stood her in good stead later in life when she had to make a living. We were living in the flat at Double Bay and I looked out of the window and there was little Ruth coming up the street. She looked up at the window with me looking out and all she called out was, "Shit".

There was a tense and difficult atmosphere at work, with incessant quarrels and shouting between Martin and Mr P. The administration of the business was difficult; in Hanna's words, "absolutely dreadful." There were four sewing machines, a large cutting out table and an ironing board and some shelves for the clothes. The floor was bare boards, and there were chairs for the girls to sit on when working. Some Australian girls were hired, and there was one Austrian woman who spoke German, who worked as a machinist. When Hanna wasn't running errands, she was allowed to do some hand sewing.

The differences between Martin and Mr P. were irreconcilable, and mainly due to the clash of personalities, no doubt exacerbated by the insecurity of being refugees, and different ideas about how they could make the business a success under wartime conditions. After a while, the partnership was dissolved, and Mr and Mrs P. left, while Martin stayed on in the premises.

He was completely dependent on having somebody who could cut and sew, and run a workroom, so he had to look for other staff. He heard of a couple called Mr and Mrs Goldstein who had their own business, and he wanted to engage them. Mrs Goldstein was the cutter; she wasn't Jewish, but her husband was, and that was why they were in Australia because he had had to leave Germany and in Hanna's words, "being a good wife," she came with him. She was the main wage-earner, because she could cut, sew and run the workroom, while her husband did odd jobs, though Mrs Goldstein had taught him how to cut and press clothes, and how to look after the stock of materials. They came to work for Martin for a salary; they didn't put money into the business, but Mrs Goldstein was more than just an employee. She was a partner in the design of the dresses, and she organised the workroom. The new partners were also difficult, and the conflicts and arguments continued, though Martin was dependent on Mr and Mrs Goldstein to run the workroom and office. He acted as the salesman, and met buyers from the main department stores, as well as designing the dresses.

The firm was called 'Continental Modes' and its clothes were aimed at the top end of the range, representing the best of European women's fashions, which became unobtainable once war had been declared in September 1939. Martin wasn't primarily a designer, but he worked in conjunction with Mrs Goldstein, although they didn't get on very well. Martin tended to bring the disagreements at work home with him, and go over them again, and Melita had to listen, while Hanna was inevitably drawn in.

Hanna described a typical working day:

> The working day started at eight-thirty and then the sewing machines were turned on. We had half an hour for lunch, and I think we had ten minutes for tea and work stopped at five-thirty. After some time, we had moved [out of Double Bay] to Pymble so

we would come in by train. Lunch was half an hour and my father and I usually took sandwiches and the Goldsteins, of course, took sandwiches, so did all the girls, but I would sit with my father and the Goldsteins in the front room round the table in the office. I had to make the tea and wash up the cups afterwards,

What made things difficult for Hanna was that, as far as the other girls were concerned, she was the boss's daughter. Martin was very concerned that no favouritism should be shown. As a result, Hanna felt that her father would lean over backwards to avoid any suggestion that his daughter received preferential treatment, and she felt she got a worse deal than the girls who just worked there as employees.

Hanna desperately wanted to continue with her education, but she wasn't allowed to, given Martin's insistence on employing her in his business. From his perspective, he could not afford to let his daughters go back into full-time education. Nevertheless, one of the things that Hanna enjoyed during her first year in Sydney was going to art lessons at the studio of a then well-known Australian portrait painter, called J.S. ('Watty') Watkins. The weekly art lessons were the highlight of her week.

As Hanna's English improved, and she became more fluent than her father, he often used her as a trouble-shooter, dealing with potentially difficult suppliers or customers. 'Continental Modes' was a luxury clothes firm, and it was difficult to justify the firm's existence, and its use of materials and labour, once the government took strategic control of the economy in February 1942, after the bombing of Darwin by the Japanese. The whole production system of the nation was placed under the direction of the government.

America was concerned to ensure that Australia did not fall under Japanese control, and with the arrival of General MacArthur in Australia in March 1942, American GIs started to be based in Australia, which was used as a 'stepping-off' point for the war in the Pacific.

From Martin's point of view, a flexible approach was required to enable him to stay in business, and he arranged to get a contract from the American army to sell overalls for them, and that counted as 'war effort'. At about this time, he got to know a Lady Anderson, a widowed Englishwoman, and he had what Hanna called "a very clever idea," which he worked out with her:

> [Lady Anderson] was very posh, pukka … between them, they worked out that Lady Anderson was going to set up a workshop, making clothes for bombed-out children in England from old army uniforms. My father supplied the machines, and some of his 'girls', including me, to sew them, and this, in addition to selling overalls for the American army, was his war effort, and so he was allowed to keep going, in spite of being classified as an enemy alien.

After 1942, when refugees were reclassified as 'refugee aliens', and were eligible to volunteer to fight, Martin would have been too old to serve in the Armed Forces (he was forty-seven) and also, the business was becoming successful. It became increasingly difficult to get permits for inter-state travel, so Martin arranged for Hanna to travel with the fashion range to Melbourne and contact the buyers. As a teenager, she was her own model and saleswoman; she had to do everything on her own.

***

On arrival in Australia in 1939, Hanna's family had made contact with the local Jewish community, and her mother joined the Sydney branch of WIZO (Women's International Zionist Organisation). Melita's desire to contribute was not reciprocated with much enthusiasm by the established members. When WIZO organized a fund-raising lunch, Melita donated one of her delicious cheesecakes. But when she arrived at the venue, she was told to do the washing-up in the kitchen and was kept out of sight. Hanna commented that she and Melita "… laughed over this many times," but it felt like a snub, typical of the disdainful attitude of the Australian Jewish establishment to the refugees.

This attitude extended to the younger generation of refugees, too. The ladies who ran WIZO in Sydney thought they ought to do something for young Jewish people, to provide them with some social activities. They weren't sure what form it should take, so they decided to arrange to an evening meeting, and ask the people who came along what they should do. When Hanna and her sister, Ruth, turned up early for the meeting, they were told to sit at the back, much to Hanna's annoyance:

> Of course, we were too naive to realise what a silly idea that was to ask the people who came early to sit at the back. Normally, the ones who come early sit at the front, so that the ones that come late wouldn't disturb the proceedings and slip in the back. So, she put us in the back, it was terribly funny – in retrospect. It was because we were 'reffos', and also, a lot prettier and nicer dressed than a whole lot of others. When Miriam S. came in, Mrs Goldberg [the organizer] said, "Ah, Miriam, how delightful to see you," and she put her in the front. I don't know why, but I suppose Miriam's parents … made donations to WIZO, I really don't know. It was so typical.

The meeting had been publicised in advance in the Sydney Jewish press, and the inaugural meeting of what became the *Shomrim* (Hebrew for 'The Guardians') youth organisation was held in late October 1939 in central Sydney. *Shomrim* had its origins in the Zionist youth movements of Europe, and appealed mainly to young refugees, as well attracting some Australian and British-born Jews.

As Hanna recalled:

> It was the beginning of *Shomrim*, I don't remember everything that happened at that meeting, except they asked people what they wanted, whether they wanted educational and cultural activities, or social activities, and ninety per cent (and they were the children of the Australian Jews) replied, "Oh, social! We want dances," and so on. That really was the beginning of some sort of organised activity among young Jewish people in Sydney.

Eventually, it became the *Shomrim* movement, though it was similar to *Habonim*, and that was when Hanna started meeting like-minded people in Sydney. There was a nucleus of activists, and before long, they rented a flat where they had regular meetings. For Hanna, membership of *Shomrim* provided a sense of belonging that had been lacking since her arrival in Australia. Most of the other members were young refugees like herself from Nazi Europe, committed to Zionism and the goal of emigrating to Palestine. This provided a degree of continuity with her idealistic commitment to *Habonim* in Berlin, and her active participation in *Shomrim* mitigated the sense of displacement and loss that she experienced as a refugee.

Shomrim started in Sydney in 1939, but it grew into an active youth organisation with over a hundred members until it merged with *Habonim* in 1944. Soon, it attracted a wide spectrum of support from the Australian Jewish community, though most of *Shomrim*'s members were critical of the perceived preoccupation of Sydney's Jewish youth with social events. They were also critical of the official Zionist leadership in Australia, with its emphasis on philanthropy at the expense of Zionist education and political activities.

These and other concerns were expressed forcibly in the *Shomrim News*, the newsletter of the organisation. The first issue, which appeared in June 1941, included brief articles of the need for a Jewish army in Palestine to contribute to the Allied war effort, and support for the internees detained in camps at Tatura and Hay in New South Wales (NSW). These internees had been shipped to Australia in appalling conditions on the *Dunera,* during the round-up of German and Austrian refugees in Britain in 1940. Many of the refugees had been interned on the Isle of Man (and later released), but over two thousand were sent to Australia, along with Nazi sympathisers and prisoners of war.

Members of the Australian Jewish establishment supported British policy and were reluctant, at least initially, to show too much public support for the detainees, unlike the members of *Shomrim*. By August 1941, when the second issue appeared, major changes had taken place in the style and size of the publication. The cover and table of contents were professionally printed, and Hanna was identified as being responsible for 'all designs'. Altogether, six issues of the *Shomrim News* were published (Issue No. 6 appeared in December 1941), but permission was refused for the publication of the next issue by the authorities; the official reason given was 'paper rationing'. At this point, the *Shomrim* committee liaised with my father, David Tabor, who was the *Habonim* leader in Melbourne, and together they produced a joint magazine entitled *The Young Zionist*.

In December 1941, the Japanese bombed Pearl Harbour, and this brought the war to Australia's doorstep. Emergency legislation was quickly enacted that restricted further the movement of 'enemy aliens' and their activities, including the right of assembly. At about this time, members of *Shomrim* were also under surveillance by the CIS (Commonwealth Investigation

Service), and many were regarded as politically suspect because they were 'enemy aliens'.

Increased restrictions on the movement of 'enemy aliens' resulted in *Shomrim* re-organising its study groups in 1942 along geographical lines, in accordance with the local police districts. These groups enjoyed considerable autonomy, and the devolved structure enabled *Shomrim* to survive the restrictions on movement. For example, Hanna was the leader of one of the largest such groups, and its focus was the study of 'Zionist ideology'.

Hanna's voice was heard in other forums. She was the youth representative on the executive of the NSW Zionist State Council. On 25 March 1942, the illegal immigrant ship, the *Struma*, was sunk in the Black Sea after being refused entry to Palestine, and over seven hundred refugees drowned. There were widespread protests from Jewish groups around the world. In Australia, Sir Isaac Isaacs, a former Governor General, and a staunch supporter of Britain and the Commonwealth, opposed those planning to hold protest meetings, on the grounds that this would show their disloyalty to the British Empire. His stance provoked a heated debate on the issue in the Australian Jewish community. The Zionist leadership, and the leadership of the wider Jewish community, were very conservative, torn as they were between their loyalty to Britain and their difficulty in expressing active support for the plight of Jews in occupied Europe and Palestine.

Hanna had no such inhibitions. At a meeting of the Executive of the NSW Zionist State Council, she advocated an active response from the Council in the form of an official reply to Sir Isaac Isaacs' letters denouncing the holding of the *Struma* protest meeting. Her efforts to encourage an 'official response' were to prove ineffectual because on being put to the vote, the motion failed. This pitiful response did not deter the *Shomrim* leadership, nor Hanna, for they had already taken action.

As the committee minutes attest:

> Miss Stillschweig reported that the Youth Council had already taken it upon themselves to reply and were about to issue five hundred circulars among Sydney [Jewish] youth, dealing with this question.' [22]

In general, *Shomrim* provided a powerful youth voice in Jewish and Zionist affairs in New South Wales at this time. It brought together alienated young refugees, like Hanna, from different backgrounds. It reinforced their sense of identity as Zionist activists, with a shared commitment to the creation of the Jewish state. *Shomrim* also provided opportunities for friendships to develop, and it was the place where some members found their future partners; its appeal was thus both ideological and social. It enabled Hanna to develop her independence and sense of self-worth, in an environment where refugees felt they were often treated with suspicion or outright hostility.

Chapter 7

Life in War-time Australia

We now have to go back to London and pick up the threads of what happened next to my father, David. As we return to his story, I am grateful for my father's diaries which included so much detail about what he did, and also how he felt. This next part of David's life covers a period from March 1940 through to the end of 1941 and I have used a number of diary entries, as well as his letters home and interviews, to help to describe his experiences. David's letters home from Australia were found in a box file after his mother (Rivka) passed away in 1970.

The letters and diary entries convey a strong sense of place, in particular the experience of living in Melbourne during the war, with its population of Jewish refugees from many parts of Europe, as well as the gifted scientific community which David was part of.

***

David left London in March 1940, embarking on what was to be the most momentous journey of his life. It was the period of the Phoney War, soon to come to an abrupt end in April, when Hitler invaded Denmark and Norway. The capitulation of France, and the Battle of Britain, were only months away, yet when David sailed for Australia, there was still a feeling of unreality about the war.

His parents, siblings and friends came to see him off on 29 March 1940 at Waterloo Station, where he caught the train to Southampton. Afterwards, he wrote in his diary:

> Dad was very confused and excited. Mum quiet but miserable … Then I said goodbye all round. It didn't seem real. Mum was anxious that I should come back. Then she began very quietly to cry. As the train moved, we all waved but whilst waving I found myself crying. I don't think they saw it. A quiet journey to Southampton …

It was the last time David saw his father. At Southampton, David quickly settled in on board the *P & O Stratheden* and prepared for departure. Though this was the period of the Phoney War, when German U-boats sank two hundred and twenty-nine British merchant ships between September 1939 and May 1940; only twelve of these had been sailing in convoy. The *Stratheden* did not have an escort, but soon after leaving Southampton, all the passengers were put through a drill, so that they would know what to do in case of enemy action.

The journey followed a route that would have been familiar to many British passengers going to India or the Far East in the nineteenth and early twentieth centuries, stopping briefly at places under British colonial rule such as Gibraltar, Malta and Port Said before going through the Suez Canal. Most of the ports the ship called at after Port Said were also British possessions, which were intended to safeguard the route east to India and beyond.

David wrote on the back of the photo:
'Dr Alice Benjamin after a dip'.

On board the ship, there was a lively social routine with the younger crowd of passengers, which included playing charades, table tennis, card games and taking walks on the sports deck. One of the young women on board was an Indian called Miss Benjamin ('Benji'), and in the course of conversation, it transpired that she was a Bene Israel, a member of the ancient Jewish community of Bombay (Mumbai). By profession a doctor, she was returning to Bombay to work in a hospital, and David wrote in his diary how much he enjoyed talking to her about Jews, Bene Israel and India.

The ship docked briefly at Malta and two days later, at Port Said, where David said farewell to two brothers, German-Jewish refugees in their teens, who were going to Palestine. They had been treated to a bottle of champagne at dinner the previous night, courtesy of one of the other passengers, which suggests that the privations of war were still rather remote. A menu which David kept as a memento of the voyage shows that the meals were lavish, although he was the only passenger who asked for a kosher diet.

The voyage out: David and friends relaxing on deck.

David's impressions of Port Said, where he and other young passengers paid a couple of brief visits, were perhaps typical of British visitors at the time, as he noted on 9 April:

Port Said is not a very fine place, but it has a certain charm about it. The kids in filthy Arab dress, the occasional native narrow streets, the richly coloured buildings and the stately palms along the pavements. Even the street vendors have a charm of their own.

Life on board continued, with its routine of meals, deck games, excursions and innocent flirtations. Home seemed far away, as did the war. On 10 April, David recorded more impressions of the Suez Canal, and a conversation with Benji, combined with one line about world events. He noted the news of the German invasion of Denmark and the attack on Norway and commented that these acts were a reminder of the existence of the war.

After passing through the Suez Canal, the ship stopped briefly at Aden, and four days later, they arrived in Bombay. David bade a rather formal goodbye to Benji (to whom he had given a book of Jewish essays); she was met by her mother and sister at the quayside. David noted in his diary that on board ship, Benji had been 'exotic'; in Bombay she slipped into the crowd, and it was 'we', the British passengers, who were out of place. There had been several discussions about the Indian independence movement on board ship, and David recorded on 18 April that one of the passengers, George,

> ... took every comment of Benji's about the British army in India as a personal sneer towards himself. He must be even more hypersensitive than a Jew.

The situation in India at the time was complex. Both Nehru and Gandhi had condemned Hitler and expressed outrage at Nazi misdeeds, but when war began between Britain and Germany on 3 September 1939, the British government declared that India was also at war. Since there had been no democratic process of consultation about this, the Congress Party resigned from the government and withdrew from the eight provincial ministries which it held. Therefore, feelings were running high about Britain's long-term intentions.

When David visited the 'Indian Bazaar', he got into conversation with a shop owner about the situation in India, which he recorded in his diary (18 April):

He said they would not help Britain in a war which was only serving her own interests. He supported Congress although he said Hindus were sacrificing a lot for it to obtain agreement with the Muslims and a United Front. He considered Jinnah a traitor encouraged by the British.

David bought a copy of Nehru's autobiography, along with a topee, for three shillings. As a socialist, he was broadly sympathetic to the Indian independence movement and, as always, was willing to discuss different points of view. David was emotionally quite reserved; he was part of a generation which did not, on the whole, talk about feelings, yet he was intellectually curious and very communicative, particularly when his interest was engaged.

Three days later, the ship moored off Colombo, and David's diary contains vivid descriptions of Colombo and the surrounding countryside, though he recorded his dislike of the large statues in a Buddhist temple, which offended his monotheistic beliefs. There was also a brief visit to Singapore to see the tourist sites, including the 'native market'. Later, the ship passed Krakatoa, and the next few days were spent eating, playing cards and table tennis, and seeing the occasional film, such as *Hound of the Baskervilles*, starring Basil Rathbone. On 1 May 1940, the ship arrived at Freemantle, the first port of call in Australia. Everyone had to get up for a 7am muster on deck. David recorded his impressions of Freemantle in his diary:

> It is a pleasant, quiet town, with shops like those in an English seaside town with sort of built-in sun blinds. The first impression was the contrast I had got to all the other ports since Marseilles. Here was a native white civilization in a natural full-sided life – not living 'on top' of a 'lower' native population. Here somehow one belonged – not so in India or Singapore. Anyhow, we changed some money and took a bus to Perth …'

On 6 May 1940, the ship docked at Melbourne in the afternoon, and David's first impression was how pleasant the city looked. He said goodbye to a couple of friends, and then saw Philip Bowden waiting for him at the foot of the gangplank. A new chapter of his life was about to begin.

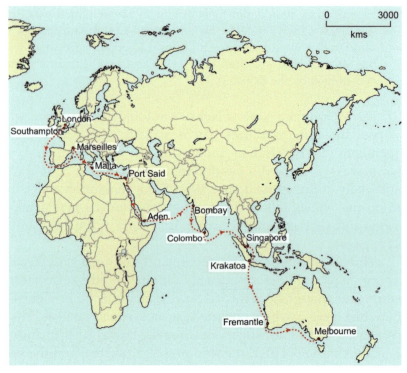

David's journey out to Australia: 1940.

***

Inter-war politics in Australia had been dominated by non-Labor parties, and in 1940, the country was ruled by the United Australia Party, a new conservative grouping that was in coalition with a number of political allies. It was led by Robert Menzies, who had become Prime Minister in 1939; he had declared war on Germany in support of Britain within an hour of Chamberlain's declaration of war. There was a widespread belief that Australia's interests, though distinctive within the Asia-Pacific region, were inextricably linked to those of Britain. Australia's reliance on imperial defence was reinforced by an economic dependence on Britain, and in the inter-war years, Great Britain had become Australia's largest trading partner and overseas investor. There was little perceived conflict between 'being British' and 'being Australian' and going 'home' to Britain was an event to be celebrated in the social calendars of Australian newspapers. Loyalty to the Empire was seen as a test of political reliability.

***

Philip Bowden had succeeded in persuading the Australian authorities of the value of setting up a laboratory which would contribute to the Australian war effort. He was appointed to the staff of CSIR (Council for Scientific and Industrial Research) in November 1939 as Officer-in-Charge of a section which was given the unglamorous title of 'Lubricants and Bearings'. By the time David arrived in Australia, the group was housed in the new Chemistry Building then just completed, where the professor of chemistry and his staff welcomed the group and co-operated fully with them. Bowden's group was not part of the University of Melbourne, but contacts with different university departments, such as metallurgy, engineering and physics, were friendly, and there was some interaction of people and ideas.

The group was highly productive and attracted a very talented team of scientists, many of whom achieved distinction after the war. Work of specific value to the war effort included the evaluation of special lubricants for machine tools and for aircraft, the development of improved casting techniques for the production of aircraft bearings, and the successful formulation of flame-throwing fuels. David was also to develop (with Bowden) fundamental lines of research on the mechanisms of metallic friction.

The initial contacts with Australian industry, particularly with those sections concerned with producing armaments or airplanes, revealed that the Australian war effort was far behind the times. For example, the practical problems of improving the production of airplanes for the war were brought home to David at the end of January 1941, when he visited the new laboratory built to house the Aeronautics section of CSIR. As he recorded in his diary for 31 January 1941, he was struck by the difficulties that the staff had in getting equipment, and the time needed to set things up to obtain useful results, which could be used to improve production.

David at work in the laboratory in Melbourne, August 1940.

David's own research continued: tests on different types of lubricants, as well as experiments on the friction between different metals. His research was innovative, and Bowden encouraged him to send a paper to *Nature* (the leading scientific journal which published the findings of original research). The paper was sent off in April, but via America, as the postal service from Australia to Britain in 1941 had been disrupted by the war.

During his research (with extra hours on Wednesday evenings, as part of the war effort), he experienced something of a breakthrough with his experiments on friction. He noted in his diary on 20 February 1941, that he did a run of silver on steel, using it as a bearing metal. David found that when sliding occurred between two clean metallic surfaces, shearing occurred at the surface layers. If one used a thin film of a softer metal on one of the metallic surfaces, shearing occurred in the softer metal, and (in the case of lead on brass) friction was decreased fivefold or more. This discovery had consequences for the production of shell casings.

On visiting a munitions factory where they were drawing brass shell cases, he asked the operator to clean all the lubricant out of his die:

> [David] then produced a brass shell case of which he had deposited a thin film of lead and asked him to draw it through the die. "You can't do that," said the operator, "because if you draw metal

without a lubricant, you will burst the die." [David] told him he had authority to do so. With incredulity, the operator put the piece in the die and activated the plunger. It went through, like a dream.[23]

This practical demonstration had two main consequences. It confirmed the idea of the mechanism of friction, and it influenced the choice of copper-lead bearings most suitable for aircraft. As a result, other members of the group collaborated with a bearing manufacturer to produce effective bearings for the fledgling aircraft industry in Australia.

David had two scientific papers published in 1941, and he found it stimulating to be part of such a gifted and hard-working team. He remembered his colleagues with affection and respect, as he recalled when I interviewed him in 1985:

> I had a number of good young research men as friends and colleagues. Abe Yoffe was there; he was a physical chemist. Alan Moore was there; he was a metallurgist and we have been friends ever since. Robert Honeycomb joined us as a metallurgist. He later became Professor of Metallurgy in Cambridge … We also had June Collins, another metallurgist who married him, and Robert and Jue Honeycomb made a very effective team in the metallurgical work at the time.
>
> Then there was [Jeofry] Courtney-Pratt, who came from Australia with a brilliant record in engineering and physics. He had won an 1851 award [a prestigious scholarship] to go to Britain but he was anti-war and refused to go … One of his great achievements was the design and construction, almost single-handedly, of a device of measuring the muzzle velocity of guns on ships while they were on the ships. … He succeeded in building a semi-portable device about ten or twelve feet long and calibrated all the ships of the Dutch navy which had escaped to Australia. … In fact, he was sent on a mission to take it [the device] to Britain to calibrate all the ships of the British fleet and after a long and arduous journey, he got to Britain. I used to say that Hitler must have heard of this and got worried because the day he arrived in Britain, Germany surrendered. But he was one of the most gifted men we ever had. Tremendously inventive in mechanical optical devices …
>
> In the midst of doing the work on applied problems, I was able to find time to do work on the basic mechanism of friction and I think

that laid the groundwork for our understanding of how friction arises, at least as far as metals are concerned. We did some work on lubrication which was a follow-up of work I had started in Cambridge in the Britannia Laboratories. … The laboratory work in Melbourne proved to be extremely successful. Bowden was very gifted in picking on people and on topics which could be fruitfully pursued. He was the sort of man who could skim the cream off an existing problem and very often find cream when nobody had found it before.

***

On arrival in Australia, David had quickly developed a routine of work in the lab, social interactions with the crowd of young singles who had rooms in Greycourt (his boarding house in Parkville, near the university), and increasing contact with the Jewish community in Melbourne, which in the 1940s, was centred on the Carlton district. He remembered it as a microcosm of Jewish life in Europe, with immigrants from different countries, and every type of Jewish political movement and activity was represented.

News about the war tended to dominate conversation, and this is reflected in David's diary, particularly during 1940. There was widespread antipathy to Jewish refugees, and this was brought home to David during his first month in Melbourne, when he was walking back to his digs from the lab with one of his colleagues.

He wrote in his diary (22 May 1940):

Intended to do a good deal of work this evening but on the way home with K., he said, "We'd have to start learning German if Hitler came and you are better off than me because you can at least read it." I then told him I was non-Aryan. He then produced some of the H. G. Wells stuff and said that the loss of Polish Jewry, except for its occasional musicians, would not be much of a loss to anybody.

He expressed his views with such complete assurance that left me furious inside. "They're not much good here anyhow," he said, "there's nothing worse than them unless it's a Russian Jew." He then admitted that what he meant was that they didn't fit in very well, and I pushed the point home. I wish he weren't so damned confident about his views – he just doesn't know a damned thing about it …

One disaster followed another in Europe, with the news on 28 May 1940 that Belgium had surrendered. Though most of the British Expeditionary Force was evacuated from Dunkirk at the beginning of June, within a couple of weeks, France had collapsed, and Petain had accepted German terms for an armistice. A few days later, David learned about the internment of German and Austrian Jewish refugees in Britain, as a result of the xenophobic reaction that occurred after the evacuation from Dunkirk. The refugees, who had fled Nazi persecution, were seen in 1940 as potential enemy agents, who might aid German plans for the invasion of England. These included people he knew in Cambridge, such as the distinguished academic, David Daube.

His diary entries for August tend to be short, recording news about the bombing of London and retaliation against Berlin, and he felt anxious because he had not heard recently from his family. Early September brought the news of the lend-lease agreement and Hitler's threat to finish off England, followed later that day, by reports of the bombing of London. News of the further heavy bombing of London, the large number of deaths and damage caused, especially in the East End and Dockland, left David feeling anxious. He wrote to his family, including notes to some of his friends, and sent the letter via America, in the hope that this would speed communications. He asked his parents to send him a cable occasionally so that he would know they were all right, even though it would cost them five shillings. At Greycourt, there was much discussion of the progress of the war, and K. (who also worked in the same lab as David) was convinced of England's imminent collapse, a view which David strongly disagreed with.

David relaxing at his digs, Greycourt, 1941.

A letter from his nephew David Lush (age nine), dated 9 September 1940, just after the heavy bombing started, revealed – to David's relief – that his family were building an Anderson shelter in the garden, with power points and lighting. Though news about the war in Europe was a source of great anxiety, yet at the same time, it seemed remote, and was often juxtaposed with mundane details. For example, on 18 November, David described eating a 'spiffing' strawberry shortbread, with five layers of strawberries and cream, prepared by one of the women at Greycourt. This was followed by a brief comment about the news of the heavy bombing of Coventry, which had been almost completely destroyed.

The war inevitably affected people around him, and a week later, he recorded that Mrs G. (another resident at Greycourt) was very depressed because she had received news that a major and a lieutenant in her husband's regiment had been killed in North Africa, where many Australian troops were serving. The war also changed people's behaviour in England, and this was brought home to David when he received a letter from a friend in London.

He noted in his diary (24 January 1941):

> She concludes with the … news that she has struck up a liaison with a married man … & carried it to its logical conclusion … This indicates to me more than anything the sort of effect the War has on people. I don't think she would ever have had the courage to go thru' with this in normal times.

America was becoming increasingly involved in the war, and on 17 March 1941, David recorded the news of a speech by President Roosevelt, promising full aid to Britain, which he described as being 'very encouraging.' News a couple of days later that some of the American Navy had visited Sydney and Auckland (New Zealand) boosted morale considerably in Australia.

In April 1941, there was news of Allied reverses in North Africa, the German invasion of Yugoslavia, and the fall of Salonika. Germany was consolidating its hold on western and southern Europe, and by June 1941, there were rumours of German troops massing on the border with Bessarabia. On 22 June, German forces invaded the Soviet Union, and David heard this news, which was to transform the course of the war, at lunch the same day. He wrote in his diary later that day: 'Almost incredible', followed by a comment after hearing the evening news, 'Even more incredible'. The effect of this news on his communist colleagues was striking, as David remembered many years later:

> One of my colleagues … was very much taken up with Marxism as a philosophy of life as a whole, not only economics but everything else, and he used to walk around with the *Handbook of Marxism* issued by the Left Book Club. It was for him, virtually a Bible and when the weather was nice, I would sometimes see him at lunchtime sitting on a park bench on the campus studying the book as though he was a Bible scholar studying the divine writ.
>
> He came to me one morning and said, "David, have you heard the radio report about the German invasion of the Soviet Union?" and I said no, I hadn't heard it. And he said, "Well, it has just come through and I believe it is an absolute lie which has been perpetrated in order to persuade the proletariat that they ought to support the war. It can't be true because there is this agreement between Stalin and Hitler and such an invasion is absolutely impossible."

The next day, everything had been changed, everybody now understood that there was war between Germany and the Soviet Union and overnight, the war became a People's War, and everybody had to support it. That was the way in which the left-wing supporters of the Soviet Union changed their tune overnight.

In a letter home a couple of months later (11 August), he described the popular dislike of the Prime Minister, Menzies, who was regarded as very egocentric and incapable of getting people to work with him. In fact, Menzies' unpopularity at the time, and his inability to form a coalition between his party (the United Australia Party) and the Labor Party led to his resignation on 29 August 1941; before the year was out, Labor was in office with Curtin as Prime Minister, and Menzies was on the Opposition benches, where he stayed until after the war.

David with Jeofry Courtney-Pratt and Abe Joffe at the Races, Melbourne Cup Day, March 1941.

The Japanese attack on Pearl Harbour on 7 December 1941, and the Japanese declaration of war on the USA and Great Britain, fuelled popular fears about a Japanese invasion of Australia. Curtin had already become Prime Minister, and later that day, David listened to his 'Declaration of War' speech, and the news of

Japan's conquest of Thailand. These events brought the war virtually to Australia's doorstep.

In a letter home written a week later (14 December 1942), David described the shock that the attack on Pearl Harbour had caused in Australia, as well as the sinking of the *Repulse* and the *Prince of Wales*. Until then, the invincibility of the British navy had always been unquestioned. He noted that when 'the full news came out', it was apparent that the Japanese attacks had been 'daringly and courageously carried out' and that the British ships had been without accompanying aircraft. This defeat gave the Japanese almost total command of the seas and changed Australian perceptions of the war.

David wrote in the same letter:

> This latest Japanese move has brought the war to the Australian public as nothing else. They have even cancelled certain horse-races, and some sports fixtures as well as future public holidays. For free and easy Australians, that is indeed something.

In a letter home, written a week later, David described how the usual 'summer' holidays over Christmas and the New Year had been cancelled, and that the government was 'really asserting itself'. It had taken over aircraft production, though David doubted that this would lead to a great increase in air strength. The government had also instructed the adult population to work on Saturday mornings, though David was unsure whether that would be maintained. The streets were blacked out, but not so completely as in England. He commented that people were beginning to realise the proximity of the war for the first time.

***

During his first year in Australia, David had joined the University Labor Club, which provided the main forum in which he could discuss political issues.

He recalled:

> That year [1940], I also would go for hikes on Sundays to various parts of the countryside or the beaches around Melbourne and I also found that I could have some sort of political discussions with

the University Labor Club. They were the only people who were at all politically conscious. Most other people had practically no interest in politics or in social problems at all. We would sometimes go to Ferntree Gully for a long weekend in which there would be debates and discussions about various policies, and we had there some very enthusiastic communists who were against the war …

I remember Ralph Gibson, a philosopher who was a very strong Marxist, and there was a Jewish man from Adelaide who was a very keen Marxist. He was also a poet and I believe now he has become a bookseller. Very lively people, but of course, the extreme left were fanatically anti-war because they regarded it as a capitalist war and should under no circumstances be supported by the proletariat …

The weekends with the University Labor Party provided David with a degree of political engagement and a level of discussion absent (on the whole) from his other social circles. The people who attended these weekends represented a range of different views, from Christian socialists and pacifists, regular Labor Party supporters, including the daughter of a local MP, and communists. He made friends with Jean Muir, who became a highly regarded educationalist and feminist after the war. David must have seemed rather unusual: British and Jewish (self-defined as 'orthodox'); socialist and Zionist; articulate but modest in his manner.

Some Australians were already talking about the shape of Australian society after the war. A few months after arriving in Melbourne, David had been to hear an annual talk sponsored by the University Jewish Society, the Monash Oration, given by the Vice Chancellor of Melbourne University, Sir John Medley, who,

… made a plea for more provocative thinking!!! And [the] need for realising that we could not return to 1939 conditions when War was over. I was very much impressed by the spirit of his talk. I wonder how well it was appreciated. The vote of thanks suggested that it wasn't …

Though the meeting was organised by the University Jewish Society there were practically no students there, and in a letter home (14 October 1940), he was critical of the students' lack of engagement with social and political issues. This was so different from the lively world of student politics he had been familiar with in Cambridge and London. His contacts with the University Labor Club continued, albeit on an intermittent basis, though he often found the discussions unsatisfactory. In a letter home (10 June 1941), David described a weekend that he had spent with the University Labor Club. He commented on how strange it was that,

> ... there was more real freedom of opinion in England than here. A large number of the left-wing publications still being produced in England would not be permitted here ... If they [the authorities] think you have been an active left-winger, they are liable to search your library and confiscate whatever they don't like. And conscientious objectors are not dealt with anything like the same liberalism as in England ... One interesting difference in background between England and Australia is that in England, there seems to be a strong widespread genuine liberal sentiment in all the political parties, and this is almost non-existent here. This no doubt explains the much freer treatment of criticism in England, (in spite of its extremely dangerous position), than in Australia.

***

As 'Dr Tabor from Cambridge', engaged on scientific war work, David was made welcome by a wide range of people in the Jewish community, especially those ministers connected to the orthodox community, and his diary contains many references to their generous hospitality, particularly during the Jewish festivals. The main divide in the community in the early 1940s was not primarily between Orthodox and Reform congregations, but between those rabbis and community leaders who supported Zionism and were sympathetic to the plight of refugees who had escaped to Australia, and those who put loyalty to King and the Empire first and opposed Zionism as being in some sense unpatriotic.

There were also a number of remarkable personalities in the Australian Jewish community at this time. The most unusual was Dr I. Steinberg, a Russian Jew who was the leader of the Freelands Movement; he advocated the settling of Jews in the Kimberley region of Australia, rather than the Zionist ideal of reclaiming the Land of Israel. He was supported by those British and Australian Jews who felt the Zionist agenda brought them into conflict with Britain, as David remembered in 1985:

Steinberg was a Russian-Jewish intellectual who had been a leading political figure in the Menshevik party, and he had actually been Minister [Commissar] of Justice in Lenin's first cabinet, though Trotsky described him as a 'fish out of water'. He came away from what he described as the 'political kitchen' of the Soviet Bolshevik movement, disillusioned with Marxism. He became – he always had been – an observant Jew, and I think he became more orthodox as he became older. He also was rather critical of the Zionist movement on the grounds that Jews ought not to put all their eggs in one basket, and he tried to revive the Freeland Movement, to acquire various territories in the world where Jews might be able to settle if they could escape from Europe.

He persuaded the Australian government to consider seriously … the [Kimberley] region in northwest Australia as a possible territory for Jewish settlement. It never come to anything, and maybe it is just as well, because they have since discovered vast diamond resources in that part of Australia, and I can't really imagine what would have happened if there had been an autonomous or semi-autonomous Jewish settlement in that part of the country. But Steinberg was a remarkable character [and] a great orator; he … captivated his audiences even when they didn't agree with him …

References to the plight of refugees in Australia occur frequently in David's diary and letters. For example, in February 1941, David visited the home of Dr R, a non-Jewish refugee from Germany living at Brighton Beach (a suburb of Melbourne) with his wife and family.

He described the visit in a letter home (3 February 1941):

The husband is remarkably Jewish looking, and yet he has not a drop of Jewish blood in his veins. He comes from an old Huguenot family which fled from France and settled in Germany; but he looks much more Jewish than many German refugees that are completely Jewish … they [i.e. husband and wife] are both rather intellectual in the Continental sense. It was amusing to hear them discussing English literature and the English stage with such assurance. I had to be very careful bluffing my way along. But I enjoyed the evening, and what is more they are keen vegetarians, and have the most amazing dishes that are at once tasty, attractive to look at, and good food.

David's account indicates the cultural sophistication that such refugees brought with them. Suzanne Rutland (a historian of Australian Jewry) has commented on the legacy of the refugees, particularly those from Germany and Austria, in creating some of the conditions for the more open, multi-cultural society that developed in Australia after the Second World War.[24]

A discussion with friends in March 1941 led to the suggestion that David should start a study group with Jewish students at the university, as he described it to me:

> I became involved in ... the formation of a Jewish students' [study] group in Melbourne. Most of the members were European youngsters who could not serve in the Armed Forces but felt the need for some form of Jewish activity and they were probably evening students or part-time students at the university. We used to meet weekly or monthly ... and have discussions on Jewish subjects and activities that were quite successful. We had some difficulty in attracting Australian [Jewish] students; many of them didn't want to join, and what is more, opposed it. Since then, Jewish student movements in Australia have multiplied and I suppose every major university has got some Jewish students' [study] group.

The Jewish Students' Study Group (JSSG) met a real need and was a success. Some of its members went on to achieve considerable distinction as leaders of the Jewish community, and in the professions. One member was Zelman Cowan, who later became Governor-General of Australia. After the war, the study group flourished for about ten years, with regular (residential) study camps which appealed to Jewish students of all religious and political affiliations, and which drew in some of the best scholars as voluntary teachers or lecturers. Many of those involved with organising the activities of the JSSG were themselves young refugees, and active in different Zionist movements.

***

The state of the Zionist youth organisations in Melbourne led David to observe in his diary (23 June) that this was 'where we were in England ten years ago'. In early July 1941, he agreed to take over the running of the local *Habonim* group, and soon, he was spending part of every weekend with his group, and at least one evening a week writing articles and liaising with Young Zionist organisations in Sydney. One of his first innovations was to run the group on the lines of English *Habonim*, and this soon became popular, as he remembered:

> The real point was that this pattern of activity was suited to Australian conditions ... Particularly in areas like Carlton, where the mixture of Hebrew songs and Jewish education and discipline appealed very much to parents and also to the youngsters themselves. Very soon, we were having groups in other parts of Melbourne. Some older people, used to youth movements in Poland, realised that this was a pattern much more appropriate to Australia than the type of youth movement they had been used to in Eastern Europe.

> The young people in Sydney also began to become active at that time. They were mainly teenagers, and they started an organisation called *Shomrim* ... We co-operated and I think they then started to form *Habonim* groups in Sydney, too. Of course, the war was in full flood. France had fallen and Japan was coming into the war so that inter-state travel became very difficult ... The only thing that was permitted was the organisation of inter-state summer camps for recognised youth movements, and indeed, we held a number of summer camps under canvas.

A pattern started to develop that was to continue until David left Australia, of meetings to organise Zionist youth work, and the regular meetings of the *Habonim* group that David was now running in Melbourne. In early September, he took a holiday in Queensland, and the last part of his trip was spent in Sydney. During his stay there, David also gave a talk to on 'Jewish youth and [the] Jewish future', though he did not realise at the time what impact his talk had had on one member of *Shomrim*, Hanna Stillschweig. Hanna was taken to the meeting by a friend, and she remembered the occasion vividly:

> We went along to this meeting, and we were just sitting in the audience, and listening to this chap from Melbourne, called Dr David Tabor addressing us ... He may have talked about *Habonim* in England, or *Habonim* in Melbourne, I haven't the faintest idea,

but as [soon as] I saw him up there on the podium, it was love at first sight, as far as I was concerned. Afterwards, I think [a friend] introduced me to him. I must have exchanged a few words with him …

I came home, talked about it to my parents, and my father obviously realised that I was rather interested, because the next day at work, he said, "Why don't you phone him up? Phone him up at his hotel." [David] must have given me the number of his hotel, the number where he stayed … He said, "I'm going back tonight or tomorrow, I've never been to Sydney before, and I was planning to go to the zoo. Would you like to come with me?"

Dr Tabor had suggested that we meet at Circular Quay, to take the ferry that went over to the zoo. We met at Circular Quay, and he said, "Could I buy you some sweets?" I was so overcome that when he said, "What would you like?" I said, "Oh well, really anything or nothing." He said, "OK, I'll get something", and he came back with a roll of cough drops (laughing). So we went on the ferry, sucking these cough drops, talking about *Habonim*, going to Palestine, and all the rest of it. We went to the zoo, and we walked around, then after a while we went back, as I had to go back to work, but I think he said, "Well, if you want to discuss this any further, you can write to me, care of the Zionist Office (in Melbourne), because I go in there every week"… and that was the start of the correspondence between us.

In his diary (3 October 1941), David wrote:

Surprise call from Hannalene Stillschweig about seeing me; so we went to Zoo together. She apparently wanted to see me about encouraging Zionists to go to Palestine either as *chalutzim* [pioneers] or otherwise …

Back in Melbourne after his month's holiday, David went straight back into his busy routine of research in the lab, social activities in the Jewish community, planning a *Habonim* camp, and fostering links with the Zionist organisations in New South Wales. On 12 December, Hanna came to Melbourne with her father on a business trip. She was the model for the fashion ranges which he was trying to sell to the buyers from local department stores.

David met her to discuss Zionist youth work, and again, six days later. After dinner, they went to see *Fantasia*.

David wrote in his diary (18 December 1941):

> I like Hannalene. She is in some ways so much older than her years. She thoroughly enjoyed *Fantasia*. … After that, coffee & a walk over Princes Bridge. Talked about ourselves. Home by twelve-thirty. To bed tired.

It was this shared interest in Zionist youth work that enabled David and Hanna to meet. How would their relationship develop?

Chapter 8

Coming Together

This chapter draws mainly on my father's diaries and letters, and the interviews I conducted with him and Hanna in the 1980s. These sources provide an evocative picture of the interaction between young Jews in Sydney, with its predominantly German and Austrian refugee population, and Melbourne, where the Jewish community consisted mainly of refugees from eastern Europe. The contrast between these two cities, and the Jewish communities that lived there during the war, underpins the story told in this chapter.

***

For Australians, the advance of Japanese forces in 1942 was the most threatening news of the war. There was considerable anti-British feeling, and David commented in a letter home in January that the Australians felt completely let down by Britain; they had sent their best troops to fight in North Africa, while their own defence had been largely neglected.

At the end of January, David recorded that advancing Japanese troops were only thirty miles from Singapore, and by the second week of February, he described the news from Singapore as very depressing. In a letter home (15 February 1942), he wrote that the one thing that had lifted morale in Melbourne, was the sight of American soldiers and airmen. After noting that he had had a full day at work, he wrote in his diary (16 February) that he was very disturbed by the news of the fall of Singapore. Churchill had given what David called an 'excellent' speech, but he asked wryly, 'What use is a speech?'

The next day, there was more news about the fall of Singapore and the surrender of sixty thousand soldiers. In his diary, David commented that everyone was very upset, and that there was a lot of anti-Churchill feeling. It was the greatest capitulation in British history, and a blow from which British prestige in the Far East never recovered. For the Australian government, which felt betrayed by the lack of British preparedness, this was the clearest signal that the country's future lay in a closer relationship with America, at least for the duration of the war. For the Americans, Australia had strategic importance as a staging post for the defeat of Japan, and over one hundred thousand American troops passed through Australia during the war.

Towards the end of February, David received a surprise visit from Reed of the Commonwealth Investigation Bureau (CIB), which had responsibility for internal security. David had sent a letter abroad that had been intercepted by the censor and was questioned about a phrase he had used. Writing to a friend in London about his involvement in Jewish youth work in Melbourne, he referred to the many young refugees, particularly those from Austria and Germany, as 'newcomers'. The Australians, with their lack of sensitivity, called them 'reffos', and they hated that. Instead, they preferred to call themselves 'newcomers', the term that David had used. The censor assumed that this referred to some sort of under-cover activity, helping pro-Japanese elements in Australia.

Looking back on this experience over forty years later, David described what happened:

> ... I was interviewed in the lab several times, much to the amusement of Philip Bowden. They enquired of the leaders of the Jewish community as to whether I was a trustworthy character or some sort of under-cover agent. Finally, the matter was resolved, and they cleared my name, explaining all the time that, of course, there was a war on, and they had to be careful that any sort of message that got out of the country might have been used to give information to people who were supporting the Japanese war effort.
>
> The thing that struck me most about it was that they were ... dedicated people who knew very little of what was going on in the world at large. They certainly knew nothing about Jewish activities, the fact that Jewish communities wrote to one another, or that there was such a thing as Zionism. Of that they seemed quite oblivious, and when one told them about this it seemed something new, that they had never heard of before.

By early 1942, the whole productive system of the nation was placed under central control and direction. The government prohibited the manufacture of unnecessary commodities, introduced identity cards and brought in a range of restrictions on consumption, employment and travel. March brought the news of further Japanese advances in Java and Burma, and the bombing of northern Australia. David participated in gas mask drill and took an ARP (Air Raid Precautions) exam, though the practical activities were difficult to take entirely seriously, as he observed in his diary (14 March):

> Good practical messing around. Lovely weather out. Played at putting fires out.

The main events of the war in 1942 were recorded briefly in David's diary, such as the American raid on the Philippines (16 April), and news of the massive bombing of Germany by Britain, which started at about the same time. News from India prompted the following comment in his diary (5 May):

> Recent statement by [the] Indian Congress Party that it would accept Ghandi's non-violent programme rather than Nehru's [support for the war effort] suggests a bad state of affairs in the war, and the thought that it would last for years left me feeling depressed.

As a socialist, David broadly supported the Indian independence movement; as a British subject, he recognised how dangerous the situation of Britain was.

Rationing in Australia was not as comprehensive as it was in Britain, but clothes rationing was introduced in May 1942. David noted in his dairy that there was panic buying of clothes, which he felt was sickening. In a letter home (12 May), he called the panic buying of clothes 'disgraceful' and commented that most people's reactions to the war were still largely self-centred. In the same letter, he wrote that the Australian forces were immeasurably stronger than six months before, largely because of the presence of American forces.

There was much local criticism of Churchill's emphasis on the need to 'beat Hitler first', a policy which he had agreed with Roosevelt. Many Australians, mindful of the threat they faced, thought defeating the Japanese should come first; David's view, expressed in the same letter, was that the two issues could not be divided. Militarily, Australia felt under attack, as the Japanese air force had bombed Darwin in the north, and their army now controlled portions of the Australian mandate in New Guinea. In early June, David recorded in his diary that three (midget) Japanese submarines attempted to enter Sydney Harbour and had been sunk, though their presence had created much alarm among the civilian population. For the remainder of the war, the defence of Australia became America's responsibility, with long-term implications for the defence relationship between Australia and Britain.

Unexpected meetings sometimes brought home the realities of war quite powerfully. For example, David took an evening train to Sydney towards the end of July so that he could visit munitions factories in New South Wales, as well as visiting Hanna. In his diary (24 July), he described the other passengers in his compartment:

> There was a nurse, a medical colonel from the Netherlands ... and then a young Australian who had lost a leg. He was terrific in height and breadth: very modest and 'normal', and then it turned out that he had just won the V.C. in Syria. Such a quiet chap (name Cutler?).

After the war, Cutler had a distinguished career as a public servant, and later became Governor-General of New South Wales.

By November, after earlier German advances had appeared to threaten Egypt, the Allies were more successful in North Africa. This culminated in an Allied victory in Libya and, at about the same time, the news of the Russian pincer movement to encircle German troops at Stalingrad. As David recorded Allied successes towards the end of 1942, he commented that the good news had boosted morale enormously. The only reference during November to war preparations in Melbourne was David's brief description (23 November), of an ARP display in the afternoon, which he considered to be more entertaining than instructive.

There are no other comments about the progress or the effect of the war in the diary for the remainder of 1942, except a reference (22 December) to a letter which David had received from his landlady in Cambridge, Mrs Searle, with the news that her son

Ronald was missing in Malaya. He learnt later that Ronald Searle had been captured by the Japanese and spent the war as a POW.

***

David continued to have some contact with the Labor Club in Melbourne, as he was also trying to gain wider support for the Zionist cause. He gave a talk on Zionism on the local radio in February, and in June, he attended the Labor Club weekend conference at Tecoma. There was a range of subjects; for example, on the first evening a Catholic gave a talk on religion and socialism (supporting both), and there was a talk on 'Music and Society', illustrated with records.

The evident change in attitude towards the war among the left-wingers present, prompted the following ironical diary entry (6 June):

> Breakfast. A short walk & then back to hear a bright talk by Ralph Gibson on the United Front. Apparently, they [the communists] have now discovered that Hitler is the greatest enemy of mankind, & socialism can wait; that there are some 'capitalists' fully prepared to fight Hitler to the bitter end: and that we must have unity! ... He thought we shouldn't try & create divisions between say Catholics & others & that perhaps Russia and the Vatican would come to some agreement!!! When I said that would mean that both of them would have to swallow a lot of words, he looked somewhat pained at my tactlessness …

Contacts with the Labor Club continued, and David attended another lively conference at Tecoma in August. The main focus was on 'The People's Wars', and there were many different perspectives, though everyone agreed on the need for a united front against Nazism. There were talks about China and India, on what the People's War meant for Russia, and the implications of the war for Australian society. What made the most vivid impression on him that weekend was the long walk that he and two friends had in the afternoon to Sharbrook, through beautiful countryside. As he noted in his diary (23 August), they had walked past…

> ... great Wattle trees pushing their golden heads up to the sky ... everything seemed gloriously exhilarating; then a mad scramble to get a bus to the nearest railway station to catch an early evening train back to Melbourne, and everyone sang revolutionary songs all the way home.

***

David often recorded in his diary the time spent in the lab, and he regularly went back there after an evening meeting and worked until the early hours of the morning. Some research was on explosives; other lines of research included developing more efficient ways of manufacturing shell casings, as well as preparing several papers for publication on the nature of friction. The work of the lab was gaining recognition, and in a letter home (7 September), he wrote that people in the munitions industry referred to the work of the lab,

> ...as having been of invaluable help, and having made a lasting contribution to the Munitions Industry here... Actually, it isn't quite as important as all that, but it is rather pleasant after having put in a lot of work at the job.

Other research during the year focused on improving the penetration of bullets, undertaken with Courtney-Pratt. David's many references in his diary to the lab, his colleagues and different work pressures or deadlines, indicate what it was like to work in a research laboratory closely linked to the war effort. The desire to solve practical scientific problems, and to combine this with fundamental research, was a central part of David's professional life.

***

Much of David's spare time in 1942 was spent on Zionist youth work. He was appointed the first Chairman of the Youth Department of the Zionist Federation and working with the support of Dr Shlomo Lowy (an emissary from Palestine who became a close friend), he was able to use this position to promote dialogue between the Jewish youth of Sydney and Melbourne. He was often called on to mediate in the often-fractious ideological disagreements between different Zionist youth groups. He edited *The Young Zionist* (the main journal of the youth movement), often writing the editorials, and when the *Shomrim News* could not be produced in Sydney due to printing restrictions, he printed some of their articles in *The Young Zionist*.

In his diary, David describes numerous public meetings, mainly in Carlton at the Kadimah (Communal) Hall, most of which were held to raise funds for *Eretz Yisrael* (Land of Israel). The meetings were often in Yiddish, and his diary entries convey the mix of personalities in the Jewish community in Melbourne at this time. Many of the ideological debates and disagreements now seem very remote. Yet some of the issues about Palestine that were discussed, in particular the relations between Jews and Arabs, still resonate today. For example, in his dairy (8 July), he described a meeting of Jews and non-Jews to discuss this issue:

> Traub [an emissary from Palestine] spoke on Palestine from 1917. He was very good. Main opposition from Badger [from the Workers' Educational Association] … His stand is peculiarly static – he doesn't like 'nationalism' or 'states' very much, I suspect. He is frightened that a J.[ewish] state will maltreat the Arabs – or that the prosperity which the Jews bring to the country will attract neighbouring Arabs & so you'll have to have more boundaries & frontiers & passports, etc – in fact since progress would create difficulties, please let us have no progress. Traub replied very well indeed. He made a good impression …

In October, he participated in a debate, speaking against the motion 'Socialism is the solution of the Jewish Question', and in a letter home (13 October), he commented on:

> … the difference in attitude of the Jewish Communists to Palestine today and say two years ago. Now, they were ready to concede that it had been all right as a refuge, but of course, nothing could be achieved so long as we were bound to British Imperialism. This is a terribly static attitude towards the whole question of one's attitude to all sorts of problems in a capitalist society. Still, I suppose that when papa Stalin hangs out a new line from the Kremlin, all the good party-members will accordingly change their tune.

The last week of December saw the first successful *Habonim* Camp at Fern Tree Gulley, under canvas. David was pleased with the excellent atmosphere, and the range of activities which engaged the children most of the time. For David, it was a positive end to the year.

***

At a personal level, David and Hanna became much closer during 1942, and they corresponded regularly about youth work.

In June, Hanna made a business trip to Melbourne and Adelaide on behalf of her father's business, showing the latest fashions from Continental Modes to prospective buyers, and obtaining orders. She was just nineteen years old. Over the next week, they met several times, after Hanna had finished work, often with a group of young Zionist activists, and had several discussions about forming a Young Zionist Federation for Australia. They also found time to be together, when David took Hanna out for dinner and to the cinema to see *Fantasia*, for the second time. He records in his diary that their conversations were mainly about youth work. Five days later, Hanna was back in Melbourne from a business trip to Adelaide, and over that weekend, they met several times, though some of the time was spent discussing youth work with other activists. At the end of the weekend, David took her to the Central Station in Melbourne, where she had to register for her journey to Sydney.

David recorded his feelings in his diary (21 June):

> There was ½ hour before the train left & this was the most pleasant period of the whole weekend. We spoke like friends of years' standing about home and family. It was very intimate and warm … Why couldn't H have stayed another week [?] I have only just begun to know her, & here she goes off … I think I have become quite fond of her.

The weekend was a turning point in the development of their relationship, and from David's diary, it is apparent that they corresponded regularly after that. In a letter home (22 June), he refers to Hanna (without naming her). It is his only reference to her in the fifty-two letters he sent home during 1942:

We had a very interesting visitor in a young girl from Sydney who was here on business and discussed youth work with a few of us. She is only about twenty, but she came alone to conduct her father's business which apparently, she did quite successfully. I noticed in discussion with her about young Zionists work that she combines the enthusiasm of a youngster with the mature judgement of somebody very much older. It was rather like a breath of fresh air …

Martin and Melita, 1940s.

Restrictions on inter-state travel due to wartime conditions made it more difficult for them to spend time together, though travel was easier for David if he was making an official visit linked to his war work. David had the opportunity to visit the Guns Ammunition Factory at Rutherford, NSW, towards the end of July, and sent a telegram to Hanna about his arrival in Sydney. The upshot was that David was invited to stay with Hanna's family over the weekend, and it was his first opportunity to meet her parents. The weekend was spent in meetings with the Zionist Youth Council and *Habonim*, meals with the Stillschweigs, and time together.

Hanna and David with friends from *Shomrim*.
At the Stillschweig home, in Pymble, Sydney, July 1942.

The correspondence between them continued after David's return to Melbourne, and there are many references to Hanna's letters in his diary, though they did not meet again until 1943. One of the few people David felt he could talk to about his feelings for Hanna was Dr Shlomo Lowy, who had become one of his closest friends in Melbourne. On one occasion, they went to a meeting together, and David described their conversation in his diary (7 September):

> On the tram, I led subject up to Hannalene again ... He said he wants to bring her to Melbourne, and I said – not knowing how to discuss something that has been so much on my mind – "I am frightened that if she comes here, I shall fall in love with her." And

he grinned & said, "An excellent solution – why not?" But an acquaintance suddenly appeared & interrupted the conversation till Lowy left and I was left with all that I had on my heart, unsaid. Ah me – let it wait.

David wrote in his diary that he was worried that the differences in their ages and backgrounds made marriage unrealistic (or possibly unworkable), though he did not discuss these concerns with any of his friends. The correspondence with Hanna continued to revolve around Zionist youth work, and the difficulties she was having with the older members of the Zionist Youth Council in Sydney, who were often antagonistic to the views of young activists.

***

January 1943 started for David with an inter-state conference in Melbourne about the Zionist Youth Movement; it was primarily a meeting of the Sydney and Melbourne groups. The *Shomrim* delegation of six from Sydney included Hanna. Over the next five days, there were meetings about the future direction of Zionist youth work in Australia, and by the end of the conference, David and Hanna had got engaged. Their friends said it was the only positive outcome of the conference. David's telegram to his parents announcing his engagement was typically to the point:

> Mum, Dad I have fallen in love getting married soon am writing via America love = Dod Tabor.

In 1987, Hanna remembered that after she and David decided to get married, they called on Mrs Lowy for lunch:

> She said later that as soon as she opened the door and saw us both standing there, she realised what we'd come to tell her. [She said] she thought that it was impossible that two such exceptional people meeting in Australia wouldn't realise that they were meant for each other … Mrs Lowy was a very good friend to us … she was Dr Shlomo Lowy's wife; he was the emissary from the Jewish National Fund, and they were his best friends.

A few days later, Hanna had to return to Sydney, and David wrote to his parents (16 January 1943) about his fiancée:

> She is several years younger than me but has lived through a lot more. She comes from Berlin and attended the Theodor Herzl School there. She is a good Zionist and wants to go to Palestine and considers England an excellent first stop. She wants to get out of Australia as soon as we can do so. She is about as *frum* as I am and knows a fair amount of Hebrew. We hope to start a Hebrew-speaking household. She is very keen on *T'nach* [Hebrew: The Bible] like me; she is also very good at art, unlike me …
>
> After all this, I haven't said much about Hanna as a person. She is charming and lovely, with a sort of inner strength about her. Anyhow, you will have to see for yourselves …
>
> Please don't worry. Everything will be all right.

The following weekend, he flew to Sydney to spend a few days with his future in-laws. The weekend provided David with on opportunity to get to know the Stillschweigs better and to spend more time with Hanna. At the end of the visit, while waiting in the airport for the plane back to Melbourne, he wrote a letter home (26 January), which included this description of his future in-laws:

> The husband [Martin Stillschweig] is in business, a clothes manufacturer. He seems a pretty likeable chap, and rather kind outside of business – I imagine he is pretty shrewd at business. Mrs Stillschweig is what her name suggests, quiet, unassertive and full of character. I rather like her. There is a younger sister, Ruth, of whom didn't see much except that she is extremely attractive: and there is my fiancée Hanna … I am sure we are going to get along together very well. We have certain differences in character and experiences of life, but underneath we have a very great deal in common. Apart from which, we are both pretty much in love with one another …

In the rest of his letter, he summarised their plans: to get married on 14 March in Sydney, followed by a week's honeymoon in the Blue Mountains. The next six weeks or so, leading up to their wedding, were busy for both of them. David and Hanna wrote to each other constantly, and occasionally talked on the phone. The wedding was going to be simple; David was going to wear a navy-blue suit, and Hanna was going to wear a short white dress. There would be a family lunch after the ceremony and no reception, because of wartime conditions.

The most pressing problem was finding somewhere suitable to live. The one flat he found was small and expensive, but given Hanna's objections to his old flat, he took it, and once the decision had been made, he felt more settled. The friendly relationship with his former landlady, Mrs Griffiths, had echoes of the relationship with Mrs Searle in Cambridge. She told David that she was sorry that he was leaving, as she had looked forward to welcoming him with his bride, on his return from Sydney.

The diary entries for the weeks leading up to their marriage reflect David's longing for Hanna, as well as his busy professional life and involvement with *Habonim*. On 9 March, he wrote, 'At lunch time, hurried to …' and there the diary ends. At this point, David stopped keeping a diary. Two days later, he left for Sydney, and on 14 March, David and Hanna got married at the Great Synagogue in Sydney, as Hanna remembered:

> It was wartime, and we didn't have a reception. We just invited a few people to the synagogue, and afterwards, we had lunch at our house in Pymble to which rabbi and Mrs Porush came, and Rabbi Falk was invited … They both officiated at the wedding and they both gave me a kiss. Then we had a lunch, [with] the two rabbis, and [close relatives] … Then, in the afternoon, my friends from *Shomrim* came for tea, and brought little presents …

David's next letter home (6 May), after they had been back in Melbourne for almost a month, described the new routines of married life:

> For the first time in six years, it means that I have a home to come back to after the day's work; regular meals and very little incentive to go out to meetings, etc. In fact, I am becoming quite a stay-at-home and rather like it. Hanna has proved to be an excellent housekeeper and whether it is the food of the company or both, I am fitter than I have been for ages, and am putting on a bit of weight. Hanna seems to be surviving pretty well, too.

He told his family that he saw no chance of returning to England before the end of the war and added that Hanna was a very great help with Zionist youth work. In a letter written a week later, David described married life:

> Here I am at home, with Hanna reading a book and knitting me a pull-over, whilst I try and keep my correspondence up to date. Gradually, we are getting used to the idea of having a home. It is a new experience for me ...

On the back of David's typed letter was a handwritten letter from Hanna:

> Dear Parents,
>
> I don't find it very hard to call you so because being married to David and knowing him well makes it seem as if I know you already a little bit too.
>
> We have been married for more than two months now and are very happy to have each other's love and comradeship. On the whole, married life seems to agree pretty well with us, and as a result of regular meals, David is actually putting on weight. I think he is looking fitter than ever since I met him about 1½ years ago in Sydney. Housekeeping is quite a new experience for me as I used to be working as a dressmaker since I have been in Sydney, but I like it and David seems quite satisfied with the results.
>
> We shall write again soon to let you know how we are keeping.
>
> With love and regards to you all
>
> Yours Hanna.
>
> P.S. Although my parents and sister live in Sydney and are not here [...] I would like to send you their best regards and wishes.

They had to move flats quite often, and it was difficult to find somewhere permanent to live, as many flats and houses had been requisitioned by the military. After a year of wandering from one furnished flat to another, Mrs Griffiths, the caretaker of the block of flats where David had lived as a bachelor, found that she had an unfurnished flat going, and she contacted David and Hanna about it. This became their first settled home, and it was in Parkville, within walking distance of the university. Though furniture was scarce, they were able to furnish their new flat, and thanks to Martin's contacts, purchase an ice box for the kitchen.

Hanna in Melbourne, 1943.

Hanna was keen to improve her English, though she was past the stage of having English lessons. David talked to someone in the English Department, and they suggested that Hanna could take the English Literature course as a part-time student. Initially, she was horrified at the suggestion, as she had learnt her English from the other girls in the factory, and at home they spoke German. She felt it would be like walking from the factory floor into a university department. After her initial hesitation, she decided to enrol. She attended tutorials, her essays were corrected, and she was allowed to sit the examinations. The experience proved to be very rewarding, as Hanna recalled:

> I enjoyed it very much. I sat the exam for the first year and I passed it. For the next year, I not only did English, I went on to English Part 2. I also took philosophy and psychology which was taught as one combined course, and I enjoyed that, and I took the exams, and I passed [them] as well. I don't think they would have ever given me a degree, because I hadn't matriculated. There was something called 'adult matriculation', but I was too young for that. I think you had to be over twenty-one, but I was only nineteen when I enrolled. I don't know what would have happened if we'd stayed on, whether the regulations would have changed…. Anyway, I enjoyed it, and became interested in the thing itself. And obviously, it helped me with my English because I remember [that when] we started the English course with Chaucer, it was like doing two foreign languages all at once. On the one hand, I had a dictionary to look up what the words meant, and then I had to translate the Chaucerian English into ordinary English. It was quite complicated, but it was good fun.

In addition to studying at the university, Hanna helped David with his Habonim activities at weekends, and for a time was a *madricha* (Hebrew: female leader) of her own group. Hanna's role in the formation of *Shomrim* in Sydney has been well documented, and there are also a number of references in studies of the period to David's pivotal role in the development of the Zionist Youth Movement in Australia during the war years.

David and Hanna, Melbourne 1943 or 1944.

Hanna with her *Habonim* group, Melbourne 1943.

***

David's father died from a heart attack on 28 December 1943, and David was keen to return to England after the war ended to see his mother and family. In early 1944, Philip Bowden paid an official visit to England, when he renewed contacts with old colleagues and began to explore the possibilities of resuming scientific activities in Britain when the war was over. During his time in London, he called on David's mother, and later wrote a letter to David (10 March 1944), about his visit. He described David's mother (Rivka) as being courageous about her husband's death, and the rest of the family were being very supportive. They were all interested in hearing more about Hanna.

In early 1945, Bowden returned again to England, to the Physical Chemistry Department in Cambridge, to recreate his research group there. David was appointed acting head of the laboratory in Melbourne, which already had a fine reputation for both its fundamental research and for its practical work. Before leaving, Bowden suggested that, for the sake of the future of the laboratory, its name should be changed to something more scientific and romantic than 'Lubricants and Bearings'. David wanted to find a name that sounded scientific, but which was so ill-understood that it would not prevent the group from continuing to work in any unconventional field that they fancied. He came up with the word 'tribophysics' (from the Greek *tribos* meaning rubbing) and was delighted when a colleague thought it had something to do with tribes and the measurement of cranial characteristics. The term 'tribophysics' has subsequently become widely used, and long ago lost its air of mystery.

***

The decision to leave Australia, and to go to England in 1946 rather than Palestine, was the result of an offer of a job from Philip Bowden. Hanna remembered this as a turning point in their lives:

> After the war, [Philip Bowden] went back to Cambridge and one day out of the blue a letter came from him, saying 'Dear David, I am very pleased to be able to offer you a position as ADR – Assistant-Director of Research – at my laboratory at £650 per annum'. We thought that was absolutely fantastic, and your father was very anxious to get back to England to see his family … I

would have preferred to have gone to Israel because England didn't mean anything to me [as] I had no relatives in England. I had never lived here, and it was just a sort of pink area on the map.

David and Hanna had to return to Britain on a converted troop ship, and the conditions were primitive. Men and women slept in separate dormitories, which they shared with the ship's rats. Their friends, the Lowys, were also on board, though they got off at Port Said, as they travelled from there back to Palestine. For Hanna, it was a ghastly voyage, and many years later, David remembered the tribulations of the journey, which was so different from his voyage to Australia on the *Stratheden* six years before:

> The trip itself was a bit horrific in a way because we had three or four sessions for each meal. We slept in bunks. I had a mentally deranged man above me who every now and again would run around with a razor threatening people and he ended up locked away in a separate room. We used to say, in fact, he was the only wise man on the ship, because he was the only person who had private accommodation.
>
> The hygiene was stretched to its limit, in fact ended by being non-existent, and the bathrooms were awash with dirty water from anything after four a.m. Anyhow, we survived that trip and got to London just in time for the first *Seder* [meal of Passover], and then went on to Cambridge. But that is now part of another story.

They had arrived in post-war, austerity Britain. It was, indeed, the start of another story.

Chapter 9

Jews of the English Persuasion

In Britain, the end of the Second World War had resulted in a landslide victory for the Labour Party, and an ambitious programme of nationalisation and reconstruction was introduced. The cost of centralised economic planning resulted in a policy of sustained austerity and self-denial, in the interests of long-term economic recovery. Rationing and price controls were introduced, and in the critical year of 1947, they were even more severe than during war. Almost everything was rationed or unavailable: meat, sugar, clothes, cars, petrol, foreign travel and even sweets were rationed. Bread rationing, never imposed during the war, was introduced in 1946, and lasted for two years, and potatoes were also rationed for a time. Basic food rationing only ended in 1954, long after the rest of Europe, but the population proved remarkably tolerant of their deprivations, in part because of a belief that they were shared fairly across the community.

For Hanna, arriving in Britain in Easter 1946, it was another new country, as alien in its way as Australia had been for her and her family in January 1939. By this stage, she spoke fluent English, but she had no ties with Britain apart from her marriage to David. For the second time in less than ten years, she had to adapt to a new country, this time without the support of her immediate family. An additional challenge for Hanna was developing her identity and role as an academic spouse in Cambridge.

What did it mean for them to be Jews in the UK after the war? Hanna was a refugee, without family in Britain, and without academic or professional qualifications. David, a brilliant young academic with a record of war work, was returning to familiar territory (his family, Cambridge). Both considered themselves to be Zionists, but how did they define their relationship to the new State of Israel? How did they respond to the aftermath of the Holocaust? How did they shape their lives in austerity Britain and embed themselves in Cambridge life?

***

Over forty years later, Hanna remembered her first impressions of arriving at Southampton in 1946, and catching a train to London:

> I think we must have travelled through the Kentish countryside; it was all green … [there] was rationing, you could get one sardine sandwich and a cup of tea, which we had on the train. And when we arrived in London, David's brother John met us, which was really very nice …

Arriving at the family home in Dollis Hill, and meeting David's mother (Rivka) was an intimidating experience. Shortly after their arrival, Hanna was quizzed by her mother-in-law, as she recalled:

> [Rivka] kept looking at David and she asked me all sorts of questions. She asked me why my mother didn't have more than two children. I said, "I don't know, I never asked." And she asked me if I ever told lies; I didn't know how to take that one.
>
> And she told me about Z.H., who your father could have married, or who he was thinking of marrying, and her father was a knight. She didn't say he worked in the Post Office, but she did say that he was a 'Sir'. I heard all about her, and all the other girls who were in love with your father, but finally, the time came round for the *Seder*, and Henry turned up [David's younger brother], now in Israel. He turned up in short trousers – I think he had just been to a *Habonim* meeting …

It was the eve of Passover, and David conducted the *Seder*, the traditional celebration of the Passover meal, as Hanna remembered:

> Afterwards, we were in our room for a little bit, I don't think we were in bed yet, there was a knock on the door, and there was Henry, ever so embarrassed, with half an orange on a plate, and he said, "Mum's sending you a nightcap." Apparently, it was a great luxury to have an orange [because of rationing], so it was shared, and we had half an orange, half a Jaffa orange. Actually, it was a lovely orange, I can still remember it …

After spending the Passover week with the Tabor family in London, Hanna and David went to Cambridge to find somewhere to live. David's boss, Philip Bowden, had found them a furnished flat, but when David's mother and John (one of his older brothers) had gone to look at it, and told the landlady that they would pay the first month's rent in advance, they were told the flat had already been let. Rivka thought it was most probably because the landlord did not want to let the flat to Jews. Instead, they took a room in a Jewish boarding-house, run by Mrs Ehrentrau, as Hannah recalled:

> She was the wife of a rabbi from Germany who had been shipped out to Australia on the *Dunera* [as an enemy alien], then sent to an internment camp. He was still in Australia … [as] it was very difficult to get a passage back.

David and Hanna soon found a one-room flat at the back of a block of flats in the Chesterton Road and started to adapt to their lives in Cambridge. Their daily routine would occasionally present unexpected surprises, as Hanna recalled:

> Sometimes, I used to catch the bus from there [Chesterton Road] into town. I went to the Technical College to an art class, and when I stood waiting for a bus, there was usually an old man standing there who came out of his front door, and somehow, I got into conversation with him. He asked me where I was from, and I said from Australia but originally from Germany, and he said, "Oh, so am I!" I said that I was from Berlin, and then he told me where he came from, and I said, "Oh, my mother comes from near there." He said, "What was your mother's name, then?" I said, "Rosenbaum." He replied, "I knew Sigmund Rosenbaum [Hanna's maternal grandfather], I was also a corn merchant in that part of Germany." So, we got nattering; a very nice old gent, Mr Mossheim …

I was born in 1947, and Hanna's mother, Melita, came over for the birth, and stayed at Mrs Ehrentrau's, which was just round the corner. There was just enough room in the one-room flat for a baisonette (travel cot) for the baby. When they had visitors, the basionette was put in the bathroom, and visitors were asked to go to the toilet beforehand. There was no room for a larger cot as well, so they decided to move. With Hanna's father giving them some money for the deposit, and Simon, David's oldest brother, lending them £500, they bought a 1930s four-bedroom semi-detached house in Windsor Road, then on the northern edge of Cambridge. It backed on to allotments, and beyond were fields that stretched all the way to Histon (now completely built-up).

At the time, it seemed to David and Hanna like a palace, but Hanna also remembered the restrictions of running a household in the post-war period:

> I had two pounds ten shillings [£2.50 in decimal currency] housekeeping money, and I thought I was ever so rich. David said that I even managed to buy him a packet of cigarettes each week out of that £2-10-0. There was rationing, [and] I had a rationing book. We got [kosher] meat sent from London, a tiny little bit wrapped in sackcloth, which came on the train. It usually arrived after the parcel office was already closed, and we had to collect it the next day, and then it often wasn't nice anymore. I remember [a friend] saying that for feeding a family of four they usually got three chops, because it went by weight. I just had to make do, and … after the War, for a short time, potatoes and bread were rationed.
>
> I was going on the bus into town [one day] and I heard some people behind me talking and saying, "Isn't it disgusting, and you know whose fault it is, don't you? It's the fault of all the Jews." They said to each other, "We ought to be allowed to go in their houses and find all the nylon stockings and silk things they've got. They've got all the money and they're taking over the country. It's all the fault of the Jews." I didn't turn round; I felt absolutely dreadful having to listen to this. Anyway, the bread and potato rationing didn't last all that long. You could buy fish, but you had to bring your own wrapping paper, so if you didn't bring your own newspaper, you had to carry it home in your bare hands. I usually had a bit of paper to take along. There was a fishmonger up the road …

While David and Hanna were starting married life in Cambridge in 1946–47, the British Mandate in Palestine was drawing to a close, and the violence between Jews and Arabs, and against the British authorities, intensified. It culminated in the blowing-up of the King David Hotel in Jerusalem by the Irgun (a Zionist paramilitary group) on 22 July 1946, with the loss of almost a hundred lives, British, Arab and Jewish. There were other outrages, committed by all sides, and Hanna remembered that during 1946–47, she could not travel on public transport without hearing anti-Semitic comments.

David and Hannah, late 1940s.

Soon after the establishment of the State of Israel in 1948, David and Hanna were still keen to go on *aliyah*, and David engaged in correspondence with Professor Sambursky of the Hebrew University to see if there might be a suitable opening for him. He paid a short visit to Israel at this time, but apparently there was no academic job available, and he did not want to teach in a high school.

The young Tabor family, Cambridge, c. 1953.

Michael with Grandma (Rivka), 1953.

My brother Michael was born in 1951, and we attended the local primary schools, in Victorian or Edwardian buildings with high ceilings and large windows. Our life as a young family was similar in many respects to other middle-class families in post-war Britain. In one corner of our back garden, there were three or four old apple trees. These were covered over with wire-netting and an enclosure was created for chickens; my parents calculated that the ration of chicken feed was a more efficient way of getting eggs than buying them from the grocer.

***

Being a Jewish refugee in post-war Britain was often not easy. Hanna had only to open her mouth for people to say, "You're German, aren't you?" She hated that, and for a while had elocution lessons, but could never quite get rid of her accent. Over time, she developed a repertoire of responses, such as "No I'm not German, I'm Jewish," or "I'm a Holocaust survivor" – to which there was never any reply. The complexities of English social codes were something she had to learn largely by herself. I remember her making only a few references to the difficulties of adjusting to this privileged but competitive academic world in the post-war period. Her lack of academic qualifications was the result of traumatic experiences which most people didn't understand or want to know about.

The synagogue in Thompson's Lane, and the Jewish community in Cambridge, formed the main focus of my parents' social life. The community had grown and changed since the 1930s, with the influx of refugees from the Continent in the late 1930s, and survivors in the 1940s. It was no longer the student-centred community it had been but was larger and more diverse in terms of membership; a suburban community similar to many found in the 1940s in other parts of Britain.

Growing up in this privileged world, as part of a traditional Jewish family, but in a small community, was different from the experience of being Jewish in North London or Manchester. Though there were academics 'of Jewish origin' in the university, who did not have any affiliation to the Jewish community or other Jewish organisations, the number of religious Jewish families in Cambridge in the 1950s and 1960s was relatively small. Within the

Jewish community, there was more understanding of what it meant to be a refugee, given that its members included refugees and Holocaust survivors. Many of them were among my parents' friends, and we learned, often indirectly or through occasional comments from our parents, of their traumatic experiences. For example, Halena – a survivor of the Warsaw ghetto and Auschwitz – was a family friend over many decades. Through her, we met Dr Alina Brewda, another survivor from Auschwitz, who in 1964, had appeared as a witness for the defence in the celebrated libel action brought by Dr Dering against Leon Uris.

Dr Dering was a retired Polish doctor living in obscurity in Hove, who sued Leon Uris for his allegedly defamatory remarks in his novel *Exodus*, about the doctor's role in performing sterilisation experiments on Jewish women in Auschwitz. Dr Brewda was a Jewish gynaecologist who cared for the women after these operations, and she appeared as a witness for the defence, in support of Uris. I remember Dr Brewda saying that she had always refused to testify at the trials of Nazi war criminals or their collaborators, but this was the one occasion when she was determined that justice should be done. The libel trial, in which Dr Dering was awarded damages of one farthing, was turned into a best-selling novel by Uris, *QB VII*, published in 1970.

***

Experiences of religious persecution or the Holocaust were something I found it impossible to talk about to non-Jewish friends for many decades. If I didn't share the sense that Ann Karpf has described of 'being an alien', I certainly felt that our family stories were very different from everyone else's. [25] When the conversation turned to the war, I could say proudly that my dad had done secret research in a lab to help the war effort. But of my mother's experiences, I felt I could say nothing, beyond admitting, when asked, that she had been a refugee.

Germany presented a particular problem for Jews of my parents' generation. David refused to accept invitations to visit laboratories in Germany and would always say why ("I'm a Jew" was his explanation). Hanna considered visiting Berlin on a scheme for former Jewish residents, but never went.

In the 1990s, David was invited to a NATO scientific conference in the Harz Mountains in northern Germany. They both decided to go; it was Hanna's first visit to Germany since 1938, and the setting was beautiful, though she discovered that there were many retired Germans on holiday there. When Hanna found herself sitting in a cafe at the same table as an elderly man with a distinct military bearing, she fled back to her hotel. Afterwards, she said that she had hated the visit, as it had churned up too many painful memories of her youth in Berlin.

***

Family group: Jerusalem 1960/61. Back row (L. to R.): Henry, Vivienne's mother, Florrie Landau; David, Vivienne, Lena. Middle (L. to R.): Ilana, Michael, Daniel. Front (L. to R.): Dahlia, Sharona, Meira, Judith, John.

In spite of returning to Cambridge in 1946, so that David could take up an academic post, my parents continued to consider emigrating to Israel. By 1960, David had become a successful and well-established academic in the field of surface physics, with an international reputation. In January 1961, my parents, with my brother and me, went to Jerusalem for eight months. David had taken sabbatical leave and was attached to the Hebrew University with a visiting professorship from UNESCO. His brief was to investigate how applied research in university laboratories could be used to help selected Israeli industries to innovate. The interdisciplinary approach to research, and the links between industry and academia, that he and Philip Bowden had developed so successfully in Cambridge, equipped David particularly well for this role.

In Israel, there was an extensive network of family and friends on both sides of the family, and there were also friends from Notting Hill days and *Habonim* in Australia who had gone on *aliyah*, with whom contact was renewed. Among the relatives on my mother's side of the family that we met and got to know, were two of Hanna's uncles: Raphael Razin (formerly Rudolph Rosenbaum), Superintendent of Police, with special responsibility for horses and dogs; and Alfred Palti (Peltesohn), who conveyed an air of quiet authority. 'Uncle Rudolph', as we insisted on calling him, was Melita's younger brother. He and his wife were very hospitable, and my brother and I thought he was an impressive figure in his uniform.

'Uncle Rudolph', 1950s.

This sabbatical leave was also an opportunity for us to see if we could settle in Israel permanently. We lived in a flat in Rehavia, the relatively affluent, bourgeois district in West Jerusalem, though that year the winter in Jerusalem was particularly cold and wet, and at times, snowy. Hanna was ill a lot of the time; my brother and I often had tonsillitis or other infections, and when the seasons changed at the beginning of summer, the hot wind – the *hamsin* – was also difficult to adjust to. David had a busy schedule attending meetings with academics and industrialists, and giving lectures in Hebrew, which he did very successfully.

Attending the local schools was a mixed experience for my brother and me; the Israeli children were friendly and welcoming, but we didn't learn much because our Hebrew was not fluent enough. In some ways, I had the most positive experience. As a gregarious thirteen-year-old, I got on well with most of my classmates, and socialised with them, while my brother Michael remembered feeling like "a fish out of water." We all had Hebrew lessons, but Michael and I continued to struggle with school. Hanna's interest in art led her, in mid-March, to visit Ruth Bamberger, a very talented local artist who agreed to take Hanna on as a pupil, and these painting lessons became the high point of her time in Jerusalem.

'Judean Hills' by Hanna, Jerusalem 1961.

The West Bank was under Jordanian control, and Jerusalem was a divided city, cut in half by barbed wire and roadblocks, and beyond the barriers, one could see the walls of the Old City, manned by Jordanian soldiers. We were warned not to go too close, in case they took a pot shot at us, and we wondered if Jews would ever be able to visit the holy places of the Old City. West Jerusalem was like an Israeli peninsular, stretching out into Jordanian territory, so there were limits on how far one could walk on nature rambles.

Palestinians were not thought of as a separate group, and we never heard the term used by Israelis. David kept a diary during our time in Israel, and there are few references in his diary to Israel's Arab population, or its Arab neighbours. Years later, I was reminded of this mutual ignorance of 'the other' when I read Sari Nusseibeh's *Once Upon a Country*, where he recalled looking across the barbed wire from Jordanian Jerusalem as a youngster, into the outpost of the 'Zionist entity' (the name 'Israel' was never used then in Arab circles) and wondering about the people who lived there.

Amos Oz's memoir *A Tale of Love and Darkness* describes how Israel in the early 1960s was emerging from a period of great economic and social difficulty. Living in Rehavia in West Jerusalem in 1961, was to be in a relatively privileged enclave, economically and socially. Most of the inhabitants were descendants of western European Jews, who had high educational aspirations for their children. Moreover, 1961 was a momentous year in Israel, as the Eichmann Trial had opened in Jerusalem on 11 April, and the sessions were open to the public. David described in his diary attending one of the sessions on 29 June:

> Very impressive, decorous but UNREAL. To hear Eichmann giving serious evidence about 100,000 Jews in France as tho' he were telling about [the] transport of 100,000 logs seemed incredible ...

I asked my father to take me to one of the sessions, but he refused, saying it was not suitable for children. He was probably right, though I thought then that the trial was a very important event, which I wanted to witness, and at the age of 13¾ you feel you are no longer a child. The trial had a huge impact in Israel, where it was broadcast live on the radio. It remains a controversial event to this day, but Golda Meir spoke for the vast majority of

Jews when she described the trial as, 'a great and necessary act of historic justice ... only the Israelis were entitled to try Eichmann on behalf of world Jewry, and I am deeply proud that we did so.'[26]

As the end of our stay in Jerusalem came closer, there were a number of discussions with Israeli academics about the possibility of a post for David in either Jerusalem or Haifa, but these discussions were inconclusive. David and Hanna had to decide whether they wanted to give up their established life in Cambridge, and the comfortable lifestyle that they enjoyed there, for the (relative) rough and tumble of life in Israel. After much soul-searching, they decided to return to England; our future as a family was going to be in Cambridge. It was a crucial decision, and though my parents made several trips to Israel in later years, the possibility of going on *aliyah* was never seriously considered again.

David with his brothers, John (centre) and Henry (right), during a visit to Jerusalem in 1976.

***

Melita came to England in 1960 for my *bar-mitzvah*, and in 1963, for my brother's. We were summoned up to the guest bedroom for rather serious one-to-one 'chats', and I learned then more about Melita's family history. It was after one of these visits that she wrote the memoir about her childhood in Giessen, which I have drawn on in Chapter 4. By this stage, she was a widow, Martin having died in 1959 at the age of sixty-four.

After the war, when communications with Europe were resumed, Martin did not adapt his *haute couture* business sufficiently to changing circumstances, and he went bankrupt. All the fair-weather friends disappeared, and at about this time, he contracted multiple sclerosis and was nursed at home by Melita. To make ends meet, she worked as the manageress of two dry-cleaning businesses, making Martin as comfortable as possible before going to work, and looking after him on her return.

It was a complete reversal of roles. Throughout their marriage, he had always been the dominant partner, but now she was the one who shouldered the responsibility for everything, and she was the sole breadwinner. In this new role, she said, "I learned my own worth." Her inner strength was impressive, and though she missed Martin, as a widow, she became more of her own person. Martin was typical of many Jewish men who had fled Germany with young families, and who died in their fifties or early sixties, their relatively early deaths brought on by the experiences of extreme stress.

Melita with her daughters, Hanna and Ruth, Sydney 1982.

Melita got on well with David's mother, Rivka, even though they were from completely different backgrounds and different generations. Melita was an educated woman who had studied chemistry at university in Germany; she had style and a reserved dignity, whereas Rivka was from a Russian-Jewish environment –

a world apart. In spite of these differences, there was a degree of mutual respect and warmth between them, and they shared a deep commitment to Judaism.

Rivka's relationship with David had always been particularly close, and a photograph of David talking to the Queen Mother at the Royal Society was proudly displayed in her sitting room, along with a much smaller photograph of her maternal grandfather, Rabbi Meir Michael Kahan. Her relationship with Hanna developed over the decades, and for many years, Rivka and her unmarried daughter, Esther, would come to stay with us at Passover and *Rosh Ha-Shanah* (Jewish New Year). Hanna organised each visit like a military campaign, and I now appreciate how much preparation went on beforehand. By the end, Hanna was the daughter-in-law 'Who Could Do No Wrong' – but it had been a long haul.

***

One story from these years was told to me by my cousin, Judith, who lives in Israel. She would come to England every year with her mother to visit relatives. Judith would often stay with Grandma Rivka and her unmarried daughter, Esther, in Dollis Hill during these trips.

One morning at breakfast, Grandma Rivka asked Judith whether she had read Tolstoy's *Resurrection*. Judith was flummoxed and didn't understand what Grandma was talking about. Some hours later, Grandma (who had clearly been thinking about this during the morning), explained the title by using a phrase from the *Amidah* prayer: *Resurrection* was (in the Ashkenazi pronunciation) *'M'cháye ha-méysim'* – 'He who revives the dead'. I can picture my formidable Russian-Jewish grandmother, trying to communicate her love of Russian literature to her Israeli granddaughter in her heavily accented English, by using a line from the Hebrew liturgy to get her point across.

***

Four generations at Vincent Gardens, Dollis Hill, 1965. Standing (L. to R.): David Lush, his parents Bessie and Hymie Lush, and Bessie's unmarried younger sister, Esther Tabor. Seated: David Lush's wife Brenda, son Dean, and Grandma Rivka.

Esther Tabor, the dutiful daughter.

***

David continued to combine two important areas of his life: Judaism and science. In 1975, David and Hanna visited Kibbutz

Kfar Ha-Nasi in northern Galilee, and he was deeply impressed by the calibre of the people running the kibbutz, people he had known as youngsters in Melbourne thirty years before. This prompted the following written comments about his relationship to the State of Israel, and how he experienced the tension between 'Jewishness' and 'Englishness':

> I remain strongly involved in the fortunes of the country [Israel] even though I do not see eye to eye with its leaders over Arab policy. But the achievements in agriculture, in building, in education and in the development of the Hebrew language are a source of great pleasure, pride and satisfaction.
>
> The problem of 'dual loyalties' has never seemed to me to be a real issue. It is rather like asking whether I am my mother's son or my wife's husband – or my children's father. Only in a truly critical situation does one have to make an agonising choice with all the anguish that [it] involves. In retrospect, it seems to me that perhaps it was the process of Zionism rather than its realisation that gave added zest and content to my Jewish interests. And even that was grounded in the religious ideals of Judaism (in its broadest, not in its fundamentalist sense) and in its eternal ethical values.

The scientific and religious facets of his character co-existed and complemented each other without apparent conflict. David saw himself as a product of Jewish values and culture, but also a product of his English education and environment, describing himself on one occasion as 'a Jew of the English persuasion.'[27]

David played an active role in the running of the Jewish community in Cambridge and was its chairman for many years. He also participated in the campaign to help 'refusniks', those Jews in the Soviet Union who were denied the right to emigrate to Israel. His support was in large part fuelled by his disgust at the way his father had been treated in Russia seventy years earlier. As the Jewish community in Cambridge grew in size, its leadership passed to a younger generation, and at the time of its split into 'Traditional' and 'Reform' congregations in the 1970s, David attempted to play a conciliatory role.

David Tabor in the 1960s.

Meanwhile, David's outstandingly successful career at Cambridge continued in collaboration with Philip Bowden, a scientific partnership which lasted until Bowden's death in 1968. Their laboratory, the Physics and Chemistry of Solids (PCS) was part of the Cavendish Laboratory. It was the first university group that was interdisciplinary in its research, long before that word became fashionable. David's early research resulted in a brilliant book, *Hardness of Metals* (1951), recently reprinted. In collaboration with Bowden, he produced their classic monograph *The Friction and Lubrication of Solids* (part 1, 1950; part 2, 1964). David was also a very good lecturer, and his first-year course of lectures eventually became a standard textbook, *Gases, Liquids and Solids*, which went through several editions, each edition updated to include topics that he and his students had pioneered. The skills of the two scientists, Bowden and Tabor, complemented each other, and it was a harmonious collaboration.

John Field wrote:

> Bowden and Tabor both had great physical insight and were sources of inspiration to their students ... Bowden found book writing a chore and was lucky to collaborate with someone as skilled in writing and linguistics as Tabor. Without Tabor, the now classic texts on friction and lubrication, and separately, hardness ... would probably not have been completed ... Tabor was no doubt happy to leave the grant acquisition and financial matters to Bowden ... To my knowledge, the Bowden and Tabor relationship was never acrimonious because each had a mutual respect for the other's talents. [28]

The range of David's research interests was remarkable: in conjunction with research students, he investigated the friction or wear properties of metals, ice, diamond, textiles, wood, and rubber. To take a few examples of other innovative lines of research: the first direct measurement of van der Waals forces between surfaces was developed by one of David's students, Jacob Israelachvili; research which David initiated with Roy Willis on the electronic properties of surfaces from the 1970s onwards led to many of the technical developments that created the field of nanoscale science; and he conducted fundamental research on the properties of colloids and polymers.

In all, eleven members of PCS were made Fellows of the Royal Society, and many became professors and Heads of Department. When Bowden died in 1968, David was appointed Head of PCS. He wrote the biographical memoir of Bowden for the Royal Society, and Kevin Kendall, then a research student, remembers David ...

> ... going round the department and personally giving us a copy of the biography with a few words on his admiration for Bowden. I still look at the memoir from time to time and reflect on the loyalty and dedication that Tabor had for his colleague and friend.[29]

David was made a Fellow of Gonville and Caius College in 1957, and a Fellow of the Royal Society in 1963. David did not involve himself directly with the running of Caius College, as his priority was scientific research, though he often took visiting scientists from around the world to Caius to dine, where his fluency in a number of languages, including French and Russian, was admired by his colleagues. In 1973, he was awarded a personal Chair in Physics; he became an Emeritus Professor on his retirement in 1980, and in 1981, he was a Visiting Professor at Imperial College. He was awarded the Royal Medal of the Royal Society in 1992, the year in which the Tabor Laboratory (for the study of colloids and polymers) was opened at the Cavendish and named after him. He took an enormous interest in the activities of the new group and continued going into the Cavendish regularly well into his late eighties; it was almost his second home.

***

For Hanna, college life could be hard going at times, particularly in the early years, and Caius was not a particularly friendly place then for non-academic spouses. Once a year, the drawbridge was let down and wives were officially allowed in for a Feast in Hall, Bishop Shaxton's Solace, which took place in mid-winter. If she sat next to a colleague of David's or someone else she knew, the conversation might be about art or literature, given Hanna's strong interest in these areas, and she enjoyed the exchange of views, but this was not always the case. Bishop Saxton's Solace was stopped in 2002. In later years, nothing about college or university life could faze her.

Hanna was determined to gain some form of higher education, and after my brother and I had left home in the late sixties, she became part of the first cohort to take an Open University degree. The Open University had recently been started when Harold Wilson was Prime Minister, and it provided an opportunity for higher education that Hanna had craved but was denied because she had not matriculated or gained the equivalent qualifications. Hanna took an honours course in humanities and studied for seven years to obtain her degree. It was a great achievement, though not always appreciated as such by those who knew her.

From her earliest years in Cambridge, Hanna continued to paint, and she sought out teachers, though very few shared her interest in abstract art. She became a member of the Cambridge Drawing Society in 1960 and was its secretary for a number of years. She formed strong friendships with some of the other members of the Society, including Joan Bevan (in whose home Wittgenstein spent his last years) and Sophie Prior (daughter of Gwen Raverat). Hanna regularly exhibited at the Society's annual exhibition, though her paintings always stood out, because they were so different from the conventional landscapes and portraits that were the norm, and over the years, her abstract style became more pared down and restrained, both in terms of form and her use of colour. Hanna's close friend, Brendel Lang, remembered Hanna's attempts to find a congenial teacher. At a talk given on 18 June 2011, the day before Hanna's tombstone-setting, she said:

> Over the years, Hanna tried out the variety of art classes Cambridge had to offer. The class that Hanna most enjoyed, and felt responded to her own artistic sensibility, was the one taught by Issam Kourbaj, subsequently Artist in Residence at Christ's College. In 1993, early in his time in Cambridge, Issam offered a class that took a theme each term but left the students to paint in any way they could find, and with general discussion at the end of the sessions. Hanna flourished in this atmosphere with the encouragement and stimulation she received, and a warm regard came to exist between Hannah and Issam.

'Composition' by Hanna, no date.

'Untitled' by Hanna, no date.

'Composition' by Hanna, no date.

Alongside the passion for art, Hanna was a voracious reader of literature, and derived much enjoyment from her membership of a U3A reading group. Her reading included eighteenth-century English novels, the works of Henry James, and much modern European literature, and she would make detailed notes on the texts she was studying.

Hanna could appear rather formal in manner, but she was a warm and loving person, committed to her family and her close friends. Her sense of style and artistic creativity reflected the world of Weimar Berlin in which she had spent her formative years, as Stefan Reif remembered in an email to me (23 August 2010):

> In many ways, you could detect the German-Jewish symbiosis that was so much as part of her character and in some respects, it complemented the Russian-Jewish background of the Tabor family … Like so many women from Vienna and Berlin, she took a great delight in running a home that was immaculate, in offering hospitality that was charming, in dressing in an elegant fashion, and in behaving as she always felt a lady should … But at the same time, we knew that such Jewish women had much to offer intellectually and culturally as well as domestically, and that part of their personalities demanded, and often gave, a straightforward answer to an honest question.

It was ironic that David and Hanna had to travel halfway around the world to meet but ended spending most of their adult lives together in Cambridge, approximately six hundred miles from Berlin. Grandma Rivka used to say that their meeting was *beshert*, a Yiddish word meaning pre-ordained.

***

For both of them, a strong sense of Jewishness, however defined, was central to who they were and how they related to others. This was not just (for example) about ensuring an adequate supply of kosher meat, important though that is in a traditional Jewish family; it was primarily about moral values.

Hanna and David, 1996.

Hanna's experiences as a refugee and an outsider gave her greater sensitively to those who struggled on the margins of society. In part, this explained the many years that she worked as a volunteer at the Citizens' Advice Bureau, concentrating on clients' legal problems. She enjoyed solving their legal problems – they were an intellectual challenge – although she was quick to deflect any suggestion that she was motivated by idealism. She also served for a number of years as the representative of the Jewish community on the local Race Relations Council.

Yet in some respects, David and Hanna were very different, particularly in matters of faith. David always felt himself to be engaged with questions of religion, and his depth of knowledge was impressive. By contrast, Hanna described herself as not religious, though she had learned what it meant to be a Jew in the twentieth century in a particularly brutal way. With their different personal qualities, they complemented each other, and they lived active, fulfilling lives into the late 1990s.

Chapter 10

Mind and Heart

Identity is one of the themes running through this book, and in Chapters 4 and 5, I explored some of the contradictions and tensions between being a German patriot, like my great-grandfather, Siegmund Rosenbaum, and being Jewish. Born in 1859, he was old enough to remember the unification of Germany and the emancipation of the Jews in 1871. The development and appeal of Zionism in the late nineteenth and early twentieth centuries threatened to undermine his sense of German identity, and his standing as a German patriot.

For subsequent generations of my mother's extended family in Germany, particularly after the First World War, Zionism provided one response to the rise of anti-Semitism, and the opportunity to develop a different type of Jewish identity.

In Chapter 5, I explained how important Zionism was for my mother in 1930s Berlin, and how it gave her a sense of self-worth and purpose. I now go back to the Berlin of that period, and in this and the subsequent chapter, I tell the stories of two of Hanna's cousins who were also Zionists, and who emigrated with their families to what was then Palestine.

In this chapter, I describe the lives of Josi Palti (formerly Peltesohn) and his wife, Nenette. Josi was a cousin of Hanna's on her father's (Stillschweig) side of the family, while Nenette was from Belgium. I interviewed Josi and his wife in Tel Aviv in July 1985, and he explained that his family's story started in Berlin in the late nineteenth-century. A brief sketch of his family's origins provides the German context to his story.

Josi's paternal grandfather, Leopold Peltesohn, owned Cassels Hotel, a kosher hotel in central Berlin in Burgstrasse, next to the Schloss. It was very popular among Berlin Jews, as it was one of the few kosher hotels in the city. The Peltesohn family were part of the bourgeois Jewish population of Berlin, engaged in a variety of businesses and trades, proud to be German and proud to be Jewish. One Peltesohn uncle was awarded the Iron Cross by the Kaiser for his bravery in the First World War.

Cassel's Hotel and Restaurant menu card, Berlin, c.1900

Leopold died when quite young, before the First World War, and his son, Alfred, then a teenager, helped his mother to run the hotel. After working in the family hotel, Alfred joined a famous Jewish metal company called 'Hirsch Kupfer' (copper); he learned the metal trade there and worked his way up until he was partner in a large Jewish metal merchant company. As a result, he could afford to get married, and he married Greta Baschewitz (a relative of Hanna's father) in 1912 or 1913. Their daughter, Paulina, was born in 1914, and their son Josi (Josef) was born a year later.

Alfred was a very successful businessman, specialising in precious metals. He had natural authority, and my mother Hanna, and grandmother, Melita, regarded him as the unofficial head of their extended family. He was the one whom relatives turned to for advice and help in difficult times, and as described in Chapter 5, it was his intervention that enabled my mother to obtain a visa to Australia in late 1938.

His son, Josi, (pronounced 'Yosi') went to a Jewish school for the first four years of his schooling, and then transferred to a general Gymnasium. Josi remembered the effects of anti-Semitism during his secondary school years in Berlin, in the late 1920s and early 1930s, when Nazi activities were on the increase. He was often harassed, intimidated or beaten up by other students. For his last two years in Berlin, he moved to a special Gymnasium, which was run by the Head of the German League for Human Rights. This was a pacifist, anti-Nazi organization, and Josi remembered the Gymnasium as a well-run school, without any Nazi influence at all.

Josi's family were traditional Jews, though not orthodox. Their social life was exclusively with other Jewish families, and they knew Hanna's family and two of her father's siblings quite well, though Josi's family lived in another part of Berlin. Josi's parents realized in the early 1930s that they had no future in Germany, and Josi's father, Alfred, had been a committed Zionist for many years. He had attended one of the early Zionist Congresses and had been very impressed by Herzl.

As a consequence of Alfred's Zionist commitment, Josi and his sister, Paulina, learned Hebrew at a home from an early age, in preparation for eventually going on a*liyah* to Palestine. They had a private Hebrew teacher, whom Paulina eventually married. Josi was also very active in the Jewish scouts and the Jewish sports movements.

His family left Germany in 1933, as soon as Hitler came to power, and moved to London. Josi was sent by his parents to the Townley Castle School in Ramsgate, which was a fairly well-known Jewish school. It had fallen on hard times, because there were hardly any pupils there. Josi was the first of about eighteen German Jewish refugee boys to go there, and this gave the school a new lease of life. He spent about nine months there to take his matriculation, which he found quite easy, along with his cousin Josef Hepner (whom we shall meet in the next chapter).

Josi's father, Alfred, opened a small business dealing in metals, with most of the capital provided by a Dutch business partner and friend. After about a year, in October 1934, the family emigrated to Palestine and settled in Tel Aviv. Alfred opened an office for his Dutch partner, specializing in precious metals, especially gold. On the one hand, he would buy gold and send it to Holland for refining, and on the other, sell dental goods which the Dutch company had produced.

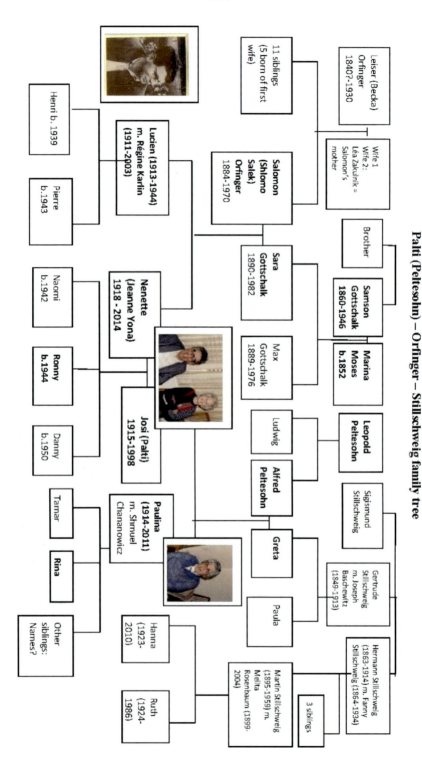

At first, Josi went to work on a kibbutz for nine months, but he became ill because of the harsh conditions and poor food. After discussion with his father, Josi agreed to study agriculture, and they took the advice of a very helpful English agricultural officer based in Jerusalem. He advised Josi to go to Reading University, where Josi later met him as a professor.

Alfred and Greta Peltesohn, c. 1940.

Josi studied horticulture at the University of Reading. At the end of his second year, he joined his parents for a holiday in Switzerland, which was to have unexpected consequences, as he remembered:

> In 1937, my parents came from Israel [Palestine] to Switzerland to spend a holiday and I met them there. Also, I met there quite a few young ladies who I had a good look at. There were two girls from [Berlin], whom my mother explained to me were actually related to us, though I hadn't seen them for many years. These were the two Stillschweig girls [Hanna and Ruth]. They were with their mother, Melita, and a cousin I knew as well, and there were also two [other] girls, one from Hungary and one from Belgium, who I found very interesting.

After two weeks in Switzerland, Josi went with the two girls from Hungary and Belgium to the festival in Salzburg, chaperoned by the Hungarian lady. Josi and the girl from Belgium, Nenette

Orfinger, fell in love. He did not propose then, but after his return to England to finish his degree, they exchanged letters, and he was invited to Brussels to meet (or rather, to be interviewed by) Nenette's parents. Nenette's mother had already written to friends in Israel to find out about Josi's family, was reassured by what she learned, and Josi was made very welcome.

***

So what about Nenette? Nenette Orfinger was born and brought up in Belgium. Her maternal family (Gottshcalk) were originally from Germany, but her grandparents moved to Belgium in the 1870s following an outburst of anti-Semitism. Her grandfather set up several tanneries in Belgium and France, which were very successful. They initially settled in Liège, and that was where Nenette's mother, Sara, was born in 1890. Later, the family moved to Antwerp. Nenette's father, Salomon Orfinger, was a Polish Jew from Warsaw, who was sent to Belgium by his mother in the early years of the twentieth century to study electrical engineering; and there he stayed.

Nenette's parents married in 1911; Nenette's older brother, Lucien, was born in 1913, and Nenette was born in 1918. Nenette did not have much contact with the Polish side of her family, but she remembered a visit she paid to Warsaw with her father in 1933, when she met her paternal grandmother:

> From time to time, they spoke Yiddish, and they also spoke Polish and French, but when they went back to Polish, I didn't understand them. … Seventeen people came to bring me to the railway when we left. Everybody [brought] presents, and it was quite a different kind of life. I was a Jewish kid, and it was very nice all of a sudden [to discover] I had lots of cousins that I didn't know really.

Nenette had been very friendly with one of her Orfinger cousins from Warsaw, who had come to Brussels to study in the 1930s. He returned to Warsaw, got married and started a family. At the start of World War Two, his wife and child were killed in a bombing raid, and after a period in the ghetto, he ran away to the Soviet Union to enlist in the Red Army. He was a communist, but he found the conditions in the army so terrible that he returned to Warsaw. He perished in the ghetto at the age of forty. Nearly every member of the extended Orfinger family in Poland was murdered during the Holocaust. Only one of Salomon's sisters survived.

Orfinger / Gottschalk family, c.1920. Front (L. to R.): Sara, Nenette, her Grandmother Marina Gottschalk; Lucien. Back (L. to R.): Salomon Orfinger; Nenette's grandfather, Samson Gottschalk and Sara's brother, Max.

Nenette had more contact with her mother's side of the family and was part of an extensive network of relatives living in Belgium and Germany. Nenette's mother had a cousin whose wife [Susan née Koch] was the first cousin of Einstein. Nenette remembered meeting Einstein in March 1933, after he had left Germany:

> He had a house at the seaside in Le Coq sur Mer, near Ostend. … He was living with his wife, his second wife, and we went to the seaside with this cousin of ours, so we met him …

> I was very proud, as you can imagine, and I photographed him; nice picture when he smiled. And then we were walking along the beach together … He was a very sweet man; he was really very nice. So that is my connection. Anyhow, this cousin had a daughter, and the one time Einstein came to sleep at their place she wouldn't change the sheets, she had to keep Einstein's sheets (laughs), [but] her mother wouldn't let her …

Nenette went to school in Antwerp, and in 1937, when she met Josi, her parents decided to move to Brussels, as it was a better base for her father's business, importing electrical components for use in factories. Brussels became the hub for Nenette's family, and when her brother, Lucien, got married, he settled there too.

***

Josi took his BSc degree in 1938 and went home to Tel Aviv. He and Nenette married in early 1939. The way it happened was that his future mother-in-law and Nenette came to Israel to meet Josi's family. While they were there, Hitler moved into Czechoslovakia, and since Nenette's mother was a lady of quick decisions, realizing that the situation in Europe could only get worse, she phoned her husband to come over to Israel because there was going to be a wedding.

As soon as Nenette's father arrived, the young couple got married, and they spend their honeymoon week together with Nenette's parents. Josi and Nenette saw them off on the ship back to Belgium and did not meet them again until 1946. Josi and Nenette saw how wise the decision was to go ahead with their marriage, when war broke out a few months later.

Josi's agricultural training in England enabled him to find a job in the Experimental Station of the Jewish Agency. He claimed that this was mainly because he was one of the few people who owned an English typewriter. One of the professors there, who later became Josi's mentor, wrote articles in English for international journals, and Josi typed them up. The professor found a space for Josi in his laboratory by shoving a few books aside, and that was how (as Josi told it) he became a plant doctor.

Josi's working life was very active:

> I spent a lot of time going up and down the country, quite literally. There was no car, so we took the bus and we started walking to the next kibbutz, because very often the bus came to the kibbutz only once or twice a day.

> It was quite some time before the Arab-Jewish troubles began. We walked along our paths sometimes for ten or fifteen kilometres

without being afraid of the Arabs; I was more afraid of the Arab dogs.

Josi had joined the Division of Phytopathology of the Agricultural Research Station and was the assistant to the Head of the Division, Professor I. Reichert, with whom he later co-authored numerous pioneering papers on plant diseases of field crops, vegetables and grapevines. The centre, based in Rehovot, was very small, but that was where Josi received his professional training in Israel. He did not enlist in the Jewish Brigade during the Second World War, because his research work and teaching were considered to be important.

In 1942, Jose and Nenette's first daughter, Naomi, was born, followed by their second daughter, Ronny (Roni) in 1946. Their third child, Danny, was born in 1950. The young children kept Nenette very busy, though during the war, she was cut off from her family and felt quite alone.

***

With the outbreak of World War Two, normal life for Nenette's family in Belgium was totally disrupted. Her brother, Lucien, was in the Belgian army, as part of the general mobilization that took place after the German invasion of Poland. When the Germans invaded Belgium on 10 May 1940, it triggered a panic among the civilian population in the path of the advancing army, and it is estimated that two million civilians fled their homes. The roads leading westward were blocked by refugees, hampering the eastward advance of French and British forces.

Nenette's parents, her grandfather and her sister-in-law, Régine, who was pregnant, were among those who fled towards France to escape the fighting. However, Nenette's grandfather was orthodox, and even though the roads to France were being bombed, he insisted that they stop travelling for twenty-four hours on *Shabbat*. He refused to move until the Sabbath was over. They reached the French border, but by that time the Belgian government had surrendered, on 28 May, and the family decided to return to Brussels, even though it was occupied by the Germans. The majority of Belgian soldiers were taken captive, as prisoners of war.

Nenette's brother, Lucien, went into the underground, along with his wife, Régine. Being pregnant with their second child, she was a useful courier, as she could conceal messages and even arms in her clothing, and because of her 'condition', she was not searched.

In 1944, Lucien was betrayed and arrested. He was imprisoned as a resistance fighter, and while he was in prison, he heard that his second son had been born. He smuggled letters out of prison, saying what his son should be called, and in one letter, he wrote that the birth of his son was 'a great victory over Hitler.' These letters were sent to an uncle in Turkey (which was neutral until 1945); he copied them and sent them to Nenette and Josi, and that was how they kept in touch with events in Belgium.

Lucien was tortured for ten months and then shot, and the trauma of his execution haunted Nenette for the rest of her life. In his letters, he described how he had been tortured. Nenette had nightmares after reading these letters, but her mother was never shown them. Lucien coped with torture by thinking about mathematical problems (he was a mathematician) and using this technique to separate the mind from the body. In his letters, he said it was possible not to feel the pain, because he was thinking of something else, and the Germans never got any information out of him.

Nenette reflected on how the war had changed her brother:

> … And that was a boy who was such a coward, because he used to be afraid to light a match. You know? It is interesting how situations change people … After the war, a lot of people who had been in prison came to my mother and told her how he had given them courses and arranged things in prison to keep them busy … My mother always said she could never understand why they didn't go away. She said they could have gone to Spain; they could have gone to the States. Why did they have to stay? It was her son … And they had him [in prison], why did they kill him? They had him; he couldn't do anything anymore.
>
> He was almost saved … There was one German soldier [and] he used to take money, a lot of money, and then he got people out of prison. We had a maid for twenty-five years who was not a Jew. So, we decided she was going to meet the German. The whole family took all the gold they had together, and they gave it to her,

and she had to meet the German in a café. She waited and waited … anyway, he never came. He had been caught by the Germans the day before. You see that is fate …

***

Josi enjoyed his work at the Agricultural Research Station, but it did not pay very well, and in 1946, he joined ICI. His job was to develop the use of ICI chemicals for plant protection in Israel, and he stayed with ICI for two years. One day, the Director of ICI called Josi, and introduced him to a young man from Holland who wanted to start an aircraft spraying company. The upshot of the meeting was that Josi was given leave from ICI to take the Dutchman round the country and see what could be done to introduce aerial spraying in Israel. At that time, only three nations did aerial spraying, Australia, England and America. It was quite new, and the Dutchman was a very go-ahead type. So, in the end, Josi was seconded by ICI to the new company, and went to America in 1948 to study the aerial application of spraying.

The end of the British Mandate was a fraught and violent time. Towards the end of the Mandate, Josi was confronted with a conflict between friendship, and his loyalty to the *yishuv* (the Jewish community in Palestine), as he remembered:

> When I came from England, I liked the British very much. They had been so helpful and so nice to me. Then I came to Palestine; the British were the enemy, and I was in a real dilemma. I once got very friendly with a British police officer and then I saw that it wasn't so popular with my Jewish colleagues …

In 1948, Josi began to work as a director of the new aircraft company. He was humorously proud that his only contribution to the Hebrew language was the name of the company, which was called 'Chim-avir', meaning 'Chemicals by Air'. Josi and his partner quickly decided that helicopters were too expensive, and that the spraying had to be done by aircraft. They demanded a monopoly, which seemed sensible in a small country, but the Minister of Agriculture, who was a good socialist, did not like the idea, though the farmers did:

There was a deadlock and then one man in the Ministry of Agriculture had a good idea. He said monopoly, never, but of course in this sort of business the Ministry of Agriculture needs a 'chosen arm' and you are the chosen arm – that solved their problem.

Josi worked for this company for four and half years, with long days, as spraying started at first light. Looking back, he felt he had never worked so hard in his life, but the work was exciting, satisfying and also effective. While running this company, Josi noticed that many kibbutzim wanted his advice about the control of weeds, as well as the spraying. In 1953, with another friend, he started a company called 'Advice to the Farmer'. It quickly became well-established, and its services were much in demand. This was mainly due to its interdisciplinary approach, as Josi recalled:

> ... In plant protection, advice was usually given by a pathologist for diseases, entomologist for pests and a weed specialist for weeds. We united all that and said that the one who has to deal with the ill-health of the crop has first of all to know the crop in health, and then has to deal with a whole range of things that can infect or limit the production. It was new at the time and it's still not the system practised in Europe ...

> Of course, there is something to be said for the specialist approach too, but our approach has been shown to be very appropriate for Israel ... We try to have our people not too specialised, but we have experts in the experimental stations, too, and that works well. This sort of system which I introduced is now being used in many developing countries, so we feel quite proud of that.

His new company was very successful, and as a result, the government decided in 1960 to create a government advisory service for agriculture, and to give the advice for free. Josi and his colleague offered their services and became directors, because they were the people with the most experience in giving this sort of advice. At the same time, Josi contributed articles to numerous journals, including the one which he edited for many years, *Ha-sadeh (The Field)*.

Josi with Ronny (right) and Naomi (left), 1950s.

Nenette with Danny, 1950s.

Josi was an innovator in developing an interdisciplinary approach to plant protection, and he received international recognition for his work. Professionally, he was a dynamic, charismatic personality who provided strong leadership to those around him, combining a hands-on approach with the writing and editing of articles, leaflets and books over many decades.

Josi, 1960s.

Josi's family were convinced Zionists over many decades, and in 1933, due to the foresight of his father, Alfred, they left Germany, settling in Palestine in 1934. The family's commitment to the ideal of building the Jewish state underpinned their lives in Israel.

By contrast, Nenette had followed her heart, and that was why she came to live in Israel. She never regarded herself as a Zionist and had what she termed an 'internationalist' outlook. Looking back, Nenette felt she would not have survived being in the Belgian resistance, and coming to Israel to marry Josi saved her life during the war. In spite of this, she was concerned about the long-term future of Israel, and the direction of its politics.

***

After the Second World War, Nenette's brother, Lucien Orfinger (1913–44) was reburied in the *Enclos des Fusillés* – 'The Park of Honour of Those Who Were Shot' – in Brussels. His grave is marked by a cross, because his widow did not want his tombstone to be different from anyone else's; it identifies him simply as a resistance fighter. His widow, Régine Karlin-Orfinger, had a brilliant career as a human rights lawyer in Belgium after the war.

Grave of Lucien Orfinger (1913-44), Brussels.

Chapter 11

Making the Desert Bloom

In the 1920s and 1930s, Zionism became important for many members of my mother's family in Berlin, as I have described in previous chapters. It enabled them to redefine their Jewish identity, and working to build the Jewish state in Palestine became a mission, in spite of the upheavals and changes this involved. The experiences of these Zionist pioneers link to the main themes of memory, identity and place, that run through this book.

In this and the subsequent chapter, I describe some of the major events in the lives of Josef and Daisy Hepner, events which are also important in the history of Israel: making the desert productive and surviving the Holocaust. In this chapter I tell Josef Hepner's story; he was one of my mother's cousins, on the Stillschweig side, and he came to Palestine with his family in the early 1930s. His wife, Daisy, was born in Budapest. She survived a period in Bergen-Belsen and emigrated to Israel after the war. I first interviewed them in 1985.

Since 1963, they lived in Givat Brenner ('Brenner's Hill'), a kibbutz in the Central District of Israel. It was founded in 1928, and with approximately two thousand seven hundred inhabitants, it is one of the largest kibbutzim in Israel today. The kibbutz grows a number of different crops, and maintains a dairy farm, though most of its industrial enterprises have been closed as they were no longer economically viable.

***

Josef was born in 1917 in Berlin, and remembered a comfortable, middle-class upbringing in a largely assimilated Jewish environment. His father, Moritz, came from Kempen in Posen, and had moved at an early age to Berlin, where he entered Jaroslaw's Mica Factory. He was active in developing the firm and became director of the plant in the north of Berlin and head of its retail branch. The firm had been founded in 1879, and in the 1920s and 1930s, it became very successful, though it was confiscated in 1940 as part of the Aryanisation of Jewish businesses.

Josef remembered his father as a quiet, introverted man, who didn't talk much but observed everything around him very acutely. He was highly respected by friends and colleagues. Josef's mother, on the other hand, had a very different personality: she was extrovert, musical, had a good voice, and danced well, and they had an extensive circle of Jewish friends. Martin Stillschweig was a cousin of Josef's mother, and Josef remembered my mother, Hanna, and her sister Ruth, and their parents, who they met occasionally at family reunions or other gatherings. The personalities of Martin and Melita made an impression on the young Josef.

Josef's maternal (Stillschweig) grandmother lived with them and was quite traditional in her religious observance, for example, only eating kosher food. His parents were not religious, and there was little or no religious education in the home. Josef recalled that his father was a German Jew, with the accent on 'German', as was the case with many of the older members of my mother's extended family. This was to change after 1933.

Josef's mother had been a Zionist from her early years, and Josef was active in the Zionist youth movement. He went on outings with his Zionist group, as well as enjoying many family holidays in the mountains, or by the seaside. With his Zionist involvement, Josef was particularly sensitive to the rising tide of anti-Semitism that became part of daily life in Berlin in the early 1930s, and in particular, the abuse he experienced at the Bismarck-Gymnasium in Pfalz Strasse, Wilmersdorf, from other pupils.

Some of his teachers behaved differently from the rest. One teacher, a Professor Lerner, though very correct and formal in his manner, encouraged and praised Josef when he did an individual project on Zionism for presentation to the class. Josef was twelve or thirteen, so this happened in 1930 at the latest, but Josef remembered his teacher's attitude as being … "very outstanding at that time." Most of the other teachers were pro-Nazi, and there was nobody on the staff who was pro-republic, supporting the democratic system that had existed during the Weimar period. Josef's school no longer exists as it was bombed during the war.

After Hitler's election in 1933, Josef's parents realised that they had no future in Germany.

As Josef recalled:

> My father said he [didn't] want to be a second-rate citizen and he believed that Hitler wanted to implement his plans, as he had said directly in Nuremberg what he wanted to do with the Jews … My father was personally harassed by the SA [Brownshirts] and we went for one month out of Germany just to be away and then we came back.

Josef's father had wanted to go to England, but his mother had made it clear that if they left Germany, the only place she would consider going to was Palestine, and subsequently, his father started to make plans for their departure. He could only take one quarter of his assets out of Germany, but he sent Josef to England to study with his cousin Josi Peltesohn in Ramsgate, as described in the previous chapter. In 1934, barely sixteen, Josef joined his parents in Palestine. His parents were already living with Josef's sister in Haifa in a flat, together with his grandmother, who had also moved to England at the same time as Josef.

Josef and his family were part of what became known as the 'Fifth Aliyah'. Approximately sixty thousand German Jews escaped to Palestine between 1929 and 1939, along with many Jews from other Central European countries.

***

In Palestine, Josef attended the Kadoorie Agricultural College, at the foot of Mount Tabor in the Lower Gallilee, which had only recently been opened in early 1934 and was still being completed. At this stage, Josef knew German and English, but very little Hebrew, and he felt an outsider to start with, particularly as there was only one other German Jewish student in his class of twenty. There were about three or four teachers, and the college was run by Shlomo Tzemach, a poet and agriculturist, who was unpopular with both the students and the teachers, and there was much disagreement about how the college was being run. Josef's account does not make explicit what the problem was, but Tzemach was regarded by the students as a divisive figure.

One evening, the school was visited by the official with responsibility for agriculture in the British administration, and Josef's fellow-students persuaded him to represent their views to the official (most probably because Josef spoke English fluently):

> I went up and presented myself to [the official] and said I should like to talk to him on a certain subject. He didn't say a word, but he stood before me and I said, "Excuse me for being so frank, but my comrades and I feel that we should tell you that we are of the opinion that our headmaster is a bad influence in the school." Something like that. "And we think that [you] should know that."
>
> I waited for an answer, but none came. Then I said, "Excuse me for taking your time. Thank you, goodnight," and bowed and went off. That's all. Half a year later, Tzemach resigned. I don't know what happened. I don't think that he really wanted to resign ...

In spite of these difficulties, the college soon acquired a reputation for the quality of its education, and other students at this time included Yitzhak Rabin and Yigal Allon. Allon, later Israeli Foreign Minister and Deputy Prime Minister, came from the nearby settlement of Kfar Tavor, and was one of Josef's contemporaries.

Josef had been a student at the college for over a year when, in 1936, there was an upsurge of attacks on Jews throughout Palestine, initially uncoordinated, which soon developed into a whole series of murderous assaults. The Arab Higher Committee, under the leadership of the Grand Mufti, declared a six-month general strike, and armed bands took up guerrilla warfare in various parts of Palestine. It was a national movement with a broad popular basis in town and country, and its effects were also felt at the college.

Kfar Tavor was very close to an Arab village, Mas'ha, and the fields of the latter village bordered the fields of the college. Some Bedouin started bringing their herds onto one of the college fields, which had not been harvested. The students, including Yigal Allon, decided to take action, and one Arab was killed, and one was seriously wounded. The upshot was that the college was closed for a time by the Mandate authorities, and the normal two-year course took three years to complete.

***

The Arab rebellion of 1936–39 was led by the Grand Mufti of Jerusalem, al-Huseini, and fed on Arab disquiet about the numbers of Jews coming to Palestine. The British government set up the Peel Commission towards the end of 1936, to investigate a solution to the problem of Palestine. Its report, published in July 1937, proposed the partition of Palestine, which would have resulted in the creation of a small Jewish state with the British retaining control over Jerusalem and surrounding areas. Though these proposals were acceptable to the *yishuv*, they were totally rejected by the Palestinian Arabs, who felt that their country was being settled by people who were energetically determined to transform it entirely.

The pro-German stance of some Palestinian leaders in the 1930s could be seen as support for anyone who was against the British, like many people in Ireland at the time, though this only served to exacerbate the atmosphere of violence and distrust between the Jewish and Arab communities. Al-Huseini, who had become pro-Nazi, was dismissed by the British in 1937, and fled to Lebanon and then to Germany, where he spent the war.

The British were determined to crush the Arab uprising, and Colonel Orde Wingate was assigned to organise and train Jewish volunteers to defend the kibbutzim, and to track down Arab raiders. These volunteers formed the cadre of the *Hagana* (Jewish Defence Force), which would later become the nucleus of the Israeli army.

***

During the time that the college was closed, Josef returned to live with his parents, who had built a house in Rishon Le-Zion, and he worked on several kibbutzim. After finishing his final year at Kadoorie Agricultural College, Josef's father gave him the option of studying at the Conservatory in Tel Aviv, where he became a student for a year and half. He studied the violin, piano and musical composition, all with excellent teachers. Josef had learned to speak Hebrew at Kadoorie, but now he studied Hebrew with a good teacher for the first time.

When he had finished his studies, Josef worked in his father's business, which produced electrical heating components. Josef found the work quite interesting, but he remembered how difficult his father, Moritz, found adjusting to the business practices that were then prevalent in Palestine:

My father was shocked. He couldn't take it; the kind of business that was done here … a word was not a word. It was not everybody. He had a few friends who held together [and] who did it like he was used to do but for most, it was quite otherwise. Now I didn't like it very much either, though the mechanics of it all interested me, but it was not for me … and I wanted to go to the kibbutz.

***

By 1939, the British policy of appeasement in Europe had failed, and the government realised war with Germany was inevitable. Arab nationalists in the Middle East, whose countries were dominated by Britain and France, watched with interest as Germany annexed Austria and dismembered Czechoslovakia in the face of British and French impotence. Chamberlain decided that Britain needed the Arab world more than it needed the Jews of Palestine.

As a result, a White Paper in May 1939 limited Jewish immigration to Palestine to seventy-five thousand over five years, and after 1944, no more Jews would be allowed to enter Palestine without Arab permission. An Arab state was to be created, including all of Palestine. In effect, the White Paper closed off Palestine to Jewish refugees from Europe on the eve of the Second World War. Strategically, the White Paper saved Anglo-Arab relations and the British Empire in the Middle East for the war years – but not beyond.

As the Arab revolt in Palestine was gradually brought under control, the co-operation offered by the Mandate authorities to the Jewish settlements changed, and British policy became more anti-Zionist. The *Hagana* was forced back into the underground, and the Mandatory authorities did their best to liquidate it. Jews discovered undergoing military training were arrested, and Jewish settlements were searched for weapons, which were confiscated.

With the outbreak of the Second World War, and the crisis of 1940, the British resumed limited co-operation with the *yishuv*, to prepare for the possibility of an Axis breakthrough in Egypt and the invasion of Palestine, while at the same time, the *Hagana* continued to come under attack.

Not much encouragement was given to the Jewish war effort in Palestine, even though one hundred and thirty-six thousand young Jews (out of a population of about four hundred thousand) had volunteered shortly after the outbreak of war to place their services at the disposal of the British military authorities. For most of the war, Palestinian Jewish units were employed almost entirely in non-combatant and ancillary tasks, for example, as drivers, mechanics, technicians and radio operators. It was not until late 1944 that a Jewish Brigade was formed and sent to Italy for the last phase of that campaign.

However, British security was threatened by the pro-Vichy administration in Syria, and a pro-German government in Iraq. In July 1941, the British, with the Free French, invaded Syria and Lebanon, having already occupied Iraq. In August, British and Soviet troops jointly occupied Iran, and the Shah was exiled. As a result, Great Britain dominated the Middle East.

The threat from German forces in North Africa, though, remained acute during 1940–42. By the summer of 1942, Rommel's Panzer Africa Corps entered Egypt on the heels of the British Eighth Army, which up to that point had been unsuccessful in halting the German advance across North Africa. It seemed possible that Alexandria and Cairo would be occupied by German forces, and that Palestine would be invaded.

In May 1941, the *Palmach* (Hebrew acronym for 'strike force') had been set up, as a small, elite force of the *Hagana* for use against anti-Jewish action by Arabs, and to provide self-defence in the event of a German invasion. Initially, it consisted of a few hundred men, and after participation in the British actions against Syria and Lebanon, training was provided in 1941 by the British military, so that it could act as a partisan army. Several hundred men were trained in guerrilla warfare and sabotage techniques in a camp set up in the forest of *Mishmar Ha-Emek* (Hebrew: Guardian of the Valley), a kibbutz in the western Jezreel Valley.

The Jewish Agency encouraged young Jews to enlist in the British Army, but when Josef went to the enlisting station in Rishon Le-Tzion (where his parents lived), he was recognised by the person in charge of registering new recruits, as they had both participated in secret weapons training with the *Hagana*. Josef was told not to enlist, as he would soon be needed in the underground Jewish army. He was recruited as a group commander in the

Palmach and became a commander of the German Brigade in *Mishmar Ha-Emek*, where training was provided by the British military. This Brigade would fight a guerilla war behind enemy lines if the Germans invaded Palestine. As Josef recalled:

> The German platoon [was] concentrated in the forest of *Mishmar Ha-Emek* ... We had a nice camp there, in tents. We were armed with German weapons and had German uniforms, talked German, liked to speak like the German enlisted men. We tried swearing and using bad language as good as we could, [singing] German songs and so on ... We kept that up for about two years until it was sure that the Germans wouldn't come.

The tide of the war changed in October 1942, after the Battle of El Alamein, and following the landing of an Anglo-American army in North Africa in November, German and Italian troops were in retreat. In May 1943, over one hundred and fifty thousand Axis troops surrendered in Tunisia. By the beginning of 1943, as the threat to Palestine receded, British co-operation with the *Hagana* and *Palmach* ceased; they were again treated as illegal organisations, and arms searches and trials were resumed, as in 1940. Both organisations went underground, and there was pressure on young Jews to enlist in the British forces.

Josef enlisted, but he didn't go into the army. Instead, as a group commander in the *Palmach*, he was appointed in 1943 to be the commander of a newly founded settlement in the Negev desert, Revivim (Hebrew: rain showers), with specific responsibility for security. The community was formed in 1938 in Rishon Le-Tzion by young immigrants from Austria, Italy and Germany, all of whom had been educated at Kibbutz Givat Brenner, though it took several years before the Jewish Agency was able to purchase a suitable site in the Negev. The settlement itself was established in July 1943 as one of three 'lookouts', which were intended to create a Jewish presence in the desert, and to demonstrate that the desert could be successfully cultivated.

Revivim was about forty kilometres south of Beersheva, in a completely new area for Jewish settlement. In the beginning, it consisted of a small hillock on a big plain, and in the hillock was a cave, in which the first settlers lived. By the time Josef arrived, they had already built a lookout tower, and a stone wall round one block, and by that wall were a few chambers that served as living quarters. Strategically, it was one of three posts of that sort in the entire Negev. As Josef remembered:

> We were the most south[erly] in line and entirely isolated. We had to go through Beersheva in order to get there. In the south of Beersheva the English put up a post [the military base of Bir 'Asluj] in order to control us, to know exactly where we are going, how many are going, then how many come back.

Revivim, September 1943.
Photographer: Zoltan Kluger.

The new settlement started with ten people, including two women, and later grew to twenty-five. Once the settlement was established, the first challenge was to discover what could be grown in this apparently barren landscape. At first, they sowed large areas with different grains, mainly barley, which was most likely to succeed in very dry conditions, but the yields were poor. The grown plants were so low they could barely be harvested with a sickle. This was the technique used by the local Arabs, and the settlers tried to harvest their crops this way alongside them. It was not a profitable approach to cultivating the desert, and after two years it was discarded.

Trees were also planted, and they were watered with sweet water brought by pairs of mules from the English camp, which was about four kilometres away. They could transport the water with two mule-drawn wagons a day, and the new kibbutz also had a small well, giving brackish water.

The desolate appearance of Revivim has been described by Golda Meir, whose daughter Sara, was one of the first settlers there:

> For miles around, there was nothing, not a tree, not a blade of grass, not a bird, nothing but sand and glaring sun. There was practically nothing to eat either, and the precious water which the settlers drilled from the ground was so salty that I couldn't drink it ... The 'settlement' consisted of a protective wall, a watch tower and a few tents. It was intolerably hot during most of the year but freezing cold in the winter.[30]

The settlers realised how conditions in the new settlement could be improved after the first winter rains. There was a rushing noise in a nearby *wadi*, and they saw a big stream of water coming down the mountain. They realized that if this water could be captured and stored, agriculture would be possible at Revivim. A water engineer was brought in, and he designed a dam, a channel and a basin, which had to be dug in order to collect water running through the *wadi*.

Josef described what happened:

> We waited during the first winter for the water to come, but it didn't come. So, we waited the entire winter, February and March, April. In May, we had a terrific downpour and a huge amount of water ... went over into the dam and filled also our basin [of the reservoir]. When we opened our eyes the next morning, we saw two white swans were swimming on the water.

This was in 1944. The settlers were very happy, but they had to act quickly to use the water to irrigate their fields. They only had irrigation channels, and though they tried to divert the water through them, it was a disaster, and most of the water was lost. But they realised that it could be done, and they prepared much better for the rains in the following year. The dam was built higher, the channel was lined with stones, the basin was enlarged and part of it was lined with tarmac ...

The next winter, there was a lot of rain, and it was stored in the enlarged reservoir. But the Arabs of the region were keen to have their share of the water, and they made a small channel in the wall for the water to flow down. The water soon cut through the wall, and it all flowed out. Next morning, there was no water left in the basin.

But one of the settlers had a lot of agricultural experience, and he realized that this disaster could be turned to good account. He saw that hundreds of *dunam*s (a *dunam* is about a quarter of an acre) had been soaked, and he recommended that they should sow the ground with winter and summer grains and wait to see what would grow. By the spring, they had a wonderful crop of different plants, and when *Pesach* (Passover) came, they held an Omer festival, which Josef described as a sort of Thanksgiving Festival:

> We invited people from all over the country to come and see the wonder of Revivim and they came, and they were really impressed. It was a wonderful day, and it was a great achievement. Now we had only to improve all these things … and we got the permission to found a real agricultural colony there, which we had not got before …

***

After the ending of the war, the full horror of the death camps was revealed, and there was increasing pressure on Britain to allow Jewish survivors in Europe to emigrate to Palestine. The Labour government, elected in 1945 with an overwhelming majority, refused to issue one hundred thousand immigration certificates to Jewish survivors in Europe, who were in Displaced Persons (DP) camps. These camps had been set up in Europe to accommodate the millions of refugees, DPs and Holocaust survivors who had been uprooted and traumatised by the war. However, illegal immigration brought seventy thousand Jews from DP camps to Palestine between 1945 and 1948, during which time there was an escalation in acts of violence committed by Jews, Arabs and some elements in the British police.

Though the British government was committed to the birth of a new Arab state in Palestine, on 18 February 1947, the British government renounced the Mandate, and referred the problem to the UN General Assembly, hoping that partition (favoured by the Zionist movement) would not be accepted. Instead, the UN created UNSCOP (United Nations Special Committee on Palestine), with the brief to report to the UN by the autumn of 1947.

The ten members of the committee arrived in Palestine in July 1947, at a time when British troops, egged on by the anti-Semitism of their officers, especially General Evelyn Barker, had gone on the rampage, creating a reign of terror in the Jewish population. They also witnessed the arrival of the *Exodus*, a ship full of Jewish survivors from Europe, who were sent back to their DP camps in Germany by the British, and in the process, created a propaganda coup for the *yishuv*.

While in Palestine, the UNSCOP committee visited Revivim, as Josef recalled:

> There came [ten] delegates … The Indian delegate, who was a Muslim, just stood outside, glared around and I offered him a drink. That he took and then he said, "Well, that is all I wanted to know," and went back into his car and off. All the others stayed and made a round walk through the gladioli nurseries with us and then we had a big banquet, in the upper story of the watchtower. Everybody climbed up the ladder and it was very cramped up there, and I gave a speech [as] … I was the only one speaking English and my English was much better than now …
>
> I said that the Jews must find a place where to settle, the emigrants from Europe, and that this is the place. It is a huge place and it's empty, and it is possible to make agriculture here, as they could see … only they have to give Negev to a Jewish state, and this they did. I don't say that they did it because we pleaded but finally, I think that it had an influence anyhow … then of course came the war [of Israeli Independence].

The UNSCOP delegation visits Revivim. Josef is on the left.

UNSCOP reported to the UN at the end of August and recommended the partition of Palestine into separate Jewish and Arab states, with an international zone to include Jerusalem and Bethlehem. The new Jewish state would include the Negev desert. With the support of the USA and the USSR, the partition proposal was passed by the UN on 29 November, and the Attlee government announced that the Mandate would end on 15 May 1948.

The British withdrew to fortified strongholds prior to withdrawal, and violent conflict between Arabs and Jews intensified. On 14 May 1948, twenty-four hours before the expiry of the British Mandate, David Ben-Gurion declared the independence of the State of Israel. On the next day, five Arab armies attacked Israel across the borders of Palestine, intent on strangling the new state at birth. The twenty-seven Jewish settlements then in the Negev seemed particularly vulnerable to attack, as described by Golda Meir:

> But who knew what would happen to Revivim or any other of the small, ill-armed, ill-equipped Negev settlements when the full-scale Egyptian invasion of Israel began, as it certainly would, within only a few hours?[31]

Josef remembered the outbreak of the war very clearly:

> Very early in the war, [and] it started really in the Negev … I was at the time in the neighbourhood kibbutz which had just been started there. I wanted to come back and couldn't come back to Revivim because of what was happening … I waited for somebody to come along to take me. And they came with a lorry with a man from our kibbutz movement, who was a supervisor in security, and he took me along. On the way, he was killed, and I was wounded in an ambush … I was brought to hospital and [that] finished my part in Revivim. I was in hospital for three months …

The five invading countries (Egypt, Syria. Jordan, Lebanon and Iraq) were disunited and hostile to one another and could not co-ordinate their military operations. The Egyptian army proved to be ineffective in the Negev, and in October and November 1948, Israeli forces seized the greater part of the Negev, except for the Gaza Strip, which remained in Egyptian hands for nineteen years.

The war was interrupted by three short truces, when each side surreptitiously rearmed and prepared for the next round, but by 1949, the third and final armistice brought an end to the fighting, and the withdrawal of the invading armies. Subsequently, over a period of several months, the UN mediator, Dr Ralph Bunche, brokered the armistice agreements between Israel and its neighbours that resulted in Israel's internationally recognised boundaries.

Josef was too badly injured to return to Revivim after the Israeli War of Independence, though he looked back on his time there nostalgically:

> It was the most exciting time of my life, and I've only given you a sketch. So many interesting people at the time came to see Revivim. Leaders [such as] Weizmann [and] Ben Gurion became very interested … Golda Meir was very often there because her daughter was a member. She lived in my room, she stayed there.
> I had met my first wife, Rachel, at Revivim. We had a small child, and when I was wounded, she was already pregnant with Hannaleh … We had to go to Kibbutz Alonim [in the Gallilee] together with other families who had children at the time. In Alonim, I spent about fifteen years, and I was in charge of the orchards for many years …

Meanwhile, Josef's first wife had died, and he married Daisy and they started a new family together. In 1963, they went to Givat Brenner, where they stayed. Josef worked in the orchards and then in 1969, he started a course at the university. Josef was fifty-three when he graduated with his first degree, and in 1975, he started work on a doctoral thesis, which he completed in 1983. He then continued working in the same laboratory with the same team of people on grapes and vine quality, research which he described as "very, very interesting."

Josef and Daisy, c.1960.

Chapter 12

Surviving Bergen-Belsen

A remarkable story of suffering, survival and resilience. This is what I discovered when I first interviewed Josef's wife, Daisy, at Givat Brenner in August 1985. Her story resonates with the main themes of this book, in particular that of identity, and the complex interaction that Daisy experienced of Hungarian patriotism, Zionism and Jewishness. Daisy's story also links to the themes of memory and place, in particular her experiences of the Holocaust in Hungary, and her life after the war. Daisy's life story reveals a trajectory of dislocation, loss and eventual renewal.

Daisy was born in Budapest in 1929; her given name was Denise, but she was always known as Daisy. Her father, Rezső Reiner, owned a dance studio, and her mother, Frida, ran a dressmaking salon, mainly making costumes for the theatre. Like the majority of Hungarian Jews, particularly those living in Budapest, they were highly assimilated. Daisy's father had no knowledge of Jewish traditions and practices, though her mother knew a little. They knew they were Jewish, but this did not affect their daily lives to any significant degree. Daisy's father regarded himself as a Hungarian patriot, and he had fought for the Austro-Hungarian Empire during the First World War, alongside many of his Hungarian compatriots.

Rezső and Frida Reiner, Daisy's parents.

Daisy's family was part of the urban middle class in Hungary, of which Jews formed a considerable part. In spite of endemic anti-Semitism, Jews were very well-represented in the professions, in industry and in commerce. The 1930 census registered that although Jews represented only 5.1% of the population, they supplied about half of the country's professional workforce (such as doctors, lawyers, graduate engineers, scientists and bankers), had the commanding role in the financial activities of the stock exchange, and virtually dominated intellectual life.[32] The other main social groups were the land-owning aristocracy, who disdained the Jews on the whole, and the peasants, often very poor, who were suspicious of those in power.

In 1920, after the First World War, Hungary was forced to cede two-thirds of its territory to neighbouring countries as a result of the Treaty of Trianon. For example, Transylvania was taken from Hungary, and made part of Romania. Under the government of the ultra-conservative Admiral Horthy (from 1920–44), Hungarian nationalism took on a more explicitly anti-Semitic tone. It was convenient to blame the Jews for the loss of Hungarian territory, and for the economic difficulties of the inter-war years.

Between 1938 and 1941, three pieces of anti-Jewish legislation, modelled on the racial Nuremberg Laws, were introduced, with the support of the Christian churches. By 1941, most of the 'lost' territories had been returned to Hungary at Hitler's behest, but there was a price to pay: support for the German war effort.

***

In the early 1930s, this was still in the future. Daisy remembered having a happy childhood; she was an only child, but she was friendly with three cousins who lived nearby on one of the main boulevards in central Budapest. Her family had an apartment in the Jókai Ház (House), on Erzsébet (Elizabeth) Boulevard, where the famous writer Mór Jókai (1825–1904) had lived. Up to the age of twelve, she attended a Scottish Missionary School, chosen in part because it did not have classes on *Shabbat*, and as a result (according to Daisy), most of the pupils were Jewish.

Daisy with her mother, Frida, c. 1933.

Initially, Daisy had no direct experience of anti-Semitism in her family circle, or with her friends, but the atmosphere changed as Hungary entered the war on Germany's side. In 1942, when Daisy was thirteen, one of her cousins took her to a meeting of a Zionist organisation, and she became increasingly involved with Zionist activities, although they were illegal. At about this time, the family had to move from their apartment into a very small flat, because the owner of the building they had lived in was Jewish; it is not clear if the building was confiscated.

From the spring of 1942, Daisy and her family became increasingly aware of the effects of the war, when Jewish refugees from German-occupied Poland, Czechoslovakia and Yugoslavia fled to Hungary, with nothing but the clothes they were wearing, and in fear of their lives. They needed to be housed, fed, and to be provided with false identity papers. By November 1943, there were between twelve to sixteen thousand refugees in Hungary. Some were taken in by local families, and for a time, Daisy's mother allowed a girl from Czechoslovakia to live in their flat.

There were at least five main Zionist Youth Movements, but by 1944, they had buried their differences, and together produced massive forgeries of protection papers, and forged large numbers of other essential documents such as ID and ration cards and supplied papers to the fledgling Hungarian resistance movement.

In the ghetto in Budapest, the Zionist youth movements took over and ran the children's houses, where the children whose parents had been deported were cared for.

From the age of fourteen, Daisy was involved in illegal work to help Jewish refugees from Czechoslovakia, as part of her membership of the *Chalutzim* Zionist youth group. Daisy's role was as a courier, delivering forged papers to refugees, which would enable them to leave Hungary and enter Romania. From Romania, the refugees would attempt to get to Palestine, either legally or illegally.

From Daisy's account, it appears that the refugees spent their last night in Budapest with the *chalutzim* in a safe house. The next morning, Daisy would go with them to the station to put them on a train to Bucharest, and as a young teenager, she was relatively inconspicuous. She had to adopt a non-Jewish identity, including learning how to say Catholic prayers. At the time, she found her clandestine activities 'very exciting', and they made her feel grown-up.

Daisy, aged fourteen, Budapest 1943.

She remembered one group of four or six young Polish *chalutzim*, who didn't speak Hungarian or German, only Polish and Yiddish. They were hidden in a bunker in Buda, in a secret room rather like the 'Secret Annex' described in *The Diary of Anne Frank*. Daisy was one of the people who brought them food, travelling there on the trams across Budapest.

In early 1944, Daisy was sent away from Budapest, perhaps to keep her out of danger. She was given false identity papers and sent to Székesfehérvár, a historic city in the centre of Hungary, about sixty-five kilometers southwest of Budapest. In the Middle Ages, it was a royal residence and was one of the most important cities in Hungary.

Daisy had (in her own words) a lot of *chutzpah* (cheek or nerve), and she was told about a farmer in the area who needed someone to look after his child. Rural life in Hungary was a shock for Daisy, and something that city life in Budapest had not prepared her for. The farm was a considerable distance from Székesfehérvár, and she travelled there across the steppe by horse and cart, as she remembered. The farmhouses were spaced out, a considerable distance from each other and the living conditions were primitive.

When Daisy arrived at the farm where she was going to be employed as a nanny, she found that they had no electric lighting and no indoor water supply. There was one good room, where the farmer and his family slept, the older servants slept in the kitchen, and the other staff slept in the stables. This was considered a rich farm.

Daisy slept in the same room as the farmer's family, and on her first morning, when she went to brush her teeth by an outside tap, everyone stood round and watched, as they had never seen anyone use a toothbrush.

There was no telephone, and no contact with the outside world, but Daisy remembered the day (19 March 1944), when the Germans occupied Hungary without opposition, to forestall Horthy's attempts to make a separate peace with the Allies:

> One morning, we heard the Germans come in. We heard it from kilometres [away] because they come on motorbikes ... We doesn't [sic] see them, we just hear the motorbikes. I never forgot it, you know, the whole earth was shaking. And then they take from the

farmers the cows, they have to sell them the cows. And then my farmer had also to sell his cows … afterwards he come home and he go to drink and [got very drunk] …

Daisy decided that she had to return to Budapest. By good fortune there was an agricultural engineer visiting the farm, and she arranged to travel with him back to Budapest. She remembered staying up all night so that they could catch the early morning train at four o'clock. There was only standing room on the train, and she slept part of the way standing up. When she arrived, she did not know if it would be safe to go home, and she was worried that she might be caught and interrogated. Daisy's narrative at this point is not clear; she may have spent one night in a shelter or safe house, but after that she went home.

***

After the day of the German occupation, the situation of Hungarian Jewry quickly became hopeless. The invading army was followed by Adolf Eichmann and his staff, and their instructions from Hitler were to liquidate the Jewish population as quickly as possible. Nowhere else in occupied Europe was this accomplished with such speed and efficiency, and this was only possible because of the whole-hearted support of the Hungarian state. There was no protest or intervention on behalf of the Jews by intellectuals or politicians. From 5 April, all Jews over the age of six had to wear the yellow star, and a barrage of laws was introduced to restrict and dehumanise the Jewish population.

The country, including the newly annexed territories, was divided into ten Gendarmerie Districts (GDs). To prepare for mass deportation, the country districts, but not including Budapest, were made *judenrein* (cleansed of Jews) in rapid succession. The operation was conducted by the Hungarian police and gendarmes, and co-ordinated by Eichmann and his team.

The Jews were herded into ghettos, stripped of all their possessions (and often tortured in the process to reveal any concealed valuables), and then shipped to Auschwitz in cattle trucks. The deportation of Jews from the country areas started on 15 May and was completed by 8 July. In less than two months, about one hundred and fifty trains left the Hungarian provinces, carrying some four hundred and fifty thousand Jews to Auschwitz.

About three hundred and thirty thousand were gassed on arrival; the others were worked to death as slave labourers. Including those who died in forced labour battalions and the death marches, and those murdered in Budapest, more than half a million Hungarian Jews were killed during the German occupation. By the end of the war, some two hundred and fifty-five thousand survived, about half in Budapest and half in the concentration camps liberated by the Allies.

One of the vexed questions about the Holocaust is how much people knew and when. In particular, this question applies to the Jewish Councils who were bullied and cajoled into co-operating with the Nazis. The most important document describing the truth about the death camps was the *Auschwitz Protocols*, produced by two young Slovak Jews, Rudolph Vrba and Alfred Wetzler, who had escaped from Auschwitz. In April 1944, they produced a detailed report describing the mass murders that had taken place between July 1942 and April 1944, and of the preparations in progress since January 1944 for the arrival of the Hungarian Jews at Auschwitz.

The document was translated into Hungarian, and circulated to Jewish leaders, church dignitaries and potentially sympathetic politicians, and eventually published in the USA. However, the Jewish leaders in Hungary and their communities continued to believe that by co-operation and submission they would eventually 'weather the storm'.

Daisy remembered that among the Jews of Budapest there was a feeling (even in 1944) that though they had learnt from refugees about the deportations to the death camps from other countries, this couldn't possibly happen in Budapest. In fact, the Jews of Budapest were due to be 'ghettoised' in July 1944, prior to deportation in August, but Horthy suspended the deportations in early July due to intense international pressure.

Some two hundred thousand Jews living in the capital were ordered to move into two thousand six hundred 'Jewish houses', identified with a large yellow star on their frontage; conditions were primitive and very cramped. Many of the Jews in Budapest who survived the war only did so because of the protective passes and protective houses provided by the Swedish diplomat Raoul Wallenberg and his Swiss colleague, Carl (Charles) Lutz.

By mid-October, with Soviet troops deep inside Hungarian territory, Horthy announced a unilateral cease-fire, but he was forced to resign by the Germans. A new government was put in place: the prime minister and head of state was the leader of the fascist and deeply anti-Semitic Arrow Cross party, Ferenc Szálasi. The final act of the Hungarian Holocaust was about to be played out. The new regime sent eighty thousand Jews on a forced death march of two hundred and twenty kilometres to Austria to work on fortifications against the Russians, without food, drink or shelter, and many thousands perished along the way.

In November, all those Jews without protection papers were forced to move into the ghetto, where conditions were worse than their previous accommodation. Gangs of killers from the Hungarian Arrow Cross party went on the rampage, murdering Hungarian Jews, wherever they could find them. Their preferred pastime was herding Jews to the Danube embankment and shooting them into the freezing river. About fifteen thousand Jews (estimates vary) - men, women and children - died in this reign of terror.

***

In 1943, an ad hoc group of Zionists had formed themselves into a 'Relief and Rescue Committee' (with the Hebrew name *Vaada*, meaning 'committee'). One member of this group was the vice-chairman, Rezső Kasztner, who organised the transport in 1944 that saved Daisy's life.

In 1944, there were two attempts by representatives of the *Vaada* to save Jewish lives. One, led by Joel Brand, was based on the proposition that a million Jews could be traded for ten thousand trucks and other commodities. The prospect of making a deal with the Germans was opposed by the British and American governments, and vetoed by the Soviet Union, and it is highly unlikely that Eichmann and his superiors thought they would succeed. By mid-June the negotiations had collapsed, Brand was arrested by the British when he crossed into Syria, and he never succeeded in clearing his name after the war as someone who had deserted the Jews of Hungary in their hour of need.

The second attempt to save Jews was led by Rezső Kasztner, a complex personality, who by this stage, had become the undisputed leader of the *Vaada*'s rescue operations. From April 1944, he entered into a tortuous series of cat-and-mouse negotiations with Eichmann, for the release of a number of Jews who had entry certificates for Palestine, or other documents giving permission to travel abroad. They would be sent to Spain and thence to North Africa, though what happened afterwards was of no concern to the Germans.

These negotiations took place against the backdrop of daily deportations of Hungarian Jews from the provinces to Auschwitz. The price agreed on was one thousand dollars per Jew, a price set by Himmler, and it was also agreed that the transport should be a mixture of Jews from the provinces and from Budapest.

The process of selecting the Jews to be saved in this way was a thankless task. A number of categories were drawn up, and the final decision was made by a small committee, though inevitably, charges of nepotism continued long after the end of the war. For those who had been chosen for the special transport, a camp was set up in the premises of the Wechselmann Institute for the Deaf-Mute in Kolumbusz (Columbus) Street in southern Budapest. For a few months, approximately two thousand Jews were able to live in relative security, while others were being deported daily to Auschwitz.

For Daisy, as a young teenager, it was a turbulent time, but her mother gave her permission to join the transport, even though she was the only child. Daisy did not talk about her illegal work, and, as far as she could tell, her mother knew nothing about it.

Daisy took the identity of a young woman called Judith who had a place on the transport but had then decided not to go. In the list of the people who were on the Kasztner transport there are approximately a dozen 'Judiths' of a similar age who could have provided Daisy's false identity. The train left Budapest on 30 June 1944, containing nearly one thousand seven hundred Jews who were meant to represent, in miniature, a cross-section of Jewry living in Hungary. Daisy was told that in two weeks' time, she would be in Palestine, though the reality was totally different.

The train journey through occupied Europe was slow, and rumours abounded on the train about what was going to happen to the deportees. On the seventh day, they arrived at Linz in

Austria and were told that they were going to be cleaned, in communal showers. There was a great panic that they were about to be gassed, as Daisy remembered:

> They make us clean, you know, they make us parade ... they separate men and women, and we were thinking ... [it is] the end ...

After the humiliation of the mass showers, the journey was resumed, and on 9 July 1944, the train arrived at the railway halt that gave access to the camp of Bergen-Belsen. For the Germans, this trainload of Jews was a valuable commodity, and for five months, they were held in the camp while negotiations continued between Eichmann and other Nazis on the one hand, and Kasztner and his associates on the other. The negotiations were about the payment of the ransom, as well as discussions about other 'deals' that might save more Jews.

In 1944, Bergen-Belsen had not yet become the hellhole that was liberated by British troops in April 1945, though it was a harsh and brutal environment. The camp was divided into five main compounds, and the Kazstner transportees were kept in a separate section, isolated from other inmates. They did not have to work and were allowed a degree of internal autonomy.

The largest compound, the 'Star Camp' (so called because the inmates had to wear the yellow star) housed over four thousand 'exchange Jews' of both sexes from various countries. In November, a group of exhausted Dutch women arrived to occupy part of the Star Camp; they had also come from Auschwitz, and one of them was called Anne Frank.

In mid-August, a group of three hundred and eighteen internees was allowed to leave and was sent to safety in Switzerland, as the result of complex negotiations between Eichmann and Kasztner, though those left behind felt totally demoralised. Daisy's main recollections of her time in Bergen-Belsen were of illness and privation:

> But this time [the departure of the first group], I do not remember because I [had] dysentery and I was unconscious ... I just remember one day when I wake up in ...[in] the barrack-like hospital there ... in the summer the camp was [bearable], but in the winter it was very wet and everybody has dysentery or something

> like this and there was just one toilet in [the] barrack … The smell – it was not nice … We had not enough food …

After further complex negotiations, the remaining Kasztner deportees left Bergen-Belsen by train at midnight on 4 December 1944, and after a slow journey across Germany, the train crossed into Switzerland in the early hours of 7 December. They had escaped from the Nazis. Kasztner courageously returned to Budapest to negotiate the release of more Jews with Eichmann, though Hitler quickly put a stop to further negotiations.

After a few days, the deportees were sent by train to Caux, seven hundred metres above Montreux on Lake Geneva. Because of the war, there were no tourists, and the refugees were distributed between two empty hotels. The Orthodox minority was housed in the Regina, the non-religious majority in the Esplanade. Though the Hotel Esplanade was a great improvement on Bergen-Belsen, it was overcrowded and there was no heating, and not enough food. After a month, the youngest children were sent to a children's home in Weggis, and the older children went to Lugano.

It was a chaotic time for all the young DPs, and for Daisy, it coincided with puberty. She wanted to find her parents by writing to the Red Cross, but initially without success. After a while, she was sent to a children's home in Bex, which was cold, dirty and infested with mice.

At Bex, the young Jews were being also prepared for emigration to Palestine, and there was competition for recruits between the different Zionist youth organisations. Daisy learnt some Hebrew, basic mathematics, gardening and how to milk a cow – part of the preparation for *aliyah*. Daisy remembered her younger self as being difficult to handle, and cheeky. She was assigned the role of cook, because the person who had been employed failed to turn up, but she had virtually no experience of cooking, let alone cooking for over fifty people.

Hepner - Reiner - Stillschweig family tree

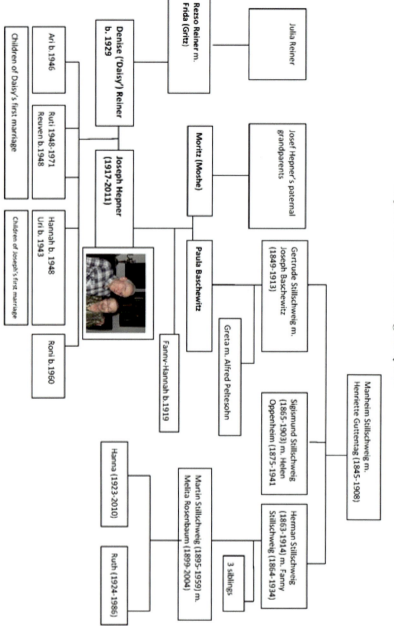

260

Cooking at the children's home in Bex was stressful, particularly when she was told to prepare a large fish for the following day's meal. Her instructions were to fry the fish, but she didn't know how to do this (there was no batter) and her attempts to cook the fish were a disaster. The young Polish survivors were particularly incensed, as they had been very keen to eat fresh fish and threatened to kill her. Daisy refused to do any more cooking at the home.

Daisy's recollections of the time spent as a DP in different places in Switzerland contain repeated references to being cold and not having enough to eat. She remembered that there was a group of boys in the home who spoke Yiddish, who had spent up to six years in Buchenwald concentration camp. They, too, were very difficult. She stole some alcohol from the pharmacy for them, but their outlook had been shaped by many years in a terrible camp, and they had come from a world that Daisy had not experienced. These survivors looked like children, but they were older, most were about twenty, while Daisy was not yet sixteen:

> Our experience [was] really not normal for this age ... we didn't know really how to handle this ... we really were confused. We were very independent on one side, [but] we have no family, nobody to [tell] us how to behave, it was hard at this critical age.

While living in Bex, Daisy met the man whom she married at the age of seventeen. Like many of her contemporaries, she was looking for emotional security through a relationship. Many of the young people rushed into marriage, most of which (according to Daisy) did not work out in the longer term.

Many of the young Jews who underwent training at Bex emigrated to Palestine, but once Daisy was married, she and her husband first lived in Montreux and then moved to Zurich. She remembered herself as being very inexperienced, not knowing how to raise a family, and she found the birth of her first three children very difficult.

Daisy was desperate to find out what had happened to her parents. She had already received a letter from relatives in Hungary saying that her mother had survived the war in the ghetto, but she only discovered what had happened to her father by chance. She found a letter in her husband's jacket which explained that her father, who had been an officer in the First World War, had joined with a group of other Jewish veterans. They had put on their uniforms and medals, and marched to the Parliament building to demonstrate that they were Hungarian patriots. They were all shot, and their bodies fell or were thrown into the Danube.

Daisy's mother visited her in Switzerland, but she was not allowed to stay, so she had to return to Hungary. After 1956, she was able to leave Hungary again, to be reunited with Daisy in Israel. Daisy and her husband had emigrated to Israel in 1949. They were idealistic, wanting to experience communal life on a kibbutz, and at first, they lived on Kibbutz Ma'ayan Tzvi (near Haifa), where other Hungarian Jews were living. But kibbutz life did not suit Daisy's husband, and they moved to Haifa. He wanted to return to Switzerland, while Daisy wanted to stay in Israel, and the result was that they got divorced.

Daisy lived on a couple of kibbutzim, and the main challenge, as a single mother, was to support herself and her three young children. She was twenty-three, and they lived in one room. She had no money, but she supported herself and her children by sewing.

Looking back, she reflected on how her generation survived and adapted to life in Israel. The main mechanism she and other survivors adopted was to live (as she put it), "on two different levels." There was the level of everyday life, where you acted normally, and the level of your former life, which you did not talk about. As she said, "You see the pictures [of your former life in the camp], but you speak about other things." The expectation she experienced in Israel was that everyone should be strong, to be *givorim* (Hebrew: heroes, strong people), and not to dwell on their previous experiences.

***

Following Daisy's marriage to Joseph, recounted in the previous chapter, she was happy and established on the kibbutz with him. She had developed a successful career as a teacher of handicrafts at the kibbutz school, and she was particularly effective with pupils with special educational needs and behavioural problems. In the kibbutz, Daisy had put down roots and flourished.

Josef listened intently to Daisy during my interview with her, and afterwards said that she had never talked about her experiences in that degree of detail before. However, during the Eichmann trial in Jerusalem in 1961, Daisy told me, she insisted that her children listen to the proceedings or reports on the radio, but she could not tell them why it was important, in terms of her own experiences.

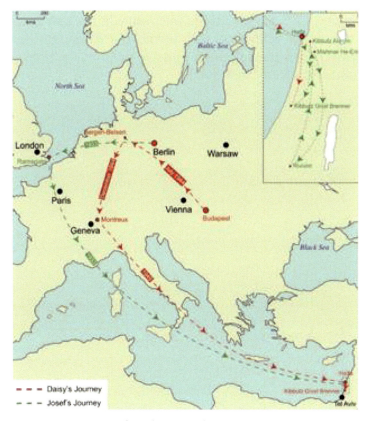

Josef and Daisey's journeys.

Daisy felt particularly angry about the way Kasztner had been treated after the war. He had emigrated to Israel in 1947 with his wife. Initially, things looked promising, and he rose to a high-ranking position in the Mapai (Labour) administration. Then a libellous slur from a disgruntled Hungarian Jew escalated into a court case that destroyed Kasztner's reputation. The accusation was that Kasztner had collaborated with the Nazis to enrich himself and to save his family and friends from the Holocaust.

The verdict of the trial, delivered in 1955, upheld the accusation of the defence that Kasztner had collaborated with the Nazis for his own benefit, and the judge concluded that in so doing, Kasztner had 'sold his soul to Satan'. The appeal, before five judges of the Jerusalem Supreme Court, took over a year. In January 1958, Kasztner was cleared of conscious and willing collaboration with the Nazis and complicity in mass murder, but it was too late for Kasztner. In March 1957, he had been assassinated by a gang of three men outside his home, and the truth about his killing is still unknown. Although Kasztner remains a controversial figure in Israel to this day, the transport he organised had saved Daisy's life.

Chapter 13

Innovators and Pioneers

I have explained how important Zionism was for my mother, Hanna, and some of her relatives in Berlin in the 1930s, and how it gave them a sense of purpose in the face of increased anti-Semitism. I have also explained how important Zionism was for my father, David, growing up in a community of immigrants in Notting Hill in the 1920s and 1930s. For David, the process of becoming a British Jew was intertwined with his commitment to traditional Judaism and political Zionism, which meant working with others for the creation of the Jewish state.

I now go back to the period immediately after the Second World War, and catch up with two of David's brothers, Henry and John. Like David, they were committed Zionists, and they made the decision to emigrate to Israel. Their stories have to be viewed against the backdrop of the turmoil in the Middle East in the post-war period.

With the end of the British Mandate in Palestine and the declaration of the State of Israel, the new state was invaded by five Arab armies in 1948. After months of bitter fighting, the invading armies were repelled, and Israel's War of Independence ended in January 1949. From the territories that became Israel, over seven hundred and fifty thousand Palestinian Arabs (some estimates put the figure close to a million) had fled or been expelled by the end of 1948, most ending up in refugee camps in Lebanon, Jordon or Gaza.

By the late 1940s, mobs had attacked the ancient Jewish communities in North Africa and throughout the Middle East, and most Jews left, by whatever means they could, many going to Israel, and others to the United States. Only Morocco offered reassurance and tried to discourage flight. Between 1948 and 1952, over seven hundred thousand immigrants (estimates vary) more than doubled the Jewish population of Israel to 1.35 million. Most of the new arrivals were totally destitute and were housed in transit camps. For a time, in the 1950s, a third of the Jewish population of Israel lived in tented cities.

Yet in spite of these problems, the creation of the Jewish state after nearly two thousand years of exile was an extraordinary event, and one that galvanised Jews around the world.

What motivated young British Jews like John and Henry to emigrate? They had witnessed the horrors of war but had been spared direct experience of the Holocaust. This chapter tells their stories, and their experiences of settling in Israel after the Second World War.

***

Henry was my father's youngest brother, a highly creative inventor and innovator, and I first interviewed him and his wife, Vivienne, in 1987. They lived in a modest flat in Beit Hakerem, a suburb in West Jerusalem. It was conveniently situated for the Hebrew University and the Hadassah Hospital, where Vivienne worked in a management role. They had two highly talented daughters, many grandchildren and, eventually, great-grandchildren.

Henry had happy memories of growing up in Notting Hill. He was regarded by his siblings as the baby of the family, and his oldest sister, Bessie, helped their mother, Rivka, in bringing up the younger children. As the youngest child in the family, Henry had little contact with his father, Chaskel, although he remembered that he was a marvellous storyteller. Looking back, Henry felt enormous respect for his father's achievements. What he admired most was his father's work ethic, as well as his determination to educate himself by reading books in English. The example of his parents had a very strong influence on Henry, and they impressed on him (and his siblings) the importance of doing things conscientiously and being of service to the community.

His two immediate older brothers, John and David, were his playmates, and he followed them to the same school, the Regent Street Polytechnic. Unlike them, once he got the Higher Schools Certificate at the age of eighteen, he decided to go to work, rather than go to university. He always saw himself as a practical rather than a theoretical person, so he decided to go into industry. He worked in the R & D departments of two organisations. The first was the Nether Research Institute Association and later, he went to work for a commercial company developing scientific instruments. However, Henry was still keen to further his education:

> I took the external degree of London University in night school, and it was actually very hard because it meant I finished work at five o'clock and I had to run like mad to get to the classes and they finished at nine o'clock[pm], and that was a pretty hectic period … I did a degree in Physics and later on, after I came to Israel, I did a PhD in Applied Physics at the Hebrew University but that was much more leisurely …

As a youngster, Henry joined a Jewish scout troop, which he didn't enjoy very much, but one day, a friend suggested that he should go to a *Habonim* meeting. The first thing that made an impression on him were the Hebrew songs. He didn't understand the words, as he didn't know much Hebrew at that stage, but as a musical young man, his interest was engaged. Later, he became more active in *Habonim*, and came to understand the ideology from what he termed "a strictly logical point of view, not just emotion."

During the war, as an applied physicist, he was in a protected profession, so he was not called up. This gave him some free time, which he used to look after several *Habonim* groups of youngsters who had been evacuated from London. Every Sunday, he would cycle thirty miles or so to places like Welwyn Garden City to run these groups. It was also through *Habonim* that he met his wife, Vivienne.

Soon after the end of the war, Henry became involved with the organisation of illegal immigration to Palestine from Europe, known in Israel as *Aliyah Bet* [Aliyah 'B']. This took place during the last years of the British Mandate, when sea-going hulks sailed secretly from French or Italian ports, carrying DPs from the camps in Europe. If these ships succeeded in evading the British navy, patrolling off the coast of Palestine, the passengers were landed on a beach, and rushed to safety in neighbouring Jewish communities. In all, over seventy thousand Jews reached Palestine by this route between 1945 and May 1948, when the State of Israel came into existence.

Henry's involvement came about as follows. Sometime after the end of the war (in 1945) Henry was approached by a secret agent from Palestine. They met in a café, and Henry was asked if he could help with facilitating immigration to Palestine, in defiance of the Mandate authorities. Henry was one of the few people in his age group who was an applied physicist, with some knowledge of engineering. Henry agreed, and his first task was to go to Foyle's bookshop and buy all the books he could find on ship architecture, because he had to work out how to construct concealed compartments in the ships.

Shortly after this meeting, Henry left his job in industry, and told his employer that he was going to get another job in France to broaden his professional experience. He went to Marseilles, though by this stage, he was engaged to Vivienne. He came back to London for the wedding, and then returned to Marseilles. Henry fitted out the boats that were intended to carry illegal immigrants to Palestine, as he recalled:

> I always remember one ship which had an American captain. It had been borrowed from America for fruit carrying, and I went around this ship with a tape measure, measuring it very, very carefully to see how many bunks I could get into it. [This was] not easy because there were posts in the middle and the posts interfere with the balance of it ... A nice job in geometry, and he [the captain] said, "I have never seen so much conscientiousness going into the shipping of fruit." And he meant it. He didn't have his tongue in his cheek at the time.

After the establishment of the State of Israel in 1948, when Jewish immigration was no longer illegal, Henry went back to his old job in London, but he only stayed for about a year, and in 1949, he decided to settle in Israel. For Henry, it was not a sudden decision, more of a slowly growing process.

It was in the immediate post-war period that Henry had first come into contact with Professor Sambursky, who was to have a decisive effect on his subsequent career. In 1945, the British Mandate authorities had set up the Board of Scientific and Industrial Research in Palestine, which was the precursor of the Research Council of Israel. The first executive director was Sambursky, a German-born Jew and scientist who had worked at the Hebrew University since the late 1920s. Sambursky also served as the Research Council of Israel's first director from 1949 to 1956, when he returned to the Hebrew University as Dean of the Faculty of Science.

Soon after the end of the war, he paid a visit to London to report to the Colonial Office about scientific progress in Palestine, and at Vivienne's suggestion (she was then working at the Colonial Office), Henry arranged to meet him, and he remembered vividly his first meeting with Sambursky. He was keen to recruit Henry, because there was a shortage of applied physicists in Palestine. Sambursky was a visionary and was already then thinking of Palestine/Israel as a kind of Switzerland with precision industries, a country which could become a hub for technological innovation.

Sambursky said he wanted to set up a National Physical Laboratory, because in Palestine at that time, people were using different British, Turkish and Arab measurements. He asked Henry if he was interested in joining his team and harmonising these different systems. Henry expressed a strong interest, but nothing happened until after the War of Israeli Independence in 1948, when Henry decided (in 1949) that he would emigrate.

Henry gave his company three months' notice, and at the end of the three months, he received a telegram from Professor Sambursky, out of the blue, asking if he would like to join his staff. Henry replied that he was on his way, as he had already packed his bags. Henry and Vivienne eventually settled in Jerusalem, and that was where they stayed.

Henry's boss, Sambursky, was the Secretary of the Research Council of Israel, and Ben-Gurion, the first Prime Minister of Israel, was its Chairman. Henry's responsibility was to organise a National Physical Laboratory, and also to act as the sort of "reconnaissance co-ordinator" (in Henry's words) for research projects in the general fields of engineering and applied physics. He didn't have any staff to start with, so he went out into the field himself to evaluate the proposals he received. At the same time, Henry was building up the National Physical Laboratory, and he slowly recruited a small staff.

Henry (in front, second from left) with David Ben-Gurion
(front right), first Prime Minister of Israel,
with members of his cabinet, late 1950s.

Inventors would write in with proposals, asking for government funding for their inventions, and Henry had to evaluate them. Most were discarded, but one very persistent inventor kept arguing the case for developing solar energy. Henry realized that he had to develop some expertise in the subject, and he read whatever literature there was at the time. As a result, he became interested in the subject. One thing that struck him was that existing solar collectors were inefficient, and the question he asked was, why? This started him off on a whole research project, and he was fortunate in having access to a laboratory facility and a couple of assistants who could help him.

He recalled:

> It was a very small team at the time. In fact, in the solar [energy] field I had almost no team at all. I had a couple of very good technicians, some of them I have worked with for twenty-five years. Then I had a piece of luck in fifty-five with this work on selective black surfaces that improved the efficiency of solar thermal collectors – it was really something new in the solar energy field.
>
> It was a mini-breakthrough and second, in 1955, they had this first world symposium on solar energy in Phoenix, Arizona and

my boss [Sambursky], with more imagination than I had, said, "Well, you must go and you must take your collector with you." I remember they had to bring a special plane from Holland with a bottom that opened because the collector was too big to get onto an ordinary plane. ... It really put us on the map for solar energy because it was something new.

Henry conducting an experiment, c.1960.

Vivienne and Henry with their two daughters,
Dahlia (left) and Sharona, 1950s.

***

There was no money in the national budget for the development of solar energy, so Ben-Gurion went to the Rothschilds, who had a fund in Israel called the Rothschild Foundation (now called *Yad Hanadiv*) and said they should support Henry's research.

Henry admired Ben-Gurion's strong leadership in the early years of Israel's existence, and his ability to take long-term decisions that determined the course of Israel's development. He compared Ben-Gurion to Churchill, as a strong leader with a marvellous sense of history.

As a result of the funding from the Rothschild Foundation, Henry was able to put together an inter-disciplinary team to develop innovative approaches to harnessing solar energy. His pioneering work on solar energy led him to travel extensively, and on one trip to America in the late 1950s, he had the opportunity to meet Einstein, in the company of a Hollendorf, a brilliant young professor of engineering from the Technion (the Israel Institute of Technology, in Haifa). Hollendorf had written a new textbook on mathematics in German, which he showed to Einstein, hoping for an approving comment. Henry remembered Einstein's reaction to the book:

> Einstein said something very serious to me ... he said, "I never write anything in German now. What the Germans did to us was for all time." I was very surprised at that statement because he was known to be a very gentle person.

Among Henry's many innovations were the use of solar-pond energy collectors, and developing highly efficient steam turbines, which enabled him to construct by 1961 a complete solar power unit using the new turbine and a new type of solar collector. Other areas that attracted his interest included the development of a 'low-loss window', comprising a plastic honeycomb sandwiched between two sheets of glass; this work eventually led to Henry receiving the 1994 PLEA (Passive Low Energy Architecture) Award for reducing energy consumption in buildings. In the 1970s, he led a successful project on electric vehicles, to find ways of improving performance. Here too, he was an innovator. What was striking was his ability to spot the potential of an idea, and to put together an inter-disciplinary team that could develop it and create something new.

In Israel, he was a well-known figure, and his solar energy water heaters are still widely used, saving the Israeli economy millions of barrels of oil each year. He was the recipient of many awards, including the ESSO Gold Medal of the Royal Society, and the Krupps Award in Germany. In January 2014, he was awarded the Presidential Medal of Distinction, Israel's highest civilian honour, for his contribution to the development of Israel's solar energy programme.

Henry with President Shimon Peres, Jerusalem, January 2014. Henry's granddaughter, Stav, is on the right.

***

Henry's wife, Vivenne, was also a Zionist from her late teens, but to understand her motivation, it is important to describe her early experiences. During the war, she was in a very secret intelligence unit of the British army. She finished school in 1942 and was recruited to the SOE (Special Operations Executive). In her unit they were dropping equipment to the Resistance in occupied Europe, particularly in France. They got first-hand information from their agents about the Jews being rounded-up and deported to the East, though initially they did not know why. The security in the organisation was very tight, to protect sensitive sources and agents who were in the field. Vivienne was practically the only Jewish person on the staff, as she remembered:

> I was on the headquarters staff in Baker Street. There I was, only a kid anyway, but ... the reports of deportations caused me very great distress. I made a resolve to myself that when the war was over – we were all sure we would win the war, now looking back I don't know why – but when the war was over, I would do something ... 'Never again'. You know? That was part of my motivation for being in *Habonim*.

M.R.D. Foot, in his history of the SOE, *SOE, The Special Operations Executive 1940–1946*, has written about the young women who were recruited,

> ... with quick brains and quiet tongues, [they] performed an essential service for SOE. They manned the base wireless stations ... Some operated the actual sets, some coped with coding and decoding ... work on which many lives depended; unglamorous, undecorated work without which everyone else's efforts at SOE would have been in vain.'[33]

When I showed this quotation to Vivienne, she said that that was exactly how it was.

Through her membership of *Habonim*, she shared the ideal of building a Jewish state, as a place where Jews could go and hold their heads up as normal people, and not be deported like cattle. Looking back, she was more critical of the ideology. She felt that her contemporaries had been brainwashed in *Habonim*, as they had expected to find all the great idealists in Israel draining swamps and planting eucalyptus trees, and the reality was rather different.

Vivienne never lived on a kibbutz, and she had never considered it, but she thought life in a town was the same sort of struggle for existence as anywhere else. In the early years, she found life in Israel difficult, without knowing much Hebrew and without the family support that she had had in Britain. While very proud of Israel's achievements in many fields, she was critical of the way the idealism of the early years had been replaced by a much more individualistic, materialistic approach.

***

Another strand in the family story is that of John Tabor (one of Henry and David's older brothers) and his wife Lena, who emigrated to Israel in 1946, with their first daughter, Judith. John and Lena died many years ago, but Judith, a retired dietician, lived in Jerusalem with her husband, Avraham, and their family, and I interviewed her in 2009 about her parents' experiences of settling in Israel.

John was an electrical engineer, but he was not such a committed Zionist as his brothers, David and Henry. He went to Palestine because he was offered a job at the Palestine Electrical Company (PEC). At the time, he was working at the Brimsdown Power Station in Enfield.

As a child, Judith remembered John's enthusiasm for living in Israel:

> Afterwards, I knew my father spoke about how happy he was that he came to Israel. He said that it was a wonderful country, and he thought everything was wonderful, and everything was just as it should be. He thought so much of Ben Gurion and the people who were in charge, you know, in the government … He felt that he had a very important job, but I don't really know if he would have come otherwise. I don't know. I was too small to know.

John and his wife, Lena, settled in Haifa, and John rose to become the Director of the Research and Development Division of the company. Lena went to Palestine because she was married to John, not because of any strong Zionist commitment. She found adjusting to life in Israel difficult, particularly in the first years, and used to go back to England every year, as she missed her family.

Wedding of John Tabor and Lena (née Silverston), June 1940

***

Judith remembered the difficulties her mother, Lena, had in getting to grips with modern Hebrew. In the beginning, she could not speak Hebrew, and when Judith's two younger sisters went to school, they complained that their mother could not talk to their friends. Lena attended an *ulpan* (a school for the intensive study of modern Hebrew), where she learnt all sorts of wonderful phrases that the rest of the family could not understand. Over time, her command of spoken Hebrew gradually improved.

Initially, Lena found some Israeli patterns of behaviour difficult to accept, and would say that it wasn't done, it wasn't polite enough, or people were not dressed the right way. Things were changed from what she was used to in England, and those conventions were not important in Israel.

In spite of these difficulties, Lena and John created a happy family environment for their three daughters. They enjoyed a comfortable standard of living in the 1950s and 1960s, as Judith recalled:

> … In some ways, we were very lucky; the other children, if they were newcomers, didn't have [much]. We had a house that was given to us by the Palestine Electric Company and my father had a

very good salary and was very well looked after, though life wasn't that easy for others … I wasn't aware of the hardship that most people had in the 1950s until many years later.

A family gathering, Haifa, c. 1960. Back (L. to R.): Vivienne, Lena, John and Ilana. Front (L. to R.): Dahlia, Meira, Judith, Sharona. Meira, Judith and Ilana were John and Lena's daughters; Sharona and Dahlia were Henry and Vivienne's.

***

I have described how Henry and John were motived by their Zionist beliefs in the immediate post-war period to settle in Israel, and to participate in the project to build the new state. They were fortunate that they were offered jobs which they felt were important. In their different ways, they were innovators and pioneers, and they made significant contributions to the development of Israel.

Judith and her husband, Avraham, regretted the passing of the pioneering spirit that had motivated Henry and John, and felt that Israel, for all its remarkable achievements, had become a different place. Judith commented:

> [People] like Henry and my father came here to build the country, to create something new. They didn't come to make money. Whenever you talk to Henry (because we always say he could have been a very rich man with his inventions) he always says, "I did it

for the State of Israel," and the same with my father, he said, "What does it matter? I built power stations because we needed power stations." ... Once things were done for the country, for everyone. Now, everyone does for himself...

Judith and Avraham, and their family, Jerusalem 2009.
Standing (from left): Judith's husband, Avraham, the author, Judith and Avraham's daughter Merav, and granddaughter, Adi.
Seated (from left): Judith, their son Ohad, and son-in-law Dorr.

Chapter 14

Lest We Forget

This is a book of memories, filtered through my narrative lens, and the stories told here are by their nature incomplete and partial. Much has been left out or forgotten or altered in the telling. The main focus of this book has been the lives of my parents, David and Hanna, but many other people have been involved, too. Older relatives, such as my two grandmothers and my great-aunt, Rosy, also made a deep impression on me, and in this chapter I will provide an update on their lives, and the lives of other family members.

David's mother, Rivka (Rebecca), lived until her ninety-fifth year, mentally alert till the end, and her passing in 1970 felt like the end of an epoch. She had grown up in the age of the horse and cart and lived to see men walking on the moon. Her powerful personality had an impact on all who knew her.

Hanna's mother, Melita, was physically and mentally active well into her nineties, and she regularly bemoaned the lack of intellectual stimulus at the Montefiore Home in Sydney where she spent her last years; she died in 2004 at the age of one hundred and five. Hanna's younger sister, Ruth, stayed in Sydney, and raised a family and had several grandchildren. She was a devoted daughter and looked after Melita. Sadly, she predeceased her mother, and died in her sixties.

Melita's older sister, Rosy, was widowed in 1957, when her husband Bernard died of a brain tumour. In 1967, she remarried; her second husband was Heinrich ('Heini') Strauss, who until 1933 had been a judge in Germany, and subsequently re-invented himself as an art historian in Jerusalem. Rosy, who had lived in South Africa for over forty years, moved to Israel to be with Heini, and they lived in an apartment in Balfour Street (where the Israeli Prime Minister also had his official residence), dispensing central European hospitality with style and charm. Rosy was always beautifully dressed and immaculately groomed; she died in her ninety-seventh year.

The last years of my parents' lives form a melancholy coda to their story. David was physically and mentally active well into his eighties, but he spent his last years in a nursing home, suffering from dementia. Even when very frail, he was able to charm those around him. He died on Saturday 26 November 2005, and was buried on 30 November, which by co-incidence, is the Founder's Day of the Royal Society. Hanna was diagnosed as having Alzheimer's at about the same time that David went into care, and eventually, spent her last years in the same nursing home and unit as David, cared for by some of the same staff. This beautiful, strong-willed woman passed away in August 2010.

Rosy and Heinrich Strauss, Jerusalem, 1980s.
A photo of Siegmund Rosenbaum is on the desk.

Of my mother's cousins, I met Josi Palti on several occasions in England and in Israel. He was always humorous, warm and welcoming, not particularly religious, and very critical of the divisive effects of *charedi* (ultra-orthodox) Jews on Israeli society. After he died in 1999, his widow, Nenette, stayed in the flat in Prague Street for a while and continued to correspond with me. A few years later, she moved to Givataim, north of Tel Aviv, to be near her daughter, Ronny.

Visiting Nenette in Tel Aviv after twenty-five years was a moving experience, as she had developed Alzheimer's, and did not know who I was. My main conversation was with her younger daughter, Ronny (Roni). She was a secular Israeli, unlike some of her religious cousins, and she was committed to living in Israel.

Ronny was proud of the achievements and progress of Israel, especially in the first thirty or forty years of the state's existence but was very concerned about the increased materialism and corruption, especially amongst the political class. She was concerned about Israel's long-term future and had made sure that her children and grandchildren had taken out German passports, as a sort of insurance policy.

Nenette passed away in 2014, after a long illness, at the age of ninety-six. I am still in touch with Ronny.

***

In 2009, I revisited Henry and Vivienne in Jerusalem. Henry was in his early nineties; Vivienne in her eighties – both amazingly alert. Though we had met several times in England during the intervening twenty-two years (since my last visit to Jerusalem), much had changed in Israel and the Middle East during that time. The hopes initially raised by the Oslo Agreement had disappeared; settlements had proliferated on the West Bank; and as a response to the Second Intifada, the 'separation wall' had been built along much of Israel's border with the West Bank. Within Israel, the population had grown considerably, partly as a result of immigration from the former Soviet Union, and economically, socially and culturally, it had become a highly developed society.

I asked Henry what he thought had been achieved in the first sixty years of Israel's existence, what he felt proud of, and what disappointed him about the country. The most striking change Henry had seen in Israeli society was the development of modern industry, though at times, he was disappointed by what he termed the 'crude' nature of some people's behaviour:

> Perhaps that's because I have a British background and occasionally, when I have a discussion with somebody, they would say to me, "Ah, your English background!"

He calculated that his contribution to Israel's industrial development was worth approximately three billion dollars, something which gave him a great deal of personal satisfaction. Both Henry and Vivienne took pride in the achievements of Israel, and the way the society had developed. At the same time, they were also concerned about the long-term future, and the sort of lives their grandchildren would have.

Henry passed away in 2015, and the then President of Israel, Shimon Peres, posted this tribute on Facebook:

> Dr Zvi [Henry] Tabor was a symbol of Israeli innovation who invented the modern solar water collector and inspired generations of scientists and entrepreneurs in the field of solar energy. (15 December 2015)

Henry and Vivienne were a remarkable couple, and I feel privileged to have known them and their family. At the time of writing (2023), Vivienne still lives in Jerusalem, at the age of ninety-nine. Her two daughters pre-deceased her.

***

I kept in touch with Josef and Daisy intermittently, but it was only in October 2009, after my retirement from teaching, that I visited Israel again, accompanied by my wife, Hazel. We went for the day to Givat Brenner. Everyone was twenty-five years older; Josef was in his early nineties, very alert but with poor vision, and Daisy was in her eighties. They lived in a modest bungalow in the kibbutz.

Looking back, Josef was particularly proud of what he called "the miracle of Revivim," as it was the first kibbutz to demonstrate that the desert could be made to bloom, and he remembered fondly the visits of Ben-Gurion, Weizmann and other leaders to the new settlement.

I asked Daisy what she felt had been achieved in the first sixty years of Israel's existence. Daisy was most struck by the changes in kibbutz life, from the primitive conditions of her first years in Israel, when there was often no electricity, and an inside shower was a novelty. She realised how much Israel meant to her when, in 2006, she went to Europe with Josef during the Second Lebanon War. Josef was giving lectures at several universities, and Daisy felt very angry when she saw the criticism of Israel in the French media. She was also shocked and angered by the anti-Semitic graffiti she saw in Budapest during that trip. She thought criticism of Israel was usually one-sided, and that Israel and the Jews were always blamed for all the problems of the region.

Daisy with Hazel, 2009.

What Daisy had learned about being Jewish, she had learned in Israel, and she had become interested in the Torah and the New Testament, from a literary point of view:

> In my eyes, Jesus was a very nice Jewish boy, really, he was never a Christian, he was always a Jew ... I like the (religious) holidays, because it is important that people have something which brings them together and to celebrate [though] not from a religious point of view. With Him [God] I have no contact.

As we were about to leave, I took some photographs, including one of Josef and Daisy together. Daisy asked Josef to stand by her side. "I have stood by you for fifty years. Why should I not stand by you now?" he replied.

In the photo overleaf, behind Josef and Daisy, against one wall, was a glass-fronted bookcase, containing (among other books) the collected works of Schiller and Heine in faded bindings, with the titles on the book spines in gold-embossed, gothic script. These too were part of their heritage, brought from Berlin in the early 1930s by Josef's parents. On another wall was a montage of family photographs: the children of Josef and Daisy's first marriages, and the children they had together, their grandchildren and great-grandchildren, totalling over fifty people. For both of them, and for Daisy in particular, this represented a triumph of survival. We walked with Daisy round the centre of the kibbutz, past an area set aside as a memorial to the members of the kibbutz who had fallen in the wars that had taken place since 1948. Daisy made one comment, "It's too much."

Josef and Daisy, 2009.

Josef led an extraordinary life. He was a pioneer, a founder of Kibbutz Revivim, and he played a significant role in the allocation of the Negev desert by UNCOP to the State of Israel. He remained alert and active till the end of his life. He died in 2011.

In 2023, Daisy is still living on the kibbutz and keeping active. We are in regular contact by email and postcards.

***

I keep in touch with my Israeli cousins, mainly by email and WhatsApp. My cousin Judith (on the Tabor side of the family) recently wrote that she thinks that Israel continues to be a materialistic society, and she is very aware of those sections of Israeli society that are poor or deprived. Though she is ashamed of what happens in Gaza and the West Bank, she thinks that most of the people she knows are wonderful, and many are outstanding in terms of their knowledge. She loves living in Israel and would not want to live anywhere else.

***

Two people I wanted to find out more about were my grandmother Melita's maid and confidante, Illi, and the Quaker teacher, Dr Zenker, who helped my grandparents learn English. During a visit to Israel, I interviewed one of my mother's cousins, Paulina (the daughter of Alfred Peltesohn and sister of Josi Palti), who lived in Tel Aviv. She provided the following information about Illi, who had worked for the Peltesohn family before coming to my grandparents, after the Peltesohns had left Germany in 1933.

Illi (Ella Hannasky), with Alfred Peltesohn (Palti), centre, father of Josi, and his daughter Paulina, Switzerland, 1955.

During the war, Illi worked for an elderly couple who owned an estate outside Berlin. They were government officials of some sort, and when Germany disintegrated in 1945, they were very worried about what the Russians were going to do. They decided to take poison and instructed Illi and the gardener to bury their bodies in the garden.

After the war, Illi returned to Berlin and lived in a rented room. She received a small pension, and renewed her contact with

Alfred Peltesohn, who regularly sent her money. In 1955, Alfred and his daughter Paulina went on holiday to Zurich and invited Illi to join them. Paulina remembered that they talked for three days non-stop, and that Illi told them that she did not know about the Nazi extermination of the Jews until after the war. My mother's comment was that if Illi had said that it must be the truth.

The photograph of the three of them shows Alfred and his daughter looking very serious. Illi is a tall, attractive woman in her late fifties with a pleasant face, smiling at the camera. I do not know what happened to her subsequently.

***

I had tried to trace Dr Zenker during a visit to Berlin in the early 1970s, without success, but the story had an unexpected sequel. Hanna was an accomplished abstract painter, and in the 1980s, attended several summer courses run by the well-known art teacher, Robin Child. At one course, it transpired that one of the other participants was a Quaker, a daughter of Corder Catchpool (a famous English Quaker and pacifist), and that she knew the daughter of Dr Zenker, now living in England. As a result, my mother made contact with Dr Zenker's daughter, and received the following letter (which I have shortened):

9 November 1988

Dear Hanna Tabor

Thank you very much for your letter. I was touched when Pleasance wrote to me to say that someone remembered my father. He died nearly thirty years ago. I often feel that people like you may have known more about him than I ever did. Family life was always disturbed for political reasons, and my father was mostly an absent father to us four children – and when I was old enough to ask intelligent questions, I no longer had the opportunity, as I came to England aged eighteen in 1950.

How difficult it must have been to bring up children in that Nazi atmosphere – making us think and understand without endangering the family even further. I remember being whisked home in Berlin when we children complained in loud voices of "all those disgusting messes in the street," pointing to 'Jude' chalked on pavements, etc. Also no longer being allowed to address friends by their surnames – suddenly only Christian names were allowed. My father had got to know many Jewish friends through his teaching. He was not allowed to teach officially, and the Quakers originally helped him to find employment as a private tutor.

We, mother and children, left Berlin soon after you did. Myers (who emigrated to Wakefield – 'Double Two' shirts) were selling a family house in Beverungen/Weserbergland, which my parents purchased and where I spent most of my childhood. Paul Meyer, the older brother of the Berliners and his non-Jewish wife were living in the house in Beverungen in an upstairs flat and were dear friends to us children. Although he was sent to Theresienstadt at the very end of the war, he returned, which was wonderful for us all.

I would like to think that it was my mother's courage which preserved us. She come from a country district near to Beverungen and would stand no nonsense from Nazi upstarts. It must have been a dangerous tightrope to tread. She always went out with two shopping bags, so as not to have to say "Heil Hitler" to anyone and raise her arm.

My father was conscripted, as a corporal, I think, in the medical corps – lying low, I suppose. Sometime during the war, he was imprisoned – tricked into too open a conversation. I well remember the terrible shock when my mother read us his letter, where he explicitly asked for his children to know where he was and that being in prison can sometimes be an honourable thing to be. My mother once travelled to see him and returned white and silent. I know so little about all these years. I think he had asked for poison.
…

… As Germany disintegrated during the latter part of the war, we had no news of my father – we did not know whether he was alive. My mother contacted the American army who were stationed along the Weser at first to try and trace him. It must have been in 1946 that a British army jeep pulled up with an army chaplain in it looking for my mother and he brought news that my father was alive and working for the British Administration in Berlin. He brought a photo – we hardly recognised him; he was so thin. Apparently, Nazi political prisoners had been given the chance to join the fighting at the Front towards the end of the war, and my father took this opportunity to get out and (he) hid in the Spreewald for many months. He was eventually picked up by the Russian army and finally handed over to the British army because of his knowledge of the English language …

He returned to us in 1947, I think. Of course, he never lived in Beverungen – he was a stranger to the small town and to his teenage children. He was also distressed about the political situation in Germany, the way all the Nazis got their old jobs back.

There was a Denazification certificate which was simply a rubber stamp and even father had to have one to teach again. He was very depressed.

He was appointed headmaster of a boys' grammar school, full of plans and idealism. He called it 'The Albert Schweitzer School' and there was a beautiful naming ceremony to which prominent musicians and poets contributed. It must have been the high point of his short professional life. He retired soon afterwards for health reasons. My parents' marriage also broke up and they were later divorced. A friend of mine once said, "Your family are like something out of Ibsen."

… Those that lived under the shadow of those events are probably affected for the rest of their lives. It was so kind of your sons to try and trace my family in Berlin. I am grateful for your kind thoughts.

[There is a brief summary of her life since the war, and some details about her married life in Britain.]

Yours very sincerely,

Hella Harris (née Zenker)

Identity card of Dr Hans Zenker, 1946.

The card above states:

Political prisoner from 3.5.1933 until 24.7.1933. Arrested for high treason. Taken into detention in K.Z. (Central Barracks) Wabern near Kassel. Arrested again on 5 August 1944 and sentenced by a military court in Berlin to 5 years imprisonment for subverting the *Wehrmacht*, this being in Dornau until 20 April 1945. Issued on 28 January 1946.

Frau Zenker, April 1959.

Though this book has focused mainly on my parents, and their families, the stories I was told about Illi and Dr Zenker moved me because of their courage, and that is why I have included them.

Chapter 15

Connecting with the Past

In this chapter I describe the physical journeys I made with my wife, Hazel, in 2009-10. I hoped these journeys would enable me recover traces of the memories, identities and sense of place that featured in some of the stories I had been told by my relatives in the UK, in Australia and Israel. I was keen to visit Vilnius, associated with my Grandmother Rivka's family, and to place her memories in the context of the city where she spent part of her youth. I also wanted to visit Smorgon (Smarhon in present-day Belarus), where my paternal grandfather, Chaskel, was born. I had hoped to visit St Petersburg, where Rivka spent her formative years, but this never happened, and at the time of writing, after the Russian invasion of Ukraine in 2022, I am most unlikely to go.

Our first stop was Vilnius, which appears like any other modern, central European city, with its heritage of beautiful baroque churches and historic buildings. It is a renewed city, different from the Vilnius that Howard Jacobson describes in *Roots, Schmoots*, just emerging in the early 1990s from fifty years of repressive Soviet rule.

However, a short journey into the countryside takes one to Ponar, the site of the killing pits in the forest, where a significant proportion of Lithuania's quarter of a million Jews were shot by the Germans and their accomplices. The memorials that have been erected, from the Stalinist period up to more recent times, reflect different political agendas. The earliest memorials were dedicated to 'the victims of fascist terror'; only since the fall of communism has the Jewish identity of the victims been acknowledged.

The majority of Lithuania's four and a half thousand remaining Jews live in Vilnius, where there is only one functioning synagogue. It is a fractured, insecure community, still traumatised by the effects of the Holocaust and the post-war period, and anxious about the resurgence of anti-Semitism in modern Lithuania. The historic Jewish Quarter was largely destroyed during the Second World War, though it has been partially restored, and it now contains shops and boutiques. Of its great spiritual heritage little remains, except for some memorial plaques.

From Vilnius to Smorgon and Oshmiany (Ashmyany in the Belarussian spelling) is a day's journey by train. These towns are in present-day Belarus, and both were largely destroyed in the two world wars. Oshmiany, where my great-great grandfather, Rabbi Kahan, lived and worked, had a population of about eight thousand at the end of the nineteenth century, of which fifty per cent were Jews, though none survived the Second World War. The population of the town today is about fourteen thousand, though many people came there from other parts of the former Soviet Union after the Second World War. Much of Oshmiany has been rebuilt several times in the twentieth century.

The central square is dominated by a large statue of Lenin on a pedestal, with an outstretched arm – a familiar icon of the Soviet era. In the past, this was the marketplace, the historic heart of the town, though nearly all the buildings there now date from after the Second World War. Before 1941, there would have been numerous small shops and businesses around the square, many of them owned by Jews. The rebuilt Catholic and Russian Orthodox Churches are nearby.

Within walking distance of the marketplace is the Great Synagogue, a decaying rectangular brick building with an open area of wasteland to one side. It was built in 1902 on the site of an earlier wooden synagogue, and adjacent to it is a brick house, which would have been the rabbi's residence. It too was most probably built on the site of an earlier wooden house.

During the Soviet era, it had been used to house an alcohol business; the same thing happened to many churches. When the Germans arrived in 1941, they created a ghetto around the Great Synagogue, containing three thousand people, including Jews from outlying areas. The ghetto survived for two years until it was liquidated in 1943.

At the time of our visit, the synagogue was owned by a state enterprise producing dairy products, and it was used as a dump for broken furniture and miscellaneous equipment. The entrance had been created in the east wall and looking back, one could see a Hebrew inscription around the circular window high up in the wall. This would have been the position of the ark; opposite was a ramshackle balcony structure supported by some scaffolding, which would have been the women's gallery. The original entrance to the synagogue, at the west end of the building, under the gallery, was not accessible.

The large octagon in the middle of the ceiling, with its central pendant, had originally been painted dark blue with stars, and there were traces of plaster mouldings and faded wall decorations that survived in parts of the interior. One can imagine the pride that the Jewish community of Oshmiany would have taken in this synagogue. Rabbi Kahan would most probably have prayed in the wooden synagogue that previously existed on this site.

Great Synagogue in Oshmiany, now derelict. Belarus 2009.

Since our visit, ownership of the building has passed to the local museum, and in 2015, an exhibition room of the museum was opened there. There were plans to convert the synagogue for use as a communal space, led by a UK-based charity, the Foundation for Jewish Heritage. However, the lack of funds and the current political situation in Belarus, have made this project impossible for the foreseeable future.

The Jewish cemetery was on the edge of Oshmiany, and it covered a large area, though it was very overgrown. The cemetery dated from the eighteenth century, though it was difficult to establish where the oldest graves were, if indeed any had survived. Most of the memorials were disintegrating and the graveyard was neglected. A ruined synagogue and an overgrown cemetery were all that remained of this once active Jewish community.

Part of the Jewish cemetery, Oshmiany 2009.

Nineteen miles away to the north-east was Smorgon, the birthplace of Chaskel Taborisky. It, too, had been destroyed during the First World War, and very badly damaged during the Second. Like Oshmiany, it consisted of wide roads in the centre, not much traffic, modern low-rise buildings and a scattering of wooden houses.

The population of the town fluctuated considerably during the twentieth century. By 1940, the population had grown to about six thousand of whom half were Jewish. In 1941, the Germans arrived. Initially, they killed those Jews who had been active in the

Communist Party or related organisations. They created two ghettos for the remaining Jews, who were then deported to other ghettos or killing sites, and the ghetto in Smorgon was liquidated in 1943.

When we visited Smorgon, its centre consisted of a small car park, with a five-story Soviet-era apartment block to one side. This had been built to house workers who were employed at a top-secret optics factory; the apartments were built on the site of the Jewish cemetery. When the authorities announced their plan to build the apartments, they gave relatives one week to move family remains, but of course, there was no one left in the Jewish community to do this.

On the opposite side of the car park was a more modern, two-story red brick building that housed a bank. This had been the site of the synagogue. During the Second World War, the Germans used the synagogue as a dairy, and it continued to be used as a dairy during the Soviet era. When a decision was made to develop the area, the synagogue was destroyed. On the front of the bank was a commemorative plaque in Hebrew and Belarussian, donated by Mordechai Taborisky, a native of Smorgon who emigrated to Palestine before the Second World War. The plaque, dated 1995, was dedicated to the memory of the thousands of Jews of Smorgon killed by 'the Germans and their helpers' between 1941 and 1943.

On the outskirts of Smorgon were the two 'Jewish' houses left in the town, near the Gerviatka river, where most of the tanneries would have been located. Once the scene of industrial activity, it was now a peaceful stream, overhung by trees and bushes, with no evidence of workshops or small factories nearby. Jews who had owned businesses, including the tanneries, would have lived near the synagogue, but the workers had to live near the factories, so this area would have been densely populated.

The two surviving 'Jewish' houses stood on opposite sides of the narrow road, near the bridge that crossed the river. These houses, built of wood to a traditional design, dated from the 1920s or 1930s. The red-painted house was called the 'Taborisky house', as before the war it had been owned by a family with that name, though not related to Chaskel's family.

Memorial plaque on the side of a bank.
Site of the synagogue in Smorgon, 2009.

The Taborisky house in Smorgon in 2009.
It had been constructed in c.1920-30.

Opposite was another wooden, single-story house, ramshackle, unpainted and locked up. It was owned by the only Jew left in Smorgon. Formerly, it would have housed several generations of one family, and possibly some of their animals. Now it was used to store manufactured goods, such as detergent and toothpaste, which the owner sold from a kiosk near the town centre. On meeting Moisei S., a man in his sixties with a non-Jewish wife, I asked him what it felt like being the only Jew in the town, and his answer was revealing, "I feel safe," he said. Though we were the same age, in almost every other respect, our lives could not have been more different.

***

On another trip, the following year, we visited Berlin, where my mother was born and spent the first fifteen years of her life, and Giessen, where my granny, Melita, was born.

Tombstone of Hermann and Fanny Stillschweig.
Weissensee Cemetery, Berlin 2010.

I also wanted to find the graves of family members who had died before World War Two, so I visited the Jewish Cemetery at Weissensee, in north-east Berlin. It was vast, much of it neglected, containing over one hundred thousand graves of Jews who had been buried there from the 1880s onwards, though it is undergoing a process of restoration. Many 'blocks' of gravestones were completely overgrown with dense shrubbery, small trees and a profusion of ivy and other creeping plants. It was a moving experience to discover the gravestone of my great-grandparents, Hermann and Fanny Stillschweig, shrouded in ivy and brambles. I am sure it had not been visited for over seventy years.

***

My mother, Hanna, had affectionate memories of her favourite great-uncle and great-aunt, Sigismund and Helene Stillschweig. This elderly, childless couple spoilt Hanna and her sister, Ruth, when they were young children. When Hanna and her sister knew them in the late 1920s, Sigismund and Helene had lived in Wormser Strasse, behind the Wittenberg Platz, not far from the iconic *KaDeWe* department store, but the section of the street where they lived had been destroyed during the war. A new road obliterated that part of the Wormser Strasse where the apartment would have been. Sigismund died in 1930; his widow Helene died in 1941 (the official cause of her death was 'a fall').

***

We visited the addresses where my grandfather Martin's brothers, Dagobert and Sigismund, had lived are in the eastern part of Berlin. They were both deported to Auschwitz, and murdered in 1942 and 1943, respectively. At each address, the buildings had been destroyed during the war. In 2010, one site was used as a car park; the other was a fenced-in area, overgrown with weeds, awaiting redevelopment.

I tried to find the apartment block in Grunewald where Hanna and her family lived in the 1930s. Some of the buildings in the complex survived the war; handsome, early twentieth- century buildings, the flats spacious, with parquet flooring, but I did not have enough information to identify the specific apartment where Hanna's family lived. The nearby synagogue had been burned to the ground during *Kristallnacht,* and it was commemorated by a plaque and an information board in an adjacent bus shelter.

The site of the apartment block where Dagobert Stillschweig, Martin's brother and one of Hanna's uncles, lived before deportation to Auschwitz. Berlin 2010.

One powerful part of Hanna's story was her account of seeing her classmates off, as they left Berlin by train from a station, the Anhalter Bahnhof, on the start of a journey that would take them to Palestine. In its heyday, this station was Berlin's 'Gateway to the South', with services to Prague and Vienna, and also to Rome, Naples and Athens.

Between 1941 and 1945, the Anhalter Bahnhof was the one of three stations used to deport Berlin's remaining Jews to a death camp. From the Anhalter alone, nine thousand six hundred left, in groups of fifty to one hundred at a time. The deportees, mostly elderly men and women, wearing their yellow stars, would have been brought to the station from an assembly point by tram or truck in the early morning, escorted by armed guards. In contrast to other deportations using freight wagons, here the Jews were taken away in third-class passenger coaches which were coupled up to regular trains. Their first destination was Theresienstadt, and those deportees who did not die there of disease or exhaustion there were sent further east, mainly to Auschwitz.

Portico and part of the facade of the
Anhalter Bahnhof, Berlin 2010.

For my mother, the idea of leaving Berlin from the Anhalter Bahnhof in the 1930s was about going to Palestine on *aliyah*, to a new life and a new identity as a pioneer in *Eretz Yisrael* (Land of Israel). Tragically, those of her relatives who did leave Berlin via the Anhalter Bahnhof were murdered soon afterwards. What remains of the station is the imposing, if somewhat battered, central portion of the original facade, and behind it, where the platforms and railway lines would have been, is a sports field.

***

From Berlin, we travelled to Giessen by train, unsure of what we would find there, though we had made prior contact with a local historian. and members of the Jewish community.

In the early twenty-first century, Giessen was a modern city of over seventy-five thousand inhabitants, in the state of Hesse, with a large student population. The Jewish community consisted of approximately three hundred souls, most of whom (about ninety per cent) were from the former Soviet Union. Many were old, living off state benefits or pensions. Those that worked were mainly doctors or engineers, and there were about twenty young people. There was a modern community building near the city centre, which contained a small *landschule*, a country synagogue, which had been reconstructed with financial help from the local churches.

Wilhelmstrasse 12 in 2010. Melita and her
family lived in the ground-floor apartment.

One of the community leaders was a woman in her early fifties, who had been born in Hamburg, and whose parents were hidden by non-Jewish friends during the war. She was the only 'native-born' Jew in the community, and thus the only link in Giessen, through her family, with the Jewish life that had existed in Germany before the Second World War.

The five-storey building in Wilhelmstrasse 12, where Granny Melita grew up, survived the bombing of Giessen in the Second World War. The spacious apartment, which the Rosenbaum family occupied on the ground floor, had become a private medical practice, and the large garden was the site of a clinic. Fifty yards back from the house was a small, single-story red-brick dwelling, which most probably had been converted from the original stable block.

Liebigschule, where Melita studied;
formerly the *Oberrealschule* for Sciences.

The route that Melita would have walked to the university passed many fine, large buildings, including stylish villas set back from the road in extensive grounds. At the first crossroad there was a left turn into Ludwigstrasse, which led towards the university. No. 42, a tall pink building which had once been the home of the orthodox rabbi, Dr Hirschfeld, was now owned by an evangelical Christian group, and was adorned with the slogan 'Jesus Lebt!' ('Jesus Lives!').

The late nineteenth-century university buildings, with the two-story chemistry building to one side (now part of the Veterinary Department) where Melita would have studied, also survived the war. The old campus, with its collection of neo-classical buildings, had a restrained and dignified appearance. Past the old university buildings, in Bismarkstrasse, there were two large cream and maroon school buildings, identical in appearance, and less than one hundred yards apart. One of them, renamed the Liebigschule, was originally the Oberrealschule for sciences, where Melita studied for her high school graduation (*Abitur*); the other school focused more on the humanities.

***

The Old Cemetery in Giessen contained, along with the Christian graves, a Jewish cemetery with a small orthodox section, and a larger liberal one. The parents of Siegmund Rosenbaum were buried in different places: his mother, Rosette, was buried in the orthodox part, while his father, Isaak, was buried in the liberal section. Several of the tombstones had been broken in the 1930s and subsequently repaired. In the liberal section, there were a number of blank tombstones or memorials that had not been used, as their owners had either emigrated or been deported.

Siegmund's brother, Samuel, was buried in the 'New Cemetery', on the outskirts of Giessen, which dated from the beginning of the twentieth century. The tombstone bore only his name, and the dates '1878–1937', which suggested that the few remaining Jews in the late 1930s could not find a suitably qualified (or willing) stonemason to engrave a traditional Hebrew inscription.

***

After returning home from eastern Europe and Germany, I reflected on my need to go back and visit the places that were significant for my grandmothers and other relatives, and which featured prominently in the telling of their life stories. I recalled the insights of Doreen Massey (quoted in the Prologue), when she wrote that a place is not 'just' a place. Rather, it should be seen in a space-time envelope, combined with the social relations that give that place its significance in people's lives, and which are constantly changing through time.

Visiting a place that was important for someone else, such as my grandmother, Melita, enabled me to connect in part with her vanished world, but also to experience a degree of detachment and distance from it. 'My' Giessen was, of course, totally different from the Giessen that Melita grew up in over a hundred years ago, even if some of the physical landmarks had survived two world wars. However, I was better able to understand her memories, and the memories of other family members, as a result of seeing the towns and cities they had lived in, as well as realising how these places have changed.

Epilogue

Looking Back, Moving Forward

My parents are at the heart of this book, but in writing it, I came to realise two things. First, how grateful I am to both sets of grandparents, who made heroic efforts to escape persecution and to start afresh in a new country. Without their courage and determination, I would not be here. Secondly, I have come to appreciate how remarkable my parents' generation was: the generation of Jews and non-Jews who grew up between the two world wars. They lived through the Depression, the rise of dictatorships in the 1930s, and the horrors of the Second World War, and in many cases, had to adjust to vast changes and rebuild their lives more than once. Their opportunities for educational and professional development were limited – though in Britain, at least, much better than before 1914.

But my family's sense of Jewish identity, however defined, had a determining effect on what happened to them, how they responded to events (within their families and the wider society), and the choices that were open to them. It is my privilege to have ties to relatives who were born or grew up in different countries: Tsarist Russia, Great Britain, the USA, Germany, Belgium, Hungary and Palestine/Israel.

The people who have a voice in this book are the survivors, one way or another, and there are many, to whom I am linked by family ties, who did not survive. Chance or fortuitous events played a large part in determining who survived. One small example, already mentioned in a previous chapter, illustrates this point. Without the intervention of Hanna's Uncle Alfred, which enabled her to be granted an entry permit to Australia, my mother would not have been able to leave Berlin in November 1938 with her family, and I would not be writing these lines now.

The compass of this book extends roughly over a period of two hundred years, from the aftermath of the French Revolution (which started the process of Jewish emancipation) to the early twenty-first century. The memories of who the early forebears were has been filtered through the stories told by my grandmothers and great-aunt Rosy, based on what they remembered their own parents (mainly their mothers) telling them, as well as stories told by other family members.

Memory thus plays a large part in this book, and the life-stories raise questions about what is remembered, and why, and what is forgotten, concealed or obliterated from memory. Memories of happy occasions, of family warmth, of the moral principles of adults who made a deep impression on other relatives, reflect the positive ways in which memory can work and shape the values of the next generation. For example, the deep respect with which my Uncle Henry remembered his father's work ethic, influenced his own values of hard work and self-reliance, and the values of his children.

Memory is closely linked to issues of identity, and this book describes some of the forms Jewish identity can take in different contexts. These life-stories describe how family members negotiated their sense of who they were, as Jews, as Germans, as British subjects, as socialists, communists, Zionists and so forth, though in Nazi-occupied Europe, Jewish identity was also defined by the racial laws of the state. The story of my great-grandfather, Siegmund Rosenbaum, a man determined to uphold his standing in the local community as a good German, encapsulates for me the tragedy of German Jewry in the twentieth century.

The sense of place has also been an important theme running through this book. In some narratives, such as the memoir of my maternal grandmother, Melita, the recollections of her hometown, Giessen, reflect her engagement with the local Jewish community and the wider society of which she was a part. German education and culture left an indelible mark on her personality, along with her deep attachment to traditional Judaism.

A disturbing experience linked to place occurred during the visit to Smorgon, the small town that was the birthplace of my paternal grandfather in present-day Belarus (described in Chapter 15). I found that there were no traces of the once-thriving Jewish community, except for a commemorative plaque marking the site of the synagogue. This pattern could be repeated in thousands of sites of Jewish settlements that had existed in the former Pale of Settlement up to 1941.

***

This book also demonstrates that one cannot write about Jews in the last hundred years or so without referring to Israel. For Jews living in the Diaspora, the link with Israel is an important component of their identity, though often quite a complicated one. Attitudes may range from uncritical support to outright criticism of the rationale for Israel's existence. For those living in Israel, the construction of identities is also complex, as is the relationship with the Diaspora.

Equally, there is a wide range of views about Israel's history and its future, and its relations with the Palestinians, as I found when talking to my Israeli relatives. One dispassionate perspective is that of Amos Oz. In a lecture originally given in 2002, he said:

> The Israeli-Palestinian conflict is not ... a struggle between good and evil, rather it is a tragedy in the most ancient and precise sense of the word: a clash between one very powerful, deep and convincing claim and another very different but no less convincing, no less powerful, no less humane claim.'[34]

However, the liberal, humanistic version of Zionism of my parents' generation seems to have receded. I find myself paying lip-service to the idea of the two-state solution to the Israel-Palestine conflict, but with increasing scepticism. A number of commentators have pointed out that it has become a mantra that the majorities on both sides say they support in theory. However, they are not willing or able to make the compromises needed for it to become a reality. The Abrahamic Accords in 2020, leading to Israel's diplomatic relations with the United Arab Emirates and other Arab countries, has also changed the dynamic of Middle Eastern politics.

Where does this leave Jews living in the Diaspora? In an article in *The Jewish Chronicle* (in 2022) to mark the fifty-fifth anniversary of the Israeli occupation of the West Bank, Jonathan Freedland wrote how the 'sheer intractability' of the occupation, combined with ongoing battles over anti-Semitism, have led to the 'numbing of our moral faculties' among Diaspora Jews. He despaired at the reluctance of many Jews in the Diaspora to see straightforward cases of unjust discrimination against Palestinians, when committed by 'our side.'

He concluded:

For years, I have feared the damage the occupation will do, and is doing, to the Israeli occupier, the way it corrodes a society's moral core. That fear has not faded. But now I see that I didn't need to look so far away. Because the corrosion is in us, too. [35]

This is a sobering assessment for Jews in the Diaspora, particularly those who care about the future of Israel. What is certain is that the human rights of both Israelis and Palestinians will be an issue for some time to come.

***

In the Prologue, I described my childhood desire to discover a secret that old people possessed, and which they could never communicate directly, but which I needed to find out by asking them lots of questions and listening very carefully to their answers.

Through my research, I came to understand the achievements of my extended family. I learnt how their lives contributed to the development of the societies in which they lived, and the ways these societies affected their own personal development.

But by the time I had finished writing *The Telling*, I realised that there wasn't a secret message from the past, waiting to be discovered. 'The secret' that I was looking for as a child turned out to be a different kind of message, as much about the present as the past. It had to do with making connections between people, within and across the generations, and between different spaces and places, which I have attempted to describe here.

In writing this book, not only did I learn to value the life-experiences of my relatives, but also to value my own. I could not have understood this as a child, even though I sensed intuitively that the old people I talked to (and they all seemed old) had something I did not have but wanted to engage with. It was the experiences of a full and varied life, which in many cases included persecution, displacement and relocation. In my seventies, I am able to empathise (at least in part) with the experiences of others, in ways I could not have done as a child.

***

It has been a humbling experience to live with the narratives of family members, many of whom are no longer alive, and to visit some of the key sites associated with them. These different experiences confronted me with the question about my own identity. In the light of my family history, how do I define my own sense of self? How do I see myself fitting into the bigger picture? There is no simple answer, but what I feel most comfortable with is my late father's statement. He saw himself as the non-conflictive product of his English education and his Jewish heritage, and once described himself as, "A Jew of the English persuasion." I can sign up to that, too.

Does this tracing of stories from one extended family over two hundred years suggest how Jewish identities might develop and change during the next hundred or two hundred years? What makes any prediction difficult is the pace of change, and the effect of new technologies, especially social media, on how people relate to each other. I have no doubt that in two hundred years' time there will be descendants of my family who will regard themselves as Jews, and be proud of their heritage, in whatever forms their Jewishness will take.

Maybe that sense of Jewishness will always be a complex and contradictory function of the three themes running through this book: how people use or discard their memories; how people define their identities through time; and how people are influenced by their places of origin, and those they are forced or choose to move to. At a personal level, writing this book has deepened my respect for the vitality and resilience of the Jewish tradition, and the different ways it has shaped the lives of my extended family over many generations.

Glossary

Unless otherwise stated, the words or phrases are in Hebrew. When a transliterated Hebrew, Aramaic or Yiddish word contains 'ch', it should be pronounced like the 'ch' in loch.

Word or phrase	Explanation
Abitur	German: high school matriculation.
Agudat Yisrael	'Union of Israel'. An orthodox anti-Zionist organisation.
Aliyah	Literally, 'going up' – emigration to Israel.
Amidah	A prayer consisting of a varying number of blessings recited while the worshippers stand.
Bar-mitzvah	Aramaic: literally, 'son of the commandment'. At the age of 13, a Jewish boy reads a portion from the Torah scroll during the Shabbat synagogue service, and this marks his transition to accepting adult status and responsibilities in the community.
Beshert	Yiddish: pre-ordained.
Bund	Yiddish: league. The name of the Jewish socialist workers' party started in Vilna in the late nineteenth century.
Chalutz	A pioneer.
Chanukah	Festival of Lights.
Chanukiah	Eight-branched candelabrum used to hold the Chanukah candles, sometimes mistakenly referred to as a menorah.

Charedi	Ultra-orthodox Jews in Israeli society.
Chazan	Cantor.
Chutzpah	Extreme self-confidence or audacity.
Cheder	Jewish primary school which taught the basics of Hebrew and religious knowledge.
Doppelverdiener	German: a person or household with two incomes.
Droshky	Russian: a type of horse-drawn carriage.
Dunam	A measure of land area used in parts of the former Turkish empire, including Israel (where it is equal to about nine hundred square metres).
Frum	Yiddish: orthodox, observant.
Gaon	An honorific title, indicating outstanding wisdom and knowledge of Judaism (especially, the Talmud), e.g. the Vilna Gaon.
Gubernia	A territorial and administrative division of Imperial Russia, similar to a province.
Habonim	Literally, 'the builders'. A Zionist youth movement.
Hachshara	Training or preparation (usually before emigration to Israel).
Hadassah	A girl's name in Hebrew, meaning 'myrtle tree'. The name of a major hospital in Jerusalem.
Hagana	Jewish Defence Force.

Hamsin	A dry, hot, sandy local wind.
Ha'noar Ha'oved	A socialist youth movement.
Haskalah	The Jewish Enlightenment, a movement that originated in eighteenth-century Germany, and swept through Eastern Europe in the nineteenth and early twentieth centuries. It introduced Jews to the world of secular knowledge, so that they could play a fuller part in Western society.
Hasidism	A pietistic, mystical movement founded in the eighteenth century in Eastern Europe.
Hechsher	Permission, usually in the context of rabbinical permission or seal of approval.
Irgun	A Zionist paramilitary group.
Judenrein	German: free of Jews.
Karaite	A sect of Jews that rejected rabbinical authority and teaching.
Kehillah	Congregation.
Kibbutz	A communal settlement in Israel, typically a farm. Kibbutzim (plural).
Kosher	Food prepared according to Jewish dietary laws.
Kristallnacht	Officially inspired pogrom against the Jewish community in Germany, 9/10 November 1938.
Madrich/madricha	A youth leader; the word also has the

	connotations of role model, inspiration and a general font of wisdom. The madrich not only leads and runs a range of activities, but also inducts his or her charges into the ideology and mythology of the movement.
Mishmar Ha-Emek	Hebrew: Guardian of the Valley. Name of a forest.
Negev	Name of the desert in southern Israel.
Omer	A sheaf of corn or *omer* of grain presented as an offering on the second day of Passover. It also refers to the period of forty-nine days between the second day of Passover and Pentecost.
Ostjude	An 'Eastern Jew'.
Palmach	Hebrew acronym for 'strike force'.
Pesach	Passover, the festival that celebrates the deliverance of the Israelites from slavery in Egypt.
Razzia	German: a raid.
Rav	A man learned in Judaism.
Rebbetzin	A title use for the wife of a rabbi, typically among Orthodox, Haredi and Hasidic Jews.
Revivim	Hebrew: rain showers. Name given to a kibbutz in the Negev desert.
Rosh Hashanah	Literally, 'head of the year', it is the Jewish New Year.

Seder	Literally, 'order', 'arrangement'. The Passover meal which celebrates the liberation of the ancient Israelites from slavery in Egypt. It involves partaking of symbolic foods, such as unleavened bread (matzah).
Shochet	Someone who slaughters animals for food according to the Jewish tradition.
Shabbat, shabbos	Saturday, the Day of Rest. Shabbos is the Yiddish form.
Shadchan	A matchmaker.
Shomrim	Literally, 'the guardians'. A Zionist youth movement that flourished before the Second World War.
Shtetl	Yiddish: a small town. The majority of Jews lived in shtetls in the Russian Pale of Settlement.
Shul	Yiddish: synagogue.
Simchat Torah	'Rejoicing of the Law' – a festival that marks the yearly completion of the reading of the Torah, and the starting of the cycle again. It occurs at the end of the Festival of Tabernacles (Succot).
Shtiebel	Yiddish: a prayer room, often in a private house.
Tallit (pl. tallitot)	Fringed prayer shawl, worn by adult Jewish males during prayer.

Talmud	The extensive commentaries on the Oral Law (Mishnah), compiled in Jerusalem and Babylon between the second and fifth centuries of the Common Era (the dates are very approximate).
Tefillin	Phyllacteries, small boxes containing extracts from the Torah, worn by Jewish men whilst saying their prayers.
Ulpan	A school for the intensive study of modern Hebrew.
Vaada	Committee.
Wadi	Arabic: a valley, ravine, or channel that is dry except in the rainy season.
Yishuv	The Jewish community in Palestine, before the State of Israel was declared.
Yom Kippur	The Day of Atonement.
Yomtov (Jontef)	Yiddish: a festival or celebration (from the Hebrew, literally 'a good day').

Notes

[1] Josipovici, G. (2020). *Forgetting*, Manchester, UK: Little Island Press/Carcanet, p.6.

[2] Waxman, Z.V. (2006). *Writing the Holocaust*, Oxford, UK: Oxford University Press, p.1.

[3] Hinton, J. (2010). *Nine Wartime Lives*, Oxford, UK: Oxford University Press, pp.17–18.

[4] Massey, D. (1995). *'Places and their pasts'*, in History Workshop Journal, **39**, p.188; p.191.

[5] De Waal, E. (2010). *The Hare with Amber Eyes,* London, UK: Chatto & Windus, pp.247-8.

[6] Hinton, op. cit., p.200.

[7] Information taken from the ShtelRoutes website, ShtetlRoutes_EN_www2_p469_476_Ashmyany.pdf, accessed 28 January 2023.

[8] The numbers of Jewish students are given by Loewe, R. (1989). 'Cambridge Jewry: the first hundred years', in Frankel, W. and Miller, H. (eds.) *Gown and Tallith*, London, UK: Harvey Miller, p.19.

[9] Bermant, C. (1971). *The Cousinhood*, London, UK: Eyre & Spottiswoode, p.1.

[10] Laqueur, W. (1989). *A History of Zionism*, New York, NY: Schocken, p.400.

[11] Tabor. D. (1982). 'Cambridge before the war. Some reminiscences' [Part 1], *Newsletter of the CTJC* (Cambridge Traditional Jewish Community), November, pp.5-6.

[12] Eban, A. (1977). *An Autobiography*, New York, NY: Random House, p.12.

[13] Tabor, D. (1983). 'Cambridge before the war. Some reminiscences' (Part 2), *Newsletter of the CTJC*, April, pp.9-10.

[14] Laqueur, op. cit., pp.506-7.

[15] Elon, A. (2004). *The Pity of it All: A Portrait of Jews in Germany 1743–1933*, London, UK: Penguin, pp.273-4.

[16] Quoted by Kitchen, M. (2006). *A History of Modern Germany, 1800–2000*, Oxford, UK: Blackwell, p.204.

[17] Klemperer, V. (1999). *I Shall Bear Witness, The Diaries of Victor Klemperer 1933–1941*, London, UK: Phoenix, p.11.

[18] Evans, R.J. (2005). *The Third Reich in Power*, London, UK: Allen Lane, p.331.

[19] Kershaw, I. (2008). *Hitler, the Germans, and the Final Solution*, Jerusalem, Yad Vashem / New Haven, CN, and London, UK: Yale University Press, p.186.
[20] Grunwald-Speir, A. (2010). *The Other Schindlers*, Stroud, The History Press, p.17.
[21] *Canadian Jewish Review*, 23 December 1938, p.3.
[22] Quoted in Gordon, G.H. (1995). *Guardians of Zion, The Shomrim in Australia 1939–1944*, Mandelbaum Trust, Studies in Judaica, No. 6, Sydney, University of Sydney, AUS: p.158.
[23] Field, J. (2008). 'David Tabor', in *Biographical Memoirs of Fellows of the Royal Society*. London, The Royal Society, **54**, p.435.
[24] Rutland, S. D. (1997). *Edge of the Diaspora* (2nd edition), New York/London, UK: Holmes and Meier, p.223.
[25] Karpf, A. (1997). *The War After*, London, UK: Minerva, p.48.
[26] Meir, G. (1976). *My Life,* London, UK: Futura Publications, p.149.
[27] From notes for a talk to the Cambridge University Jewish Society, 'What Judaism means to me,' 3 November 1972.
[28] Field, op. cit., p.451
[29] Kendall, quoted in Field, op. cit., p.452.
[30] Meir, op. cit., p.149.
[31] Ibid., p.184.
[32] Kaposi, A. (2020) *Yellow Star, Red Star*, Manchester, UK; i2i Publishing, p.69.
[33] Foot, M.R.D. (1999). *SOE, The Special Operations Executive 1940–1946*, London, UK: Pimlico, pp.75–6.
[34] Oz, A. (2012). *How to Cure a Fanatic*, London, UK: Vintage Books, pp.4–5.
[35] Freedland, J. (2022). 'The 55th anniversary of the Six Day War merits no celebration', *The Jewish Chronicle*, 26 May, p.18.

Bibliography

This is a list of the books and articles that I have referred to, as well as titles which relate to the subjects raised in the book, should readers wish to find out more.

Prologue

De Waal, E. (2010). *The Hare with Amber Eyes.* London, UK: Chatto & Windus.

Grele, R. J. (1998). 'Movement without aim', in Perks, R. & Thompson, A. (eds.) *The Oral History Reader.* London, UK: Routledge, pp.38-52.

Hinton, J. (2010). *Nine Wartime Lives.* Oxford, UK: Oxford University Press.

Josipovici, G. (2001). *A Life.* London, UK: London Magazine Editions.

Josipovici, G. (2020). *Forgetting.* Manchester, UK: Little Island Press/Carcanet.

Maalouf, A. (2003). *In the Name of Identity.* London, UK: Penguin.

Massey, D. (1995). 'Places and their pasts', in *History Workshop Journal*, **39**, pp.182-192.

Portelli, A. 'What makes oral history different', in Perks & Thompson, op. cit., pp.63–74.

Sebald, W. G. (1996). *The Emigrants* (English translation by Michael Hulse), London, UK: Harvill Press.

Sebald, W. G. (2001). *Austerlitz* (English translation by Anthea Bell). New York, NY: Random House.

Waxman, Z. V. (2006). *Writing the Holocaust*. Oxford, UK: Oxford University Press.

Chapter 1 Golden Years

Austin, P. B. (2000) 1812: *The Great Retreat* (Book Three), pp.337–372, in *Napoleon's Invasion of Russia*. London, UK: Greenhill Books.

Bieder, A. (2008). *A Dictionary of Jewish Surnames from the Russian Empire*: Revised Edition, Bergenfield, NJ: Avotaynu.

Beizer, M. (1989). *The Jews of St. Petersburg*. Philadelphia, PA: The Jewish Publication Society.

Berenbaum, M. & Skolnik, F. (eds.) (2007). *Encyclopaedia Judaica*. Detroit, MI: Macmillan.

Nathans, B. (2002). *Beyond the Pale: The Jewish Encounter with Late Imperial Russia.* Berkeley, CA: University of California Press,

Nathans, B. (2006) *The Jews*, in Lieven, D. (ed.) *The Cambridge History of Russia*, pp.184-201, Volume II. Cambridge, UK: Cambridge University Press,

Petrovsky-Shtern, Y. (2009). *Jews in the Russian Army, 1827–1917: Drafted into Modernity*. Cambridge, UK: Cambridge University Press.

Tobias, H. J. (1972). *The Jewish Bund in Russia*. Stanford, CA: Stanford University Press.

Zamoyski, A. (2004) *1812, Napoleon's Fatal March on Moscow*. London, UK: HarperCollins.

Chapter 2 Home in Notting Hill

Alderman, G. (1987). *The Federation of Synagogues 1887–1987*. London, UK: The Federation of Synagogues.

Bourke, J. (1994). *Working-Class Cultures in Britain, 1890-1960*. London, UK: Routledge.

Cesarani, D. (ed.) (1990). *The Making of Modern Anglo-Jewry*. Oxford, UK: Blackwell, pp.93–4.

Endleman, T. M. (2002). *The Jews of Britain, 1656 to 2000*. Berkeley, CA: University of California Press.

Feldman, D. (1994). *Englishmen and Jews: Social Relations and Political Culture, 1840–1914*. New Haven, CT & London, UK: Yale University Press.

Gartner, L. P. (1960). *The Jewish Immigrant to England, 1870–1914*. London, UK: Simon Publications.

Howe, I. (1980). *World of Our Fathers*. New York, NY: Bantam Books.

Kaplan, M. (1983). *Young Zionism and Jewish Youth in London between the Wars*, (typed m.s.). Queens' College, Cambridge, UK.

Lasserson, M. (ed.) (2005). *Sascha Lasserson, Portrait of a Teacher*. London, UK: Kahn and Averill.

Lipman, V. D. (1990). *A History of the Jews of Britain since 1858*. Leicester, UK: University of Leicester Press.

Shaw, H. (1959). 'The Other Notting Hill', *The Jewish Chronicle*, 19 June, p.15.

Tabor, D. (1996). 'Reflections: when two Palestinian soldiers held a spirited Chanukah party for a group of children in Notting Hill', *The Jewish Chronicle*, 13 December, p.25.

Chapter 3 A Cambridge Rarity

Bermant, C. (1971). *The Cousinhood*. London. UK: Eyre & Spottiswoode.

Block, G. D. M. (1942). 'Jewish students at the Universities of Great Britain and Ireland – excluding London, 1936-1939', *The Sociological Review*, 34, pp.183-97.

Chertok, H (2006). *He Also Spoke as a Jew*. London, UK:, Vallentine Mitchell.

Eban, A. (1977). *An Autobiography*. New York, NY: Random House.

Frankel, W. & Miller, H. (eds.) (1989). *Gown and Tallith*. London, UK: Harvey Miller.

Green, A. (2010). *Moses Montefiore: Jewish Liberator, Imperial Hero*. Harvard, CT: Harvard University Press.

Kushner, T. (2006). *Remembering Refugees, Then and Now*. Manchester, UK: Manchester University Press.

Kushner, T. & Lunn, K. (eds.) (1989). *Traditions of Intolerance*. Manchester, UK: Manchester University Press.

Laqueur, W. (1989). *A History of Zionism*. New York, NY: Schocken.

Parkes, J. (1934). *The Conflict of the Church and the Synagogue: A Study in the Origins of Anti-Semitism*. London, UK: Soncino Press.
Parkes, J. (1938). *The Jew and His Neighbour* (2nd revised edition). London, UK: Student Christian Movement Press.

Richmond, C. (2005). *Campaigner Against Antisemitism*. London, UK: Vallentine Mitchell.

Rose, J. (2010). *The Intellectual Life of the British Working Classes* (2nd edition). New Haven, CT & London, UK: Yale University Press.

Srebrnik, H. F. (1995). *London Jews and British Communism, 1935–1945*. London, UK: Vallentine Mitchell.

Tabor, D. (1969). 'Frank Philip Bowden, 1903–1968', in *Biographical Memoirs of Fellows of the Royal Society*. London, UK: The Royal Society, **15**, pp.1-38.

Tabor, D. C. (2017). 'An Unlikely Friendship: James Parkes and David Tabor, 1939-40', *Jewish Culture and History*, pp.255-273.

Weizmann, C. (1949). *Trial and Error*. London, UK: Hamish Hamilton.

Wendhorst, S.E. (2012). *British Jewry, Zionism, and the Jewish State, 1936-1956*. Oxford, UK: Oxford University Press.

Chapter 4 Germans of the Mosaic Persuasion

Benjamin, W. (1997) 'A Berlin Chronicle', in *One-Way Street and other Writings*. London, UK: Verso, pp.293-346.

Elon, A. (2004) *The Pity of it All: A Portrait of Jews in Germany 1743–1933*. London, UK: Penguin.

Garland, H. & Garland, M. (1997). *The Oxford Companion to German Literature*. Oxford, UK: Oxford University Press.

Kalmar, I. D. (2001). 'Moorish Style: Orientalism, the Jews, and Synagogue Architecture', *Jewish Social Studies*, 7, 3, Spring/Summer (New Series), pp.68–100.

Kitchen, M. (2006). *A History of Modern Germany, 1800–2000*. Oxford, UK: Blackwell.

Knauss, E. (1987). *Die jüdische Bevölkerung Giessens 1933–44.* Weisbaden, Kommission für die Geschichte der Juden in Hessen.

Steil, D. (1997). 'Zur Geschichte der Juden in Giessen'. In: *800 Jahre Giessener Geschichte 1197–1997*, Brake, L. & Brinkmann, H. (eds.), Giessen, University of Giessen, pp.394–5.

Wasserstein, B. (2012). *On the Eve.* London, UK: Profile Books.

Chapter 5 Weimar and After

Burleigh, M. (2000). *The Third Reich: A New History.* London, UK: Macmillan.

Evans, R. J. (2003). *The Coming of the Third Reich.* London, UK: Allen Lane.

Evans, R. J. (2005). *The Third Reich in Power.* London, UK: Allen Lane.

Gay, P. (1998). *My German Question: Growing Up in Nazi Berlin.* Yale, CT: Yale University Press.

Grunwald-Speir, A. (2010). *The Other Schindlers.* Stroud. Cheltenham, UK: The History Press.

Hughes, W. R. (1964). *Indomitable Friend, Corder Catchpool 1883–1953.* London, UK: Housmans.

Klatzo, I. & Zu Rhein, G. (2002). 'Cécile and Oskar Vogt: the visionaries of modern neuroscience', *Acta Neurochirurgia*, Supplement 80, Springer, Vienna/New York, NY, pp.1–130.

Gilbert, M. (1987). *The Holocaust.* London, UK: Fontana/Collins.

Klemperer, V. (1999). *I Shall Bear Witness, The Diaries of Victor Klemperer 1933–1941.* London, UK: Phoenix.

Kershaw, I. (2008). *Hitler, the Germans, and the Final Solution.* Jerusalem, Yad Vashem, New Haven, CT and London, UK: Yale University Press.

Nachama, N., Schoeps, J. H. & Simon, H. (eds.) (2002). *Jews in Berlin* (English translation). Berlin, GER: Henschel.

Scholem, G. (1988). *From Berlin to Jerusalem: Memories of My Youth.* New York, NY: Schocken Books.

Chapter 6 Newcomers Down-Under

Benjamin, R. (1998). *A Serious Influx of Jews: A History of Jewish Welfare in Victoria.* St Leonards, NSW: Allen & Unwin.

Blakeney, M. (1985). *Australia and the Jewish Refugees 1933–1948.* Sydney, NSW: Croom Helm.

Medding, P. Y. (2006). 'Zionism and Australian Jewry before 1948: the battle for ideological and communal responsibility', *Jewish Political Studies Review,* **18**, pp.99-118.

Freilich, M. (1967). *Zion In Our Time.* Sydney, NSW: Morgan Publications.

Gordon, G. H. (1995). *Guardians of Zion, The Shomrim in Australia 1939–1944.* Mandelbaum Trust, Studies in Judaica, No. 6. Sydney, NSW: University of Sydney.
Hyams, B. (1998). *The History of the Australian Zionist Movement.* Victoria, MEL: Zionist Federation of Australia.

Langfield, M. (2009). 'Lost Worlds': Reflections on home and belonging in Jewish Holocaust survivor testimonies', in Cesarani, D., Kushner, T., & Shain, M. (eds.) *Place and Displacement in Jewish History and Memory.* London, UK: Vallentine Mitchell, pp.29-42.

Lee, G. S. (1985). 'The battle of the scholars – the debate between Sir Isaacs Isaacs and Julius Stone over Zionism during World War II', *The Australian Journal of Politics and History*, **31**, 1, pp.128–34.

Liffman, H (1985). 'In search of my identity,' *The Australian Journal of Politics and History*, **31**, 1, pp.10–28.

Rutland, S. D. (1985). 'Australian responses to Jewish refugee migration before and after World War II', *The Australian Journal of Politics and History*, **31**, 1, pp.29-48.

Rutland, S. D. (1997). *Edge of the Diaspora* (2nd revised edition). New York/London: Holmes & Meier.

Chapter 7 Life in War-time Australia

Beaumont, J. (ed.) (1996). *Australia's War, 1939-45*. St. Leonards NSW: Allen and Unwin.

Calvocoressi, P., Wint, G., & Pritchard, J. (1999). *The Penguin History of the Second World War*. London, UK: Penguin Books.

Field, J. (2008) 'David Tabor' in *Biographical Memoirs of the Royal Society*. London, UK: The Royal Society, **54**, pp.425-459.

Greenwood, N. N. & Spinks, J. A. (2003). 'An antipodean laboratory of remarkable distinction', in *Notes and Records of the Royal Society of London*. London, UK: The Royal Society, pp.85–105.
Refaeli, Esther (Shapiro) (2007). 'My Jewish Carlton – recollections' in Jewish History Australia, at www.ajhs.info/jha.

Rutland, S. D. (1997). *Edge of the Diaspora* (2nd edition). New York/London, UK: Holmes and Meier.

Tabor, D. (1951). *Hardness of Metals*. Oxford, UK: Oxford University Press.

Tabor, D. C. (2012). 'The general awakening of Jewish consciousness: The development of the Jewish Students' Study Group in Melbourne', *Australian Jewish Historical Society Journal*, XX1, Part 1, pp.61–85.

Taylor, A.J.P. (1965). *English History 1914–1945*. Oxford, UK: Oxford University Press.

Chapter 8 Coming Together

Weinberg, G. L. (2005). *A World At Arms* (2nd edition). Cambridge, UK: Cambridge University Press.

Chapter 9 Jews of the English Persuasion

Arendt, H. (2006). *Eichmann in Jerusalem: A Report on the Banality of Evil*. London, UK: Penguin Classics.

Judt, T. (2005) *Postwar*. London, UK: Heinemann.

Karpf, A. (1997). *The War After*. London, UK: Minerva.

Minney, R. J. (1966). *I Shall Fear No Evil: The Story of Dr Alina Brewda*. London, UK: Kimber.

Nusseibah, S. (2007). *Once Upon a Country: A Palestinian Life*. London, UK: Halban.
Oz, A. (2004). *A Tale of Love and Darkness*. London, UK: Chatto & Windus.

Thomson, D. (1966). *Europe Since Napoleon*. London, UK: Penguin.

Uris, L. (1958). *Exodus*. New York. NY: Doubleday.

Uris, L. (1970). *QB VII*. New York, NY: Doubleday.

Chapter 10 Follow Your Heart

Cohn-Sherbok, D. & El-Alami, D. (2001). *The Palestine-Israeli Conflict*. Oxford, UK: Oneworld Publications.

Foot, M.R.D. (1976). *Resistance: An Analysis of European Resistance to Nazism, 1940-1945*. London, UK: Methuen.

Hertzog, C. (2004). *The Arab-Israeli Wars* (updated by Gazit, S.). London, UK: Greenhill Books.

Isaacson, W. (2008). *Einstein, His Life and Universe*. London, UK: Simon & Schuster.

Lagrou, P. (2000). 'Belgium', in Moore, B. (ed.) *Resistance in Western Europe*. Oxford, UK: Berg, pp.27–64.

Michman, D. (1999). *Belgium and the Holocaust: Jews, Belgians, Germans*. Bar-Ilan University/Yad Va-Shem Publications.

Morris, B. (2008). 1948, *A History of the First Arab-Israeli War*. New Haven, CT & London, UK: Yale University Press.

Pappe, I. (2006). *The Ethnic Cleansing of Palestine*. London, UK: Oneworld Publications.

Weiner-Henron, J. (2005). 'Régine Karline-Orfinger, 1911–2003', *Jewish Women, A Comprehensive Historical Encyclopedia*, in: http://encyclopedia/article/karlin-orfinger-regine.

Chapter 11 Making the Desert Bloom

Ben-Dror, E. (2015). *Ralph Bunche and the Arab-Israeli Conflict: Mediation and the UN 1947–1949*. London, UK & New York, NY: Routledge.

Blumberg, A. (1998). *A History of Israel*. Westport, CN: Greenwood Press.

Garcia-Granados, J. (1949). *The Birth of Israel*. New York, NY: Alfred A. Knop.

Lazar, H. (2012). *Out of Palestine*. New York, NY: Atlas & Co.

Near, H. (1992). *The Kibbutz Movement* (Vols.1 & 2). Oxford, UK: Oxford University Press.

Chapter 12 Surviving Bergen-Belsen

Bogdanor, P. (2016). *Kasztner's Crime*. London, UK: Routledge.

Cesarani, D. (ed.) (1997). *Genocide and Rescue: The Holocaust in Hungary 1944*. Oxford, UK: Berg.

Löb, L. (2008). *Dealing with Satan*. London, UK: Jonathan Cape.

Wetzler, Alfred (2007). *Escape from Hell: The True Story of the Auschwitz Protocol* (translated by Ewald Osers). New York, NY & Oxford, UK: Berghahn Books.

Wiesel, E. (2006). *Night* (translated by Marion Wiesel). London, UK: Penguin Modern Classics.
Zsolt, B. (2005). *Nine Suitcases* (translated by Ladislaus Löb). New York, NY: Schoken Books.

Chapter 13 Innovators and Pioneers

Foot, M.R.D. (1999) *SOE, The Special Operations Executive 1940–1946*. London, UK: Greenwood Press.

Jorisch, A. (2018). *Thou Shalt Innovate*. Jerusalem/New York, NY: Gefen Books.

Chapter 15 Connecting with the Past

Grade, C. (1987). *My Mother's Sabbath Days* (Translated by Channa Goldstein and Inna Grade). New York, NY: Schocken Books.

Gryn, H. (2001). *Chasing Shadows*. London, UK: Penguin Books.

Jacobson, H. (1993). *Roots, Schmoots: Journeys Among Jews*. Harmondsworth, UK: Viking Books/Penguin.

Kruk, H. (2002). *The Last Days of the Jerusalem of Lithuania*. New Haven, CN and London, UK: Yale University Press.